Archival Storytelling

Fully revised and updated, *Archival Storytelling* second edition is a timely, pragmatic look at the use of audiovisual materials available to filmmakers and scholars, from the earliest photographs of the 19th century to the work of media makers today.

Whether you're a top Hollywood filmmaker or a first-time documentarian, at some point you are going to want to find, use, and license third-party materials—images, audio, or music that you yourself did not create—to use them in your work. This book explains what's involved in researching and licensing visuals and music, and exactly what media makers need to know when filming in a world crowded with rights-protected images and sounds. Filled with insights from filmmakers, archivists, and intellectual property experts, this second edition defines key terms such as copyright, fair use, public domain, and orphan works. It guides readers through the complex archival process and challenges them to become not only archival users but also archival and copyright activists.

This book is an essential resource for both students and professionals, from seasoned filmmakers to those creating their first projects, offering practical advice for how to effectively and ethically draw on the wealth of cultural materials that surround us.

Sheila Curran Bernard is an Emmy and Peabody Award-winning filmmaker and writer with credits on nearly fifty hours of theatrical and television programming, and the author of *Documentary Storytelling*, now going into its fifth edition. She is an associate professor in the Department of History at the University at Albany, State University of New York.

Kenn Rabin is a consulting producer for narrative features and documentaries and an internationally-recognized expert on the use of archival materials in film storytelling, with over one hundred credits on projects including *Troop Zero* (Bert & Bertie), *Selma* (Ava DuVernay), *Milk* (Gus Van Sant), and the acclaimed PBS series *Eyes on the Prize* and *Vietnam: A Television History*.

Praise for *Archival Storytelling*, 1ˢᵗ edition

"The excellent new resource, *Archival Storytelling*, is really two books in one: a detailed how-to guide for filmmakers on the process of researching, acquiring, and clearing rights to archival materials; and a deeper exploration of the implications, ethical and creative, of using these materials to tell new stories."

—Grace Lile, *American Archivist* (The Society of American Archivists)

"Kenn Rabin and Sheila Curran Bernard have written an important book, one that will serve as the definitive text on archive-based filmmaking for years to come ... I have been working with film and video archives for over twenty years, and I understand the hunger for this information in the production communities. This book delivers the information, but also reinforces why the archive-based program, done right, is a critical part of our cultural conversation."

— Matthew White, Filmmaker

"This book is a great resource because it surveys the entire landscape from ethical/ creative considerations, to fair use and to changes in the digital age, and the focus is always on the importance of telling stories."

— Ingrid Kopp, *Shooting People*

"I am often asked how to work with archival materials. Now I have an easy answer: Get a copy of *Archival Storytelling* and read it. Everything's there—how to use archival materials, acquire them, and most of all, how to think about them. *Archival Storytelling* is indispensable."

— David Grubin, Filmmaker

"This is it, the book that will save you thousands of dollars and untold hours of frustration. It will be the single best purchase your production company will make. *Archival Storytelling* clearly explains the entire process of researching, acquiring and licensing archival footage and music. Included are time-tested tips and techniques for efficiently managing the work flow and negotiating rights."

— Ann Petrone, Archival Supervisor

"One of the best—and most needed—texts I have seen in a while. The challenge is to keep what is a fairly technical aspect of filmmaking interesting, without compromising the quality and depth of information. The authors have done an exceptional job in this regard... There is the strong sense of being in the presence of experienced filmmakers and researchers who accept that while there are standard practices, archival use and intellectual property laws, etc. are contingent fields in which each case must be assessed and dealt with on its merits."

— Bruce Sheridan, Chair, Film & Video Department, Columbia College

"I've been making historical documentaries for many years, yet I learned new things from this book. This is the definitive guide for archival research for documentary filmmakers. An invaluable resource."

— Mark Jonathan Harris, Filmmaker and Distinguished Professor, School of Cinematic Arts, University of Southern California

Praise for Bernard's *Documentary Storytelling*

"An extremely useful book for those who want to know more about how to make a documentary film is Sheila Curran Bernard's comprehensive *Documentary Storytelling: Creative Nonfiction on Screen*... It stresses the use of narrative techniques in documentary production, provides examples of treatments, and includes interviews with a number of important filmmakers."

— Bill Nichols, *Introduction to Documentary*, 3rd edition

"With the availability of high-quality affordable cameras and editing equipment, documentary filmmakers today enjoy a freedom in shaping their films that their counterparts a decade ago couldn't have imagined. As the new aesthetic is shaped, Sheila Curran Bernard's brilliant and effective *Documentary Storytelling*... aims to guide the Errol Morrises of tomorrow with great advice and practical knowledge that every documentarian would benefit from."

— *BackStage*

"With all the buzz over blockbuster docs, Focal Press serves up a perfectly timed winner in a much-neglected area. True to the nature of the beast, the book is more about filmmaking as a whole, and how and where storytelling weaves into the overall process. It succeeds in covering every aspect without belabouring any. Not only does Bernard write from the viewpoint of an award-winning filmmaker (she's a writer, director, and producer), but the last 100 pages include extensive interviews with a wide range of acclaimed documentarians."

— *Canadian Screenwriter* (Writers Guild of Canada)

"[A] pragmatic exploration of the role of narrative in nonfiction filmmaking... In writing this volume Bernard demonstrates to documentarians how story can be more effectively incorporated into every level of nonfiction filmmaking from conception to development and pre-production, in the field and in the editing room. Her discussions incorporate many examples from contemporary documentaries to illustrate a variety of salient points."

— *Documentary* (International Documentary Association)

"While documentaries are nonfiction, they are certainly not objective, and even the smallest choices in writing, filming, interviewing, narrating, or scoring can drastically alter the perspective of the film, and in turn, the audience. Bernard is keenly aware of the power of persuasive images, and her insistence on complexity and integrity is a consistent theme throughout the book."

— *The Independent* (Association of Independent Video and Filmmakers)

Archival
Storytelling

A Filmmaker's Guide to Finding, Using,
and Licensing Third-Party Visuals and Music

Second Edition

Sheila Curran Bernard
Kenn Rabin

Routledge
Taylor & Francis Group

NEW YORK AND LONDON

Second edition published 2020
by Routledge
52 Vanderbilt Avenue, New York, NY 10017

and by Routledge
2 Park Square, Milton Park, Abingdon, Oxon, OX14 4RN

Routledge is an imprint of the Taylor & Francis Group, an informa business

First edition published by Focal Press 2009

Library of Congress Cataloging-in-Publication Data
Names: Bernard, Sheila Curran, author. | Rabin, Kenn, author.
Title: Archival storytelling : a filmmaker's guide to finding, using, and licensing
    third-party visuals and music / Sheila Curran Bernard and Kenn Rabin.
Description: Second edition. | London ; New York : Routledge, 2020. |
Identifiers: LCCN 2019052869 | ISBN 9781138915046 (hardback) | ISBN 9781138915039
    (paperback) | ISBN 9781003026204 (ebook)
Subjects: LCSH: Documentary films--Production and direction. | Archival materials.
Classification: LCC PN1995.9.D6 B393 2020 | DDC 070.1/8--dc23
LC record available at https://lccn.loc.gov/2019052869

ISBN: 978-1-138-91504-6 (hbk)
ISBN: 978-1-138-91503-9 (pbk)
ISBN: 978-1-003-02620-4 (ebk)

Typeset in Giovanni and Optima
by Servis Filmsetting Ltd, Stockport, Cheshire

Paperback cover image: Women workers employed as wipers in the roundhouse having lunch in their rest room, C. & N.W. R.R., Clinton, Iowa. April 1943. Photograph by Jack Delano for the Farm Security Administration-Office of War Information. Marcella Hart at left; Mrs. Elibia Siematter at right. (Collection USW361-644, Library of Congress Prints and Photographs Division, https://www.loc.gov/pictures/item/2017878365/.)

Contents

Acknowledgments

We remain grateful to the Graduate Program in Journalism at the University of California, Berkeley; the MFA Program in Documentary Film and the Film and Media Studies Program, both at Stanford University; and the Center for Internet & Society at Stanford for their help with the first edition. We are also grateful for ongoing guidance from the Center for Media & Social Impact at American University. Our thanks to those with whom we met and/or otherwise communicated during the preparation of both editions, including Claire Aguilar, Patricia Aufderheide, Hubert Best, Ronald Blumer, James A. DeVinney, Michael Dolan, Michael Donaldson, Jon Else, Anthony Falzone, Kevin Green, Sam Green, Roberta Grossman, Justine Jacobs, Peter Jaszi, Alexander Kandaurov, Elizabeth Klinck, Rena Kosersky, Debra Kozee, Jan Krawitz, Lawrence Lessig, Muffie Meyer, Susan McCormick, Dale Nelson, Stanley Nelson, Bill Nichols, Polly Pettit, Rick Prelinger, Jay Rosenblatt, Bonnie Rowan, Kristine Samuelson, Lisa Savage, Patricia Shannahan, David Thaxton, Mauro Tonini, and Geoffrey C. Ward. For this edition, we are grateful to Sir Peter Jackson and editor Jabez Olssen for permission to quote from Jackson's "making of" featurette that accompanied the U.S. preview screenings of *They Shall Not Grow Old*. We are also grateful to Focal Press and its talented editorial and design teams. For this second edition, we thank Alyssa Turner, Lusana Taylor, Emma Tyce, Priscille Biehlmann, Laurie Fuller, and John Makowski.

Sheila: First and foremost, thank you to my amazing family and, of course, Joel. Thank you to the colleagues and friends with whom I've worked over the years, and to opportunities at Westbrook College, Princeton University, and since 2008, the University at Albany, State University of New York, especially the Department of History, the Documentary Studies Program, the College of Arts and Sciences, and the New York State Writers Institute.

Kenn: Many thanks to all my teachers and mentors along the way. I send especially fond thoughts and special thanks to Sara Altherr, Richard Berge, Jon Else, Lynn Farnell, Raye Farr, Vanessa Gould, Jerome Kuehl, Lawrence W. Lichty, David Loxton, Bill Moyers, Martin Smith, Judith Vecchione, and the late Richard Ellison. I would like to dedicate my work on this edition to the memory of Henry Hampton, who gave me the best job of my life, and to the late David Thaxton—researcher, filmmaker, teacher, and friend.

Sheila Curran Bernard
Kenn Rabin
October 2019

CHAPTER 1

Introduction

We are surrounded by images and sounds that have been shaped by others into content intended to entertain, inform, educate, sell, persuade, and even mislead. Much of this visual and aural record has been and will continue to be preserved for future reference, including use by filmmakers, journalists, historians, educators, and others. The purpose of this book is to offer insight into:

- How archival materials came into being;
- Where these materials can be found;
- How they can be acquired and used in today's digital editing workflow; and
- What's involved in acquiring the rights needed to use this material in your own film or other media project, and the challenges—ethical, historical, and creative—that should be considered when drawing upon this audiovisual heritage.

"Archival" materials is a term we're using to loosely mean any audiovisual material not created/originated by you. It may have been captured today, or a decade ago, or even in the mid-19th century, at the dawn of photography. By the 1890s cameras could capture motion and recorders could capture sound. By the mid-20th century, both image and sound could be transmitted over the air to receivers—television sets and radios—in people's homes. By the late 20th century, cable technology and the internet had again transformed the audiovisual landscape. Now, as we enter the third decade of the 21st century, images and sounds can circumvent the globe in a matter of seconds.

There is a unique power to the audiovisual record: it seems to capture reality itself. Still and motion picture photography, along with recorded sounds, speech, and music, have long been tools for documenting our world, sharing stories, and selling products. And yet as we explore in this book, recorded images and audio, including those created for purposes of journalism or documentary, are *not* reality: they are representations of it, and their authenticity requires analysis and interpretation. Who created this material, for what purpose? What is beyond the frame? Does the image accurately represent the event, person, or place? How accurately does the spoken word reveal the circumstances in which the recording was made, or the purpose and selection of what was recorded, or what was edited out? Have these materials been altered or falsified in some way, whether at the point of creation or later? And what about events, people, or places that were *not* documented in some way? All of these questions apply, whether the material was generated a century ago or yesterday, although today the rise of increasingly sophisticated "deepfake" technology gives a new and troubling urgency to the need for media literacy.

When we first published *Archival Storytelling* in 2008, our primary goal was to engage and serve filmmakers, including those working on projects intended for Hollywood, broadcast, and streaming media; dramatic or documentary; and single films or multi-part series. These filmmakers weren't necessarily focusing on "historical" stories. Projects often utilize at least some material not created by the filmmaking team. It was also our intent, however, to engage media makers who specifically *do* seek to interrogate the historical record through their work, challenging them to consider this material in its context and consider how they are using it as audiovisual evidence of the past.

The response to that book, not only from new and established filmmakers but also from readers working in a range of disciplines, led us to realize that this information has a broader use. For that reason, in addition to significant updating, this second edition was written to serve not only filmmakers but also media professionals in general (including those who deal routinely with issues of intellectual property), as well as historians, curators, and other scholars who rely on third-party materials in their research. We especially hope to reach public historians, a group that the National Council on Public History (ncph.org) describes as including "historical consultants, museum professionals, government historians, archivists, oral historians, cultural resource managers, curators, film and media producers, historical interpreters, historic preservationists, policy advisers, local historians, and community activists."

In addition, we seek to inform an argument for the importance of ongoing preservation of audiovisual records, as well as to call attention to obstacles regarding access to some of these important archives, including, but not limited to, the rising cost to license materials. Media makers are free, of course, to eschew the use of archival materials and instead rely on re-enactments, generic imagery, and perhaps animation to convey historical stories. These choices, however, should be made for creative and content purposes, and not because access to archival material is restricted or licensing costs prohibitive. In some cases, of course, use of third-party materials may *not* require licensing, as we discuss in chapters dealing with the *public domain*, and with *fair use*, a legal exception to U.S. copyright law.

Lastly, we hope that this book may help to raise awareness among funding organizations, policymakers, elected officials, and especially entertainment industry executives that quality programming requires resources. Much has changed since the first edition was published, and there has been an encouraging increase in venues through which top-notch independent programming can reach audiences. With that said, the push to turn out media "product" faster and cheaper has also intensified, and we hope that this book offers a reminder that good, ethical, effective media production—especially when it seeks to tell the stories of history—takes time, expertise, and money.

3

What Are "Archival" Materials?

The range of acquired images and sound generally described in this book as archival audiovisual materials includes:

■ *Illustrative* moving images, such as "beauty" shots of famous landmarks, sunsets, time-lapse photography (such as flowers opening, or the sun rising), weather photography, and aerial photography (such as footage shot from a helicopter or drone). These are often owned by commercial enterprises and sometimes by the individuals who shot them.

■ *Historical and news-related* moving images, such as footage of newsworthy events. In general, the greater the importance of the moment and those involved, the more likely it is that you can find this material at commercial entities, such as television networks or newsreel houses. But historical moving images exist for a wide range of events, some of which may have never reached the national news and instead were documented by local crews and archived at local television stations, libraries, universities, historical societies, and even in personal collections.

- *Industrial and educational materials*, which have long been and continue to be created by industries and social organizations all around the world for purposes of advertising, sales, and education. These can afford a fascinating look into the past (as well as the present) and include every possible genre.
- *Government-produced materials* from around the world, including important works of record, such as those created by branches of the military. Government works have documented wars; social programs and movements; federally funded projects including infrastructure projects; public art of various kinds; advances in medicine and science; and, of course, government-produced propaganda (which could include any of the above).
- *Personal* moving images and still photographs, an ever-expanding body of materials created by individuals and families that reflects ongoing changes in technology, from tintypes to Kodachrome slides, Super 8 home movies to cell phone videos and stills.
- *Commercially-owned or produced* photographs of any kind, generic or specific, including news photos from newspapers and magazines, stock photos from agencies, wire service photos, Hollywood publicity portraits, celebrity service photos, and others.
- *Graphics* such as antique maps, fine art (including paintings, textiles, and such), editorial cartoons, lithographic illustrations, movie posters, and newspaper headlines. Flat art may be used to augment visuals for events that predate the invention of photography or to provide context and commentary on historical events; a newspaper headline may serve when there is no film or still coverage of an event, and it can also efficiently push the story ahead.
- *Music*, including music not created expressly for your project (as a "work for hire" by a composer, for example), and preexisting recordings that come from downloads, CDs, LPs, or other sources not originally recorded by you.
- *Sound*; for example, the "wild" (unsynchronized) audio of events in lower Manhattan on September 11, 2001, or a radio broadcast of Edward R. Murrow reporting on the London blitz in the 1940s, or the early recordings made on wax cylinders by folklorists eager to preserve traditional cultures.

Who Uses Archival Materials?

When people think of archival use, they often think first about historical filmmakers such as Ken Burns and Lynn Novick, who co-directed the 2017

PBS series *The Vietnam War*. But a surprisingly diverse group of people uses archival materials, including not only documentary filmmakers but also advertising agencies, public relations firms, news organizations, fiction filmmakers, historians and makers of educational material, students, and the general public. Any time you order a photograph from the collection of ship images at Ellis Island, search through military records at Ancestry. com, or visit a local museum or historical society, you're benefiting from the preservation and accessibility of archival materials.

In some cases, as noted, archival material adds real-world verisimilitude to fictionalized storytelling. For example, director Ava DuVernay's Academy Award-nominated *Selma* (2014) dramatized the 1965 civil rights march from Selma to Montgomery, Alabama. In the film, as the march reached its conclusion with the protesters' arrival in the city of Montgomery, the visuals shifted from the present-day actors to archival footage of the real marchers, filmed 50 years earlier by newsreel cameras and network news crews. The fictional AMC television series, *Mad Men* (2007–2015), set in the 1960s and 1970s, at times showed their characters watching televised, actual news reports of events from that era. For the Oscar-nominated *Straight Outta Compton* (2015), a fictionalized drama about the musical group N.W.A., director F. Gary Gray evoked the 1980s and 1990s through the use of period news footage from CNN, NBC, and ABC; music video clips from MTV; film clips from director John Singleton's 1991 feature *Boyz n the Hood*; and clips from a 1970s TV sitcom, *What's Happening!!*

In documentary programming and in academic scholarship, archival materials may be used as visual and aural evidence of the past. This was the case with *Eyes on the Prize*, the 14-hour archival history of the modern U.S. civil rights movement that was broadcast on PBS in two parts (1987 and 1990). Director Werner Herzog's *Grizzly Man* (2005) relied on a video diary shot by naturalist Timothy Treadwell before his death in 2003, in his efforts to understand why Treadwell would risk his own life—and others'—to live among wild bears.

At other times, archival materials are used to fill a general need for visuals that evoke a specific time or place. This can provide a valuable context for a subject. Filmmaker Raoul Peck, for example, used home movies, talk show clips, and period footage of New York, Paris, and other cities in *I Am Not Your Negro* (2017). The documentary is built upon a book that author and activist James Baldwin began in 1979, in which he pays tribute to three close friends who were assassinated in the 1960s: civil rights leaders Medgar Evers, Malcolm X, and the Rev. Dr. Martin Luther King, Jr. (The book remained unfinished at the time of Baldwin's death, in 1987.)

5

Among the most influential users of archival materials are advertising agencies, whose (relatively) high budgets have shaped today's market and, to a large extent, driven prices up from what they were just a decade or two ago. These agencies tend to rely on commercial stock houses, whose fees may be higher than elsewhere but whose material may be available almost immediately: a simple click and download after a credit card payment. In contrast, independent filmmakers may have less money but more time to do the digging that's often required to find material in alternative, less expensive places—and to dig deeper for material that may be less well-known or more relevant, or that might push their research in new directions.

Nearly *all* media makers, at some point in their careers, will want to use third-party materials. Despite perceptions, this use does not need to destroy your budget or schedule. With some creative thinking and perseverance, even those with limited funding should be able to find useful and affordable materials. Additionally, you'll be better informed when asked to license your own work to others.

Who Owns Archival Materials?

The short answer is: everybody, from you and your family (those boxes of photographs you've been meaning to sort, along with home movies, audiotapes, school papers, and more) to some of the wealthiest individuals, institutions, and corporations in the world. Getty Images, the U.S. government, and the British Crown are just a few of the world's notable collectors.

Challenges of Archival Storytelling

The complexity of finding, using, and (as needed) licensing archival images and sound can be daunting. The following are some of the challenges media makers routinely face:

- The rights holder to photos, footage, or music you want to use refuses to grant a license, or is charging a fee so high you can't possibly afford it;
- You found footage that was perfect, but in it, people are singing a song, which may mean that you need to also negotiate permission to use the song;

- Although you cleared the necessary rights for your project five years ago, some of them were time limited and are now expiring, so you can no longer sell or distribute your work;
- You found material that you want to use on YouTube, but have no idea how to locate the rights holder;
- You've discovered that someone else has incorporated portions of your work in their program without your consent.

We'll address these issues and others in the following pages, drawing not only on our own experiences but also those of other media professionals, legal experts, film and music researchers, insurance executives, archivists, and others.

The Importance of Access

Although it can be difficult to find and use third-party sounds and visuals, it's our hope that in offering strategies for doing so effectively and economically, we can encourage filmmakers to continue to make the effort. This is *our* heritage, and filmmakers have a right and even, arguably, a responsibility to draw on that heritage in the creation of new work. "When we stop allowing each generation to be actively involved in interpreting and reinterpreting history, then we're creating a real disservice for everyone involved," Orlando Bagwell, filmmaker and former director of the documentary program at the UC Berkeley Graduate School of Journalism, has said. "That's when history is really exciting; when each generation has its chance to consider it in terms of their times and needs and experiences." The good news is that a lot of talented, determined people are working to find effective and creative ways to resolve many of these issues, as we explore in these pages.

7

The Impact of Technology

Before the internet, a researcher had to visit an archive to see what material was available. Today, researchers do a good deal of their investigation online, where they can find an unprecedented variety of elements for audiovisual storytelling: old newspapers, music and other audio, high-resolution digital photography, artwork, and moving images. These materials can often be *ingested* directly from the cloud and then added into any project, editing timeline or playlist, using software that, until fairly recently, was expensive, complex, and reserved for professionals.

The resulting edited or "mixed" images and sound—in other words, the finished film or project—can be saved and shared virtually or physically (such as on a drive or disk), and increasingly, creative work goes directly to audiences without passing through the traditional "gatekeepers" overseeing content on behalf of a broadcast or streaming entity or studio. Such freedom requires responsibility, and it's our hope that this book can better prepare media makers, educators, and students to protect their own creative rights while also respecting those of others.

Reading Between the Images

An interesting aspect of archival footage is the information it unintentionally conveys. Some of the earliest surviving snippets of captured movement depict intimate and ordinary moments of daily human life. These were created as "tests" for the newly invented medium of motion pictures: a sneeze, a kiss, a train pulling into a station, an image of New York Harbor from a circling vessel. Almost immediately, however, the power of film to record larger events, such as the aftermath of the 1906 earthquake in San Francisco, was recognized. Looking more closely at these early motion pictures, today's viewers may discover unexpected information. Edwin S. Porter's early drama, *The Great Train Robbery* (1903), reveals information about the geography of Essex County, New Jersey, where the exteriors were filmed, even as it tells a fictional story of cowboys and train robbers in the "Wild West." Filmmaker D.W. Griffith's early short, *The New York Hat*, offers a look at the clothes, traffic, and even the way shadows fall on a New York street in 1912, while it also exhibits the talents of screenwriter Anita Loos and actors Lillian Gish, Lionel Barrymore, and Mary Pickford.

Any visual record of the past is likely to have value. A colleague in charge of a local television news archive (1950s through 1970s) in a major American city was running out of storage space for her collection. She was encouraged to eliminate such items as the evening news stories about random apartment fires from over 50 years ago. She refused. "How are we going to know what a city fire truck looked like 50 years ago, or the firemen's uniforms, or what equipment they had and didn't have?" she argued. Archival materials can provide the historian, film historian, sociologist, art director, and others with unexpected treasures.

On the other hand, archives are forced into difficult choices due to real and pressing challenges. Even as collections continue to grow, space is limited, money and time are tight, and technology continues to evolve, rendering materials in one format obsolete and requiring their

8

migration to another. In addition, all audiovisual materials deteriorate over time, so archivists must be concerned with their preservation. At times, this goal may be viewed as conflicting with pressure to make—or keep—collections accessible for use by scholars, filmmakers, and others.

The Camera Can Lie

As discussed throughout this book, even though archival images are used as evidence of the past, they require careful scrutiny. Many film-makers use mid-20th century newsreel footage, for example, without knowing that it was sometimes staged, with actors portraying figures of recent history. Some of the world's most iconic images, now presented as authentic, were actually created for the purposes of propaganda or public relations. Issues of bias, privilege, distortion, and exclusion come into play. And oddly, there are moments that people believe they've seen on film, and that archivists and researchers tear their hair out trying to find—but if visuals exist, they are still photographs, not motion picture. They've become part of our collective memory as we imagined them.

Audiovisual materials should be fact checked, regardless of what they claim to show. Sent to shoot a mob but not actually finding one, for example, a newsreel camera operator may have shot tight and close, creating an impression of a crowd where none existed. Intent on portraying an individual's guilt, a news photographer may have used unflattering angles and harsh lighting or perhaps worked in a darkroom to juxtapose two unrelated images. Farm Security Administration photographers, sent out in the 1930s to capture images of farmers and laborers, often photographed them from low angles to make them look more noble. In addition, users of archival visuals—moving images in particular—can and often do alter color, speed, even background sound. With added sound effects, a peaceful archival street scene can become the site of conflict, as shots and screams are heard. This footage, with its new audio track, may then be picked up by other film researchers. Unless they sufficiently authenticate the archival find, the facts of the original scene may become even further distorted.

Who Owns the Past?

Some media makers, especially those who've been priced out of using third-party images and music that they believed were critical to their projects, are angered by the notion that these materials can be protected for many decades as "intellectual property." In time, however, many of these same creators struggle to determine what to charge when others want to use *their* original material as third-party content, or they're dismayed to find that their images or audio were used in ways they didn't authorize and for which they weren't compensated.

One of the trends over the past couple of decades has been larger archives buying up smaller ones. Getty Images, which is among the world's leading sellers of archival materials (as well as creators of it), is a good example of this. Since its founding in 1995, the company has bought entire collections, such as the Bettmann Archive, which at one time was the largest still image library in the world, Hulton Archives, WireImage, Image Bank, and Corbis (which until it was bought by Getty had been its largest competitor). Getty has also gained exclusive representation rights for numerous other collections. For example, just in the sports genre, and just in the first half of 2019, Getty renewed its exclusive rights to represent images owned by the International Paralympic Committee, the World Surf League, and the Fédération Internationale de Football (FIFA). Getty also has an international team of photographers and other media makers creating new exclusive content for them. As an example, Getty is now the official photographer for the Met Gala, the Tribeca Film Festival, and the BAFTA Awards, and their huge collection of red carpet photographs of celebrities are among their biggest sellers.

When Do You Need to Think About Archival Materials?

For historians and educators, digging into the archival record may be ongoing. For media makers, archival use varies project by project. In general, a film starts out as an idea or concept, or perhaps a broad attraction to a situation or subject. An experienced filmmaker begins to narrow the focus, considering story, subjects, themes, and creative approach. Will it be a dramatic film with actors? A biopic? A documentary? An experimental work? Are archival visuals and/or music necessary, or might they contribute in some way? If so, how critical is it that the images and sound *exactly* depict a place, event, or time period?

It's fair to say that most media makers think about archival images and music later in a production than they should. This is a problem for two main reasons. First, archival materials can often inspire new or different thinking about a film's subject or story. Second, the route to finding, licensing, and acquiring masters of third-party materials can be complicated and costly. The more time you leave for this work, the better able you'll be to handle obstacles and the more likely it is that you'll be able to find suitable, lower cost, or even rights-free alternatives where necessary.

Ideally, you should be thinking about third-party materials from the start of a project. In many cases, a beginning awareness of archival resources informs your project's storytelling even at the outline and treatment stage. If you're going to write fundraising proposals or present "pitch" documents to production executives or others with the power to *greenlight* (give the go-ahead to) your film, you need to know if your plans are realistic. Does footage of that deep-water archeological excavation even exist? Do you anticipate a wide commercial release for your film, and if so, do you expect to be able to raise enough money to pay rights fees for expensive Hollywood clips? You also may want to refer to archival materials as you write and shoot your work. Historical photographs, for example, can be used as references for costume designers and art directors. And if you are actually including archival content in the production itself—such as having it appear on a television a character is watching—it may need to be available on the set, unless you use technology to add it later. You will likely be making archival choices and conducting additional research as your storytelling goes in unanticipated directions.

In other words, archival use should not be an afterthought. Don't censor yourself by presuming that you can't afford the materials you need. Instead, become informed enough to know what obstacles you may face, while you have time to explore creative, lower cost alternatives. One of the *least* effective ways nonfiction filmmakers use archival materials is to wait until the last minute and then just grab generic stand-ins. Think more organically about third-party materials as a component of the overall work.

About the Book

While we have tried to be as comprehensive as possible, no single book can cover a topic as complex as this. Both technology and archival holdings change rapidly, so any comprehensive list of resources will soon be out of date. If you plan to work with audiovisual archival materials on a regular basis, we encourage you to investigate and consider joining professional organizations such as The Association of Moving Image Archivists (AMIA), the Federation of Commercial Audiovisual Libraries (FOCAL International), and the Fédération Internationale des Archives de Télévision/International Federation of Television Archives

11

(FIAT/IFTA). Also, while we tend to use terms such as *filmmaker* and *media maker* fairly loosely, we mean them to include any media professional who incorporates third-party material in their work, for whatever venue.

International Issues

We began the revised edition with every intention of making it as international in scope as possible. However, intellectual property laws are not only mind-bogglingly complex, they also vary from nation to nation (and even U.S. state to state). For this reason, our primary focus is on American intellectual property law as it pertains to archival use, including copyright, public domain, and fair use. Where possible, though, we've also discussed these terms as they may apply or have some form of counterpart elsewhere, especially in Europe and among the Commonwealth Nations. We've also noted where clearance of rights in the United States may be insufficient if you want to distribute your film elsewhere. We're hoping that by at least starting to untangle the web of rights and licenses in the United States, which has a news and entertainment industry that continues to be globally powerful (and is uniquely litigious), we've gotten the conversation going. We certainly hope this book helps when you want to research, acquire, and license footage *from* the United States. American archives, both public and private, are unusually unrestricted when it comes to foreign use.

Disclaimer

While we have made every effort to be accurate and current in the information contained in this book, *we are not lawyers* and do not intend that anything contained in this book be construed as legal advice, which we are not qualified to give. Before entering into any kind of legal arrangement, you are advised to seek qualified legal counsel.

Sources and Notes

The interview with Orlando Bagwell appears in Bernard's "Eyes on the Rights," *Documentary* magazine (June 2005). The cast of *The New York Hat* (1912) is listed on IMDb, www.imdb.com/title/tt0002391/. The archivist quoted was a colleague of Kenn's in San Francisco. For the Getty Images information, see "Getty Announces Additional $100 Million Investment by the Getty Family and Koch Equity Development," January 31, 2019, on the PR Newswire site, at press.gettyimages.com (Getty's own press releases) and "Koch Industries unit invests $500 million in Getty Images," *Reuters*, November 26, 2018. See also the "About" page at gettyimages.com.

PART 1

ABOUT
ARCHIVAL
MATERIALS

CHAPTER 2

Still and Motion Picture Photography: A Brief History

As noted in the introduction, "archival" visuals can refer to a broad range of items, including artwork, maps, newspapers, print documents, artifacts, and more. This chapter and the next focus more closely on the changing technologies behind the creation of today's audiovisual heritage—photographic images and sound. We look at what the technology was meant to achieve; how the results were used by people at that time; and how further innovation has continued to affect how people capture, share, and preserve the sights and sounds of the world around them.

Still Photography

As a component of recorded history, still photography is a fairly recent invention. But non-photographic visual representation of events has long existed, including paintings and sculptures. One of the key elements missing with these "visuals," however, was the ability to produce multiple copies of the same image. For that reason, the emergence of still photography might be described as having some roots in *lithography*, a printing process that emerged in the 1790s and was increasingly refined in the first decades of the 19th century. By then, *engraving* had been around for about 350 years. Engraving involves carving a pattern into wood or metal, which is then inked and pressed to paper. Lithography was different, because it offered a way for artists, technical illustrators, travel writers, mapmakers, music publishers, and others to *draw* visuals, rather than carve them. As explained on the website of the Metropolitan Museum of Art in New York (see end notes), the process involves using an oil-based crayon or ink to draw on a flat stone, such as limestone, or on a prepared metal plate. The drawn areas hold ink, allowing the image to be transferred to paper. Lithographs are often a visually compelling and useful record of 19th century life, used in newspapers and magazines throughout that era. But to French inventor Nicéphore Niépce, they weren't enough.

Heliography: The First Photograph

Born in 1765, Niépce was reportedly captivated not only by the possibilities of lithography but also by the *camera obscura*. The device is based on an ancient understanding that light traveling from a source through a small hole into a darkened space, such as a box or room, will project an inverted image of the source onto the opposite side or wall. The image can then be righted using mirrors. With a chemically treated plate, would it be possible to capture, or *fix*, the projected image? In 1827, after a decade of experimentation and frustration, Niépce created a heliograph (literally, "sun drawing"). The original is in the collection of the Harry Ransom Center at the University of Texas, which describes its production:

> To make the heliograph, Niépce dissolved light-sensitive bitumen in oil of lavender and applied a thin coating over a polished pewter plate. He inserted the plate into a *camera obscura* and positioned it near a window in his second-story workroom. After several days of exposure to sunlight, the plate yielded an impression of the courtyard, outbuildings, and trees outside. Writing about his process in December 1827, Niépce acknowledged that it required further improvements, but was nevertheless "the first uncertain step in a completely new direction."

Daguerreotypes

While Niépce's accomplishment is significant, it was Louis-Jacques-Mandé Daguerre who created the first practicable photographic technology, changing the chemical process in order to significantly reduce exposure time. Around 1839, he invented the *daguerreotype*, a means to fix highly detailed, one-of-a-kind photographic images onto copper

18

plates. "Within a few years, daguerreotype studios appeared in United States cities [and in Europe] and the popularity of the medium grew through the 1850s," notes the U.S. Library of Congress, which holds a number of daguerreotypes in its collection. Over time, the process grew more refined, and exposure times continued to shorten. In some cases, daguerreotypes were shot outdoors.

Ambrotypes and Tintypes

Available since 1851, *ambrotypes* (also known as *collodion positives*) used chemically treated glass plates, rather than metal ones. The exposure time was far quicker, and the cost to produce them cheaper. Over the following decade, the technology was improved to allow for contact prints to be made on paper from these glass negatives. This was the technology used by Matthew Brady and the photographers who worked for him during the American Civil War.

Tintypes were developed a couple of years after the ambrotype, based on similar technology. These aren't actually images printed on tin, but

Unidentified soldier in Confederate uniform with shotgun sitting next to a dog; hand-colored ambrotype. U.S. Library of Congress.

on thin sheets of iron. They were inexpensive and quick to make, and became popular for mid-19th century portraiture. If you have a photo album handed down in the family, there may be tintypes in it.

Matthew Brady

American photographer Matthew Brady opened his first studio on Broadway in New York City in 1844, where he created daguerreotype portraits. He adopted new technologies as they emerged, and soon his business grew to include a gallery in Washington, D.C. In 1861, with permission from U.S. President Abraham Lincoln, he set out to photograph the Civil War. And so, as historian Ted Widmer noted in *The New York Times*, "a remarkable effort began that would ultimately exhaust all of Brady's resources, leave him bankrupt and result in one of the most important photographic archives in history." Over the next four years, teams of photographers—some working directly for Brady, and some whose work was later acquired by him—traveled with cumbersome cameras and processing equipment to document the war.

The Metropolitan Museum in New York, which holds some of these plates in its collection, describes the process of making the images:

Matthew Brady's photo outfit, Petersburg, Va. (ca. 1864). U.S. Library of Congress.

When the photographer was ready for action, a sheet of glass was cleaned, coated with collodion, partially dried, dipped carefully into a bath containing nitrate of silver, then exposed in the camera for several seconds and processed in the field darkroom tent—all before the silver collodion mixture had dried. Given the danger of their situation and the technical difficulty of their task, front-line photographers rarely if ever attempted action scenes.

The resulting archive is vast. As Widmer notes, "Brady did not capture all of it—only one photograph of a battle scene survives. But thanks to his team, we have a remarkable trove of tens of thousands of images, only a tiny percentage of which have been published." Brady spent a fortune to create the archive. "Creditors claimed some of the archive, but in 1875 the U.S. government bought most of it," Widmer adds. That collection is now in the U.S. National Archives.

Celluloid

The challenges of working with heavy glass plates led inventors to search for a different medium on which to capture a photographic image. In 1888, American inventor George Eastman, working with undergraduate chemistry student Henry Reichenbach, began to experiment with *celluloid*. Merriam-Webster defines celluloid as "a tough flammable thermoplastic composed essentially of cellulose nitrate and camphor." As a photographic medium, it worked. In 1889, the Eastman Company brought its "flexible transparent film" to market. It could be wound onto reels, making possible the development of motion picture film as well as roll film for still photography.

Starting in the early decades of the 20th century, Eastman Kodak's celluloid film products were available in sheets (most often 4" × 5" or 8" × 10", but also larger and smaller sizes) as well as in rolls of film in a format known as *620 film* (similar to the 120 film still used today). All of these film stocks were capable of rendering a black-and-white, or *monochrome* image.

Sheet film was used by professional press photographers, working with cameras such as the *Speed Graphic* (a somewhat bulky hand-held camera with a bellows) or with *view cameras*, which were even bigger and bulkier, necessitating a tripod. Professionals also used view cameras for studio portrait and still life work, and on location for landscape and architectural photography. Each exposure was a cumbersome process, involving inserting a *film holder* into the back of the camera, removing a *dark slide*, and shooting one sheet at a time. If a photographer was traveling, the weight and space required for film holders could be substantial, depending on the size of the sheets, although they were a vast improvement over the glass plates.

The so-called "medium format" roll films, such as 620 and (later) 120, on the other hand, were a big hit with consumers in the early part of the century, along with a variety of simple and relatively inexpensive cameras, such as Kodak's Brownie series of *box cameras*, introduced in 1900. Refined over the next several decades, these small cameras (which didn't require a tripod) had only a few controls for exposure and focus; they relied on approximate settings as being "close enough," in order to make them consumer-friendly. Instead of yielding a very detailed image on 4" × 5" or 8" × 10" sheets, the roll film yielded a negative of approximately 2.25" × 2.25" square (or, with some cameras, a 2.25" × 3.25" rectangular negative). While smaller, these negatives were still capable of rendering high-quality prints at a reasonable size of enlargement. Serious hobbyists, and sometimes fine art photographers, also used these rolls, shooting with a more professional *twin-lens reflex* camera. These were lighter and smaller, and photographers could take multiple exposures with them simply by rotating a dial or winder on the camera after taking an exposure—the next film frame would then be queued up and ready for exposure. Usually, a dozen exposures could be made before needing to change rolls. Professionals and hobbyists would process the film in a home darkroom, while amateurs would send their film to a lab for processing.

Color

In 1907, French brothers Auguste and Louis Lumière introduced the first publicly displayed still color images, called *autochromes*. They weren't the first to bring color to photography, however. In 1908, the Nobel Prize in Physics was awarded to French inventor Gabriel Lippmann "for his method of reproducing colours photographically based on the phenomenon of interference;" a breakthrough he'd made in the 1890s.

The ability to shoot color photographs didn't generally reach consumers until the 1930s, when Kodak began selling Kodachrome and, later, Kodacolor film stock in various sheet and roll film formats. Kodachrome film, when processed, resulted in a transparent "direct-positive" image—known as a *diapositive, transparency* or, colloquially in consumer formats, a *slide*. Slides were mounted individually, in glass, metal, or cardboard, so that they could be inserted into a projector and seen on a large screen. Kodacolor, when processed, yielded a color negative, which, like the black-and-white negative films, could then yield any number of prints.

Introduction of 35mm Still Photography

In the late 1920s, the German manufacturer Leitz developed a still camera that used a small, light-tight cartridge of celluloid, 35 millimeters (35mm) wide, the size of standard movie film but turned on its side. By the 1930s, their Leica—small cameras with excellent lenses and sophisticated controls—was revolutionizing both consumer photography and photojournalism. Kodak quickly began marketing the 35mm roll film cartridges that yielded either 24 or 36 negatives or transparencies that were just 1" × 1.5" each. Very soon, 35mm cartridge film became the standard for most new film cameras. Camera brands including Nikon, Canon, Pentax, and Minolta adopted this standard, and companies around the world, such as Agfa, Ilford, and Fuji, began manufacturing both black-and-white and color film cartridges alongside Kodak. Not coincidentally, some of the great photojournalism magazines began publication, including the enormously popular *Life* and *Look* magazines, which debuted in the United States in 1936 and 1937 respectively.

Polaroid

Today, it's worth remembering that film requires chemical processing in a darkroom to make the *latent image* on the film visible and stable. While many professionals and even hobbyists set up their own darkrooms, they generally did so to process black-and-white still images, whether on sheets or rolls. Otherwise, people sent exposed stills and movies to labs for development. During the period from the 1950s to the 1990s, however, professionals and consumers alike also enjoyed *Polaroids*, invented by Edwin Land. This technology allowed photographs to be processed within a minute of snapping the shutter. It involved a *film pack*, meaning that the film for a single exposure was packaged along with chemical developer and paper on which the exposed image would appear. The photographer took a shot and then pulled the film pack out of the camera; the film pack served as its own darkroom. After 60 seconds, the photographer peeled the print from the rest of the pack and quickly coated the image with a fixative solution provided by Polaroid.

In the early 1970s, Land marketed a new process, called SX-70 Time Zero. The camera was flat when stored; the user would unfold it, aim, and shoot. With a *whrrr*, the exposed film slid from the camera and the image slowly appeared, with no additional work needed. Polaroid images couldn't compare in quality to those from more traditional still cameras, but the immediacy was enormously popular in business as well as family settings. Neither technology could compete, however, when digital photography emerged.

The original model Polaroid SX-70 Land Camera, folded and unfolded. Photo: Kenn Rabin.

Image Transmission: Stills

For those seeking to use archival media, it can be useful to understand the transmission of images. This may be helpful in finding copies or prints of images if the originals have been lost or destroyed.

Wire Services

In the 1830s, inventors in the United Kingdom patented the first commercial electrical telegraph, a device for transmitting text over long distances by wire. Independently but simultaneously, American inventor Samuel F.B. Morse also patented an electrical telegraph, and by the 1840s he had convinced the U.S. Congress to wire the nation. The organization that became the Associated Press was formed in 1846, and by the time of the U.S. Civil War, AP reporters were using the telegraph to communicate in real time with their home newspapers. By the early 20th century, telegraph wires spanned the globe.

Until 1880, photographs could not be reproduced in newspapers. Instead, articles might be illustrated with woodcuts or engravings, sometimes rendered after a photograph. That year, the invention of the *halftone process* enabled photographs to be converted into thousands of dots of varying sizes for reproduction in newspapers. In 1921, for the first time, halftone images could be transmitted via telegraph, and in 1935, the Associated Press began WirePhoto, the first wire service for photographs.

Motion Picture Photography

Early Efforts

Perhaps inevitably, the advent of still photography gave rise to the invention of motion picture photography, which exploits a phenomenon known as "persistence of vision." A series of stills (frames), when observed in rapid sequence, are perceived by the human eye and brain as being in motion. Inventors early in the 19th century created entertainment devices, such as the Zoetrope, Thaumatrope, and Fantascope, that exploited this phenomenon. Anyone who's drawn on a stack of cards to create flip animation will also recognize the phenomenon.

Eadweard Muybridge

In 1878, working in Palo Alto, California, still photographer Eadweard Muybridge used multiple cameras to photograph a horse in motion. Reportedly, he hoped to prove that a running horse might have all four legs in the air at once. Using a number of cameras placed at intervals along a track and triggered by wires, he created a series of images—including one with the horse fully off the ground.

The Edison Studio

Building in part on Muybridge's work, Thomas Edison and other inventors in his New Jersey laboratory, established in West Orange in 1876, set out to develop a single camera that might accomplish what multiple cameras were doing. They created a flexible "strip" of photosensitive celluloid with *perforations* (sprocket holes) down each side. Unlike various experimental formats being developed in Europe, Edison's strips were 35mm wide. Mechanical sprockets, catching the holes on the film, were used to guide the strip through the camera. As it passed through the gate, it would stop for a fraction of a section, and the shutter would open to expose one frame of film. The shutter would then close, the film would advance, and the process would repeat until the full strip was exposed. There was much experimentation with a suitable *frame rate* (speed), so that when played back at the same speed, the images would appear to show natural motion and not flicker. The studios' debut efforts included *Dickson Greeting* (1891), a silent camera test in which fellow inventor William K.L. Dickson tips his hat. Two years later, lab assistant Fred Ott sneezed on camera, and *The Edison Kinetoscopic Record of a Sneeze* (1894) became the earliest surviving copyrighted motion picture in the United States.

With no suitable method of projection, associates set up viewing parlors, or *arcades*, where each film was played in its own viewing box,

From *Fred Ott's Sneeze*, filmed January 7, 1894. U.S. Library of Congress.

with an eyepiece at the top. These devices were called *mutoscopes* or *kinetoscopes*, depending on the technology used. The novelty of being able to watch images move made these very popular.

Global Developments

Worldwide, other inventors were also perfecting motion picture technology. In France in the 1890s, brothers Auguste and Louis Lumière were recording and projecting the first true *vérité* motion pictures. Their early films were short "takes" of everyday life, such as workers leaving a factory, a couple feeding their baby, and trains arriving at various stations. The films of the Lumière brothers were shown in China in 1896, and by 1905 China was producing its own films—the first was a recording of a Peking opera. India, likewise, was introduced to the Lumières' work in 1896, and Russian cinema also emerged at around this time.

Projection

Initially, the *projection* of film was a novelty event, sometimes accompanied by live vaudeville-style novelty acts. As the technology of film advanced, though, so did its use as a medium for storytelling. In 1903, Edison produced *The Great Train Robbery*, a dramatic film written, directed, and filmed by Edison camera operator Edwin S. Porter. Projected at proper speed, its length is about 14 minutes. The film was shot in black-and-white, but some scenes were hand-colored. Two years later, in 1905, the first *nickelodeons* opened in the United States. These were movie theaters in which audience members each paid a nickel to sit together in a darkened theater while a film was screened, usually accompanied by piano music.

Early Content

Filmmakers today are often delighted to discover that motion picture from the 1890s onward exists from all over the world. Content includes politics, sports, and entertainment; there is footage of vaudeville and Wild West acts, prize fighters, immigration, travel footage, and more. It's

26

important to remember that these films reflect the biases of their times and makers. Stereotypes of race, gender, and class are often evident, yet when considered within a wider context (including the venues in which they were shown and the audiences with whom they were popular), they can be illuminating in ways not imagined by their original creators.

The Growth of an Entertainment Industry

Hollywood

Movies as a form of both entertainment and business grew rapidly during the first decades of the 20th century. In the United States, the film industry was initially centered in New York and, to a lesser extent, Chicago. In addition to actuality films, producers began to shoot short comedies and dramas as well as early experiments in animation. An important early studio was the American Mutoscope Company, founded in 1895 by William K.L. Dickson and partners as a principal competitor to Edison. The company would later become the American Mutoscope and Biograph Company, and in 1908, filmmaker D.W. Griffith joined its ranks. Soon after, Biograph and other companies began to film in the newly incorporated town of Hollywood, which became part of Los Angeles in 1910. By then, theatrical motion pictures had reached "feature" length—still silent, of course, but gaining in technical, visual, and storytelling quality.

In 1915, with the release of Griffith's *The Birth of a Nation*, theatrical feature films had come into their own in the United States. A three-hour silent epic that was presented in larger theaters with live orchestral accompaniment, the film is based on a stage play, *The Clansman*, adapted by Thomas Dixon from his novel of the same name. The book, play, and film were condemned then, as now, as a deeply racist misrepresentation of the post-Civil War era known as Reconstruction. The National Association for the Advancement of Colored People (NAACP), founded in 1909, was among those trying to have the film banned. But with its breakthrough dramatic film storytelling, the movie was a hit, serving an industry dominated by white leadership, talent, and storylines, and playing to often segregated audiences. Yet even in these early days, alternatives were emerging. For example, "race movies," as they were called at the time, began to be produced by and for African Americans. Among these filmmakers was Oscar Micheaux, who directed more than 40 films, including the features *Within Our Gates* and *The Symbol of the Unconquered*, both in 1920.

Worldwide, cinema too was quickly growing as a source of entertainment, propaganda, and documentary. Researchers seeking still and motion picture footage, working with experts within countries of interest, are likely to find a wide range of materials. Even in countries where social and political turmoil led to the destruction of materials, many gems remain.

Why Does Action In Old Footage Seem To Move So Quickly?

Today, the standard rate at which motion picture film is shot and projected is 24 (or in Europe, 25) frames per second (fps). Footage from the earliest years of motion pictures, however, was mostly shot at about 14–16 fps, even up through *The Birth of a Nation* (1915). Over time, the standard rate increased to about 18 fps, and remained so through the 1920s. (In fact, even 8mm home movie cameras, if they didn't record sound, ran at 18 fps as late as the 1960s.) But until the 1920s, when the use of motor-driven cameras became standard, most footage was hand-cranked through the camera at a speed approximated by the time it took for the handle to make a full rotation.

For this reason, viewing these old films today at a higher projection speed can make their motion seem accelerated. If this footage is projected at the same rate at which it was filmed, the motion looks normal, which is also how it would have appeared to audiences at the time. As discussed in Chapter 9, this "correction" can be seen in Peter Jackson's documentary *They Shall Not Grow Old* (2019), which is built on hand-cranked footage shot during World War I (1914–1918), but re-mastered and colored to appear shockingly contemporary.

As noted, the development of "talking pictures" (discussed in the next chapter) led to current frame rate standards.

20th Century Nonfiction Footage

Newsreels

Some of the early actuality films might be considered news reports, in that they presented short clips of political and sporting events and travelogues. But *newsreels*, created specifically to provide current events to the public in cinemas, were introduced in 1909 by Pathé, a company founded in France in 1896. Newsreels grew increasingly popular in Europe and the United States during World War I, and by the end of the 1920s almost every major studio in Hollywood released weekly or biweekly newsreels, such as *Paramount News*, *Universal Newsreel*, and *Fox Movietone*. Others outsourced this work: Hearst Corporation, for example, produced Metro-Goldwyn-Mayer's newsreels (called *News of the Day* and, later, *Hearst Metrotone*). RKO and, later, Warner Brothers, both released American versions of Pathé newsreels under the Pathé name. Newsreels were shown in movie theaters until about 1967, creating a substantial archival treasure trove, some of which is in the public domain.

As journalism, newsreels varied significantly in quality and authenticity. Many totaled seven or eight minutes. They included a variety of short stories on politics, natural disasters, entertainment, sports, fashion, and other topics, and were generally narrated in urgent, stentorian, or sometimes patronizing tones. While they can be a useful source of audiovisual content, the tone and often very narrow point of view of these stories merits close research and a questioning of their journalistic value. Additionally, some of what's presented as on-the-scene coverage is actually (and not always obviously) re-enactment, involving actors and film sets. One of the newsreels most noted for this technique was Time, Inc.'s *The March of Time*, exhibited monthly between 1935 and 1951 (it had previously been a radio program). Rather than rush out a handful of stories each week, *March of Time* producers covered fewer stories at greater length and in a more polished form, more akin to the Hollywood feature that would be projected after the newsreel had ended.

Some newsreels were specialized. In 1935, for example, Paramount Pictures premiered *Popular Science* (1935–1950), named after the magazine. Between 1942 and 1946, the U.S. Office of War Information created *United News* to counter propaganda from Axis countries. Also in the 1940s, producers William Alexander and Claude Barnett created *All-American News* to offer an African-American perspective to targeted audiences, primarily in black theaters and churches.

Government-Sponsored Documentary

Beginning in the late 1920s, much of the world succumbed to the Great Depression, which lasted throughout most of the 1930s. Many of the strongest nonfiction films of this era were made with government support. In the United Kingdom, filmmaker John Grierson's GPO Film Unit, which operated between 1933 and 1939 under the direction of the General Post Office, and then as the Crown Film Unit under the Ministry of Information, turned out numerous acclaimed works. These include *Coal Face*, a celebration of Welsh miners, and *Night Mail*, following the mail train that traveled from England to Scotland. Merging filmmaking and the arts, these films feature music by classical composer Benjamin Britten and a narrative written by poet W.H. Auden.

In the United States, the Resettlement Administration and the Farm Security Administration, and later, the Office of War Information oversaw a remarkable campaign to use radio, still photography, books, theater, and motion picture to document and celebrate American life and, not coincidentally, keep a significant number of artists employed. Between 1935 and 1944, still photographers Dorothea Lange, Walker Evans, Jack Delano, Russell Lee, Marion Post Wolcott, and others created about 250,000 images of the American landscape and people, of which about 164,000 are held in the American Memory Collection at the U.S. Library of Congress. Filmmaker Pare Lorenz created various films, including *The River* (1938), a poetic tribute to the Mississippi River and an argument for the work of the Tennessee Valley Authority. The script for *The River* was nominated for the Pulitzer Prize for poetry, and composer Virgil Thomson's score for the film is still played in concert halls today.

Other U.S. government initiatives, including the Works Progress Administration (WPA, later known as the Works Projects Administration), funded a range of civic projects, from the construction of libraries, schools, post offices, and other buildings to the performing arts. The WPA records are vast. At the National Archives alone, more than 94,000 still photographs, 100 films, and 400 radio broadcasts survive from the 1930s. WPA-sponsored murals decorate the walls of government offices, libraries, schools, and post offices across the country. Because they were created under the auspices of the government, much of this material is in the public domain.

Military Collections

Each branch of the U.S. military—Army, Navy, Air Force, and Marines—has its own collection of material, and in most cases, this material is in the public domain. For example, Army Signal Corps materials form Record Group 111 at the U.S. National Archives and Records Administration (NARA). The earliest military footage dates back to World War I; these military sources include still photographs, audio recordings, and oral histories. Specific information about obtaining footage from these sources can be found in Chapter 6.

Miscellaneous and Ephemeral Films

Ephemeral films is a term coined by archivist, filmmaker, and educator Rick Prelinger to describe "films made for a specific purpose at specific times, such as advertising, educational and industrial films"—although as he notes in Chapter 5, he would now describe them as "useful cinema." Many of the films in his collection are available

Frame grab, *Dial Comes to Town*, an AT&T/Bell Systems film on how to use a rotary phone, b/w, 20 minutes, undated. From the Prelinger Collection at Internet Archive.

online, to be viewed or downloaded free of charge, at Internet Archive (archive.org).

Many films purportedly created for educational use and distributed to schools for 16mm projection were, in fact, advertising for featured products. For example, *Molly Grows Up* (1953), an educational film about menstruation, prominently featured the Modess brand. Many of these films were also designed to teach social skills and acceptable or conformist behavior to teenagers, such as *Dating Dos and Don'ts* (1949) and *The Prom: It's a Pleasure!* (1961). Others addressed social and political issues, including racial integration in neighborhoods and the workplace; labor and productivity; and civil defense and the atomic age.

Motion Picture Film Technology

Those working with footage that pre-dates the 1970s—and in fact, most footage shot before about 1990—should understand the basic differences between *film* and *video* production. Those seeking an understanding of both processes, including both analog and digital video, are advised to get a copy of *The Filmmaker's Handbook*, written by Steven Ascher and Edward Pincus and updated and expanded over several editions by Ascher. Here, we offer a brief overview.

One key aspect of motion picture film is that, as with film-based still photography, its creation involves chemical processing. Motion picture stock cannot be exposed to light, other than through the camera lens, or it will be ruined. Footage that has been "shot" or exposed is sent to a lab (or taken into a darkroom) in sealed containers for processing, thus delaying the availability of the viewable image.

Cellulose Nitrate and Cellulose Acetate

For the first half of the 20th century, motion picture film technology was based on the use of *cellulose nitrate*, the flexible plastic base material that had been a big improvement over the use, in still photography, of glass plates. Furthermore, cellulose nitrate allowed for the development of motion pictures with an exceptional depth of grey-scale range, and, in the case of three-strip Technicolor, a richness of color. Unfortunately, cellulose nitrate was also highly chemically unstable. Before and after exposure, cellulose nitrate stock needed to be stored within a narrow range of temperature and humidity or it would break down and the *emulsion*, which held the image, would literally slide off the clear backing. Worse, cellulose nitrate film is highly combustible (one of the main reasons so many early films are lost to us), and so by 1948, industry safety requirements led to the development and adoption of an alternative: *cellulose acetate film*, commonly known as *safety film*. It was a significant improvement, but film stock (exposed and unexposed) remained vulnerable to deterioration. This is why film preservation (and where possible, transfer of decaying material to more stable formats) is a priority for groups including the American Film Institute, the U.S. Library of Congress, and others.

Independent Field Production and Cinema Vérité

In the 1950s and early 1960s, important technological changes impacted both the quality and style of independent filmmaking, both fiction and nonfiction, as well as the gathering of television news. Professional-quality 16mm cameras had proven their durability through military use during World War II, and the technology had continued to improve. The popularity of 16mm filmmaking continued as lighter-weight cameras were developed that could be carried on a person's shoulder, enabling freer movement.

A few of these cameras, such as the Auricon, could record *single-system sound* directly onto special film stock that included a thin strip of magnetic audiotape between the image and the sprockets (a *mag stripe*). But more often, a separate audiotape recorder was needed to capture sound (*double-system sound*). While magnetic tape recorders had existed for some time (see Chapter 3), a system for synchronizing the recorder and camera in the field wasn't available until the 1950s. In Germany, a system called *Pilottone* (often referred to as *cable sync*) was developed, and the technology rapidly spread to the United States and elsewhere. With this system, the camera could be connected by cable to a separate (magnetic) tape recorder, carried by a *sound person*, who also held the microphone. The cable carried a reference tone (*pilot tone*) that enabled the audio and footage to be recorded separately but synchronously. With a slate or other point of reference, these could then then be synchronized in the editing room.

The problem with cable sync was that the cameraperson and sound recordist were physically connected. This issue was resolved around 1960, with the development of *crystal sync*. Installed in each device, oscillating crystals maintained identical recording speeds for both, which freed up the movement of the film crew. In fact, several cameras that are outfitted with crystal sync can shoot simultaneously and independently, and all will synchronize correctly with the sound

Production still, *Salesman*, 1968, showing portable sync sound recording. Filming Bible salesman Paul Brennan (left) are David Maysles (recording sound on magnetic tape) and Albert Maysles (16mm camera).

that's being recorded. This allows for a variety of camera angles that can be cut together in the edit room. Look at the concert films of the 1960s and 1970s, such as *Gimme Shelter* and *Woodstock*, to see the results of this major shift.

Portable 16mm technology, both before and especially after the development of crystal sync, gave new energy to independent cinema. It also fueled the emergence of a form of observational filmmaking, known in Europe as *cinema vérité* and in the United States either by that name or as *direct cinema*. One of the first U.S. films to use the crystal sync technology was Robert Drew's landmark documentary, *Primary* (1960), which followed Democratic candidates John F. Kennedy and Hubert Humphrey during the 1960 Wisconsin presidential primary. Other notable examples include *Dont Look Back* (1967), directed by D.A. Pennebaker, and *Salesman* (1968), directed by Albert Maysles, David Maysles, and Charlotte Zwerin.

Advances in Film Technologies Other than 16mm

By the 1960s and 1970s, Super 8 replaced the old "standard 8" in popularity for consumers wanting to shoot home movies, because of its enhanced frame size and sharper image. Adding to Super 8's popularity as a consumer product, starting in 1965 the film was sold pre-loaded into easy-to-use cartridges. By 1973, it was also possible to record Super 8 sound with images on stock that used a mag stripe, like the ones available on 16mm film. *Super 16* became popular with independent filmmakers whose budgets required that they shoot in 16mm, but who wanted to be able to create high quality 35mm "blowup" prints for theatrical screening.

Image Transmission: Motion Photography

The lineage of television dates back to 1909 or earlier, but the technology didn't become practicable until the 1920s, when American inventor Philo T. Farnsworth developed a way to scan and transmit images electronically, rather than mechanically. After some further development, these images could then be received and reassembled on a screen. By 1938, the first television sets were being sold to consumers, albeit in very limited numbers, not least because there was almost nothing being broadcast. In a feat of promotion, on April 30, 1939, RCA carried a live broadcast of U.S. President Franklin Delano Roosevelt speaking at the opening day of the 1939 World's Fair in New York City. A few weeks later, on May 17, NBC brought baseball to television, carrying the Princeton University team as they played a double-header against Columbia University in New York. (Princeton won both games.)

As the United States entered World War II in December 1941, there were just two broadcast networks: NBC and the Columbia Broadcasting System (CBS, expanding from its earlier radio broadcasting interest). Two more followed: the American Broadcasting Company (ABC) was established in 1943 and began television operations in 1948. The DuMont Television Network operated from 1946–1956. There would not be another fourth network until 30 years later, with the launch of the Fox Broadcasting Company in 1986.

The production of television sets for a consumer market was delayed by World War II, but by the late 1950s, television ownership in much of the industrialized world was becoming commonplace. Programming was needed to fill expanding hours of broadcast time. At first, some of television's content migrated in from cinemas. In the aftermath of the war, for example, newsreels such as *Movietone News* and, for a time, *All-American News* found a secondary home on the airwaves. Programs such as *NBC Saturday Night at the Movies* and *The Late Show* broadcast theatrical films in local and national markets. By 1949, NBC was creating its own 15-minute news program every night, named for its tobacco company sponsor: *The Camel Caravan of News*. "Game shows" (also known as "quiz shows") also migrated from radio, and sporting events dotted the schedule.

In the early days, when television was broadcast directly from a studio, the signal was sent out live, so that in many cases, no recording remains. (This is also true of some early radio.) Programming that has survived was preserved in its time on *kinescopes*. These were created by using a motion picture camera to *film* what was on the television monitor. This method of preservation was in use in the 1940s and 1950s, because prior to the practical availability of videotape, it was the only way to save programming. While kinescopes are not high-quality, they are precious because they are the only record of many early live television broadcasts, including shows from the so-called "golden age" of television in the 1950s.

By 1960, according to Reuters, 90 percent of U.S. households owned a television set, compared to just nine percent a decade earlier. In the interim, CBS reporter Edward R. Murrow, who had begun his career in radio (his radio news series, *Hear It Now*, became the television series *See It Now*), was among those exploring the power of this new medium. His March 1954 "A Special Report on Senator Joseph McCarthy," offered an evidence-based condemnation of the senator's scaremongering and

35

unwarranted attacks on Americans, helping to sway public opinion against the senator.

Beginning in the 1950s and running through the 1970s, the networks created full-length stand-alone documentaries and news series, such as *See It Now*'s successor, *CBS Reports*, NBC's *White Paper*, which aired from 1960 to 1980, and *ABC Close-Up!*, which premiered in 1960. These long-form series (shot and edited on film and then aired on television) provided in-depth coverage of issues and individuals, and they've proven to be a boon to scholars and filmmakers in the decades since. Initially, they were filmed in black-and-white, but as color television sets became increasingly popular in the mid-1960s, the networks began to use color film. By around 1980, many had also begun to move to video.

In the meantime, as part of his Great Society initiatives and in an effort to support the development of non-commercial television and radio, U.S. president Lyndon B. Johnson signed the Public Broadcasting Act of 1967. The act created The Corporation for Public Broadcasting (CPB), a non-profit funded by the federal government to support National Public Radio (NPR) and the Public Broadcasting Service (PBS), both launched in 1970. PBS is not a network, but rather a consortium of member stations. Programming is produced by member stations, independent producers, and producing organizations worldwide, whether through origination or acquisition, and then presented to the network—a bottom-up rather than a top-down model. In the years before the emergence of commercial cable (and now, streaming media), PBS was where viewers could turn for programming on gardening, cooking, the arts, science, public affairs, long-form documentaries, drama and comedy, educational children's programming, and more.

Video Technology

According to Merriam-Webster, "video" as an adjective ("relating to, or used in the transmission or reception of the television image") was first used in 1934. As a noun, "a recording of a motion picture or television program for playing through a television set," it was first used in 1935. Today, people often use "video" to describe *all* moving image. But in terms of technology, video is very different from film and was developed much later. Unlike film, which captures images photochemically, video captures images and sounds electronically. With *analog* video, that capture is onto magnetic tape. With *digital* video, the capture is the 0s and 1s of computer technology, which may also be recorded on tape, or, increasingly, stored as a digital file on a memory chip or hard drive.

Analog Video

In the 1950s, overlapping the era of kinescopes and continuing, in some cases, to the present, television studios used magnetic videotape to record studio programming. The basic technology involves the use of magnetic reel-to-reel tape, similar to but more complex than the use of magnetic tape solely to record audio. At first, broadcast videotapes were big, heavy reels, generally 2″ in width, called Quad videotape. The tape stock proved to be relatively unstable, unfortunately. Although Quad tapes that were stored under good conditions can look good, if preservation is important they should be dubbed to another, more modern format. Additionally, because video technology and formats evolved so quickly, machines capable of playing back older formats have become much harder to find and maintain. Quad tape was replaced by the more stable reel-to-reel 1″ Type C videotape during the second half of the 1970s, and most television shows from this era and later were mastered on Type C.

Portable Video Technology

In 1967, Sony introduced a portable video recorder and camera combination called the Portapak. It was battery powered and relatively lightweight. The system was really two main pieces: a camera (that could only shoot black-and-white) with an attached microphone, and a tape deck that, in the Portapak's first iteration, held 1/2″ reel-to-reel videotape. It wasn't cheap; the listed price in 1970 was $1,495. Still, the new technology gave rise to what was dubbed *guerilla video*, a new-technology take on *vérité* production—not least because a single person could record camera and sound simultaneously. The image quality was far inferior to that of 16mm film, which many independents still used, and the built-in microphone (or microphones attached with cable) did not offer the sound quality of a professional recorder. But video had some notable advantages. Because it was shot on magnetic tape, no processing was needed, so sound and picture could be played back right away, in sync. Once the Portapak was bought, the cost of tapes was minimal and the tapes reusable. Video collectives emerged to create documentaries and/or *video art* with this new technology, and within a short period of time video makers began to receive mainstream recognition. However, unlike the physical process of editing together pieces of film, videotape, with its electronic signal, was difficult to edit, and often involved copying (dubbing) a repeated number of times, resulting in a loss in quality each time.

Video and News Gathering

As video technology continued to evolve, *professional* portable video recording became possible, with Portapaks using 3/4″ color U-matic video cassettes. Television news directors attracted to video's immediacy could now use it to create, what was at the time, broadcast-quality color images with no need to wait for film processing. Electronic news gathering, or ENG, was hyped to the public by the television news media beginning around 1974. Local stations' news units moved to video as they could afford to, between the mid- and late 1970s. This changeover also coincided with the general movement of commercial networks away from in-depth coverage of news and current events in documentary form. In the United States, public television became, for a time, the primary source of long-form coverage, while commercial networks shifted their focus to news and entertainment "magazines," following the lead of *60 Minutes*, launched by CBS News in 1968.

Those researching changes in television content of this time, or relying on television news, will also notice a significant shift in how stories are covered. Network news reports from the 1950s and 1960s, shot on film, tended to cover stories visually as well as verbally, meaning that scenes and even sequences could be edited together, movie-style. As long-form documentary work migrated to PBS (and independent filmmaking), and as networks began to shoot on video, an era of sound bites and cutaways shortened stories and tended to reduce the quality of visual storytelling, at least at the networks.

Commercial Cable

Analog television technology depends on the transmission of radio waves, or signals, through the atmosphere, where they are picked up by customers' individual receivers. But even the growing use of satellites to aid in the transmission of analog signals didn't solve a basic problem with the technology: a weak signal meant poor reception. Commercial cable in the United States emerged, in part, to bring analog television signals into homes located in remote or geographically difficult areas, such as mountainous regions. A central antenna was placed where it could receive a strong signal, and from there cables carried the content into homes. With the advent of satellite technology (and regulatory changes), the path was cleared for the launch in 1972 of Home Box Office (HBO). In 1976, the Turner Broadcasting System (TBS) was started, followed in 1980 by the Cable News Network (CNN). The cable industry grew rapidly, providing new platforms for distribution and new sources of news and entertainment programming. At the same time, ownership of many of these diverse platforms became increasingly centralized. In 1983, according to the website for *Democracy on Deadline*, "50 corporations controlled most of the American media, including magazines, books, music, news feeds, newspapers, movies, radio and television. By 1992 that number had dropped by half. By 2000, six corporations had ownership of most of the media."

Digital Video

Digital video emerged in the 1980s as a higher-quality alternative to analog video. Steven Ascher explains digital recording in *The Filmmaker's Handbook, 4th edition*:

> The video or audio signal is represented by a set of numbers, which are recorded as simple on-off pulses. Digital information is very 'robust'—it is not susceptible to tape noise and you can make many generations of copies without any loss in quality (digital copies are called *clones*). Because digital data is what computers use, once a video or audio signal is in digital form, a whole new world of possibilities is opened up for storing, editing, and manipulating sounds or images.

Digital technology rapidly changed the production and transmission of audiovisual media. By the summer of 2009, all major broadcasters in the United States were required by Congress to switch to digital transmission. Once this conversion was complete, the way was clear for stations to begin sending more information in the same bandwidth, which in turn allowed for both production and display of higher definition picture and multi-channel sound. A decade later, in 2019, feature films with relatively high technical quality are being shot on hand-held smart phones, streaming media threatens to bypass the networks altogether, and digital sounds and images circle the globe at unimaginable speed.

Just 50 years earlier, in the summer of 1969, the world watched and listened, live, as humans first stepped out onto the moon. Images of that unique historic event were beamed to Earth via satellite, over a distance of 238,000 miles. By today's standards, the transmission was terrible: black-and-white video images that were often jittery or blurry, and audio that was distorted and interrupted by static. Still, the idea that in real time we could see and hear Neil Armstrong as he stepped off the lunar module was then almost unimaginable. In 2019, audiovisual media—past and present—still holds that tremendous power.

Sources and Notes

For more about the process of lithography, including video demonstrations, see www.metmuseum.org/about-the-met/curatorial-departments/drawings-and-prints/materials-and-techniques/printmaking/lithograph. Information about Niépce's heliograph can be found at www.hrc.utexas.edu/niepce-heliograph/. There is also interesting research on it from the Getty Conservation Institute, www.getty.edu/conservation/our_projects/science/photocon/photocon_component3.html. Additional information about daguerreotypes can be found on the website of the Library of Congress, www.loc.gov/teachers/classroommaterials/connections/daguerreotype/history.html. Non-studio exterior images can be found at www.loc.gov/pictures/item/2004664596/. Discussion of the Brady photographs comes in part from Ted Widmer's "The All-Seeing Eyes," *The New York Times* (July 25, 2011). Civil War photographs can be found at the Library of Congress's American Memory website, http://memory.loc.gov. For more about autochromes, see https://blog.scienceandmediamuseum.org.uk/autochromes-the-dawn-of-colour-photography/. Getty has published a pamphlet about the halftone process, www.getty.edu/conservation/publications_resources/pdf_publications/pdf/atlas_halftone.pdf. The Thomas Edison National Historical Park is in New Jersey, www.nps.gov/edis/index.htm. Information about the Edison company and examples of films, including *Dickson Greeting*, can be found at the Library of Congress, www.loc.gov/collections/edison-company-motion-pictures-and-sound-recordings/articles-and-essays/history-of-edison-motion-pictures/. Information on the American Mutoscope and Biograph Company from Paul C. Spehr, "Filmmaking at the American Mutoscope and Biograph Company, 1900–1906," in *The Quarterly Journal of the Library of Congress* (vol. 37, no. 3/4, Summer/Fall, 1980). A five-disk collection of restored early films by African-American filmmakers is available from Kino Lorber, in collaboration with a handful of organizations. Two of the best books about American newsreels are by Raymond Fielding, *The American Newsreel 1911–1967, 2nd edition* (McFarland & Company, 2011), and *The March of Time 1935–1951* (Oxford University Press, 1978). For a definitive guide to film and video production, see Steven Ascher and Edward Pincus, *The Filmmaker's Handbook, 5th edition* (Penguin Random House, 2019). Information about CPB funding can be found at www.cpb.org/funding.

An example of a film shot in "three-strip Technicolor" is MGM's 1939 *The Wizard of Oz*. For a list of film preservation groups, see www.loc. gov/programs/national-film-preservation-board/resources/film-preserva tion-and-cultural-organizations/. For more on the Dumont Network, see David Weinstein, *The Forgotten Network* (Temple University Press, 2006). Statistics on television ownership are from the Library of Congress's Moving Image Section.

CHAPTER 3

Recorded Sound: A Brief History

The first surviving recording of sound was made in 1860 by French inventor Édouard-Léon Scott de Martinville. For several years, he'd been toying with an idea: if a camera used the basic technology of the human eye to capture and preserve images, why not a machine that could emulate the human ear, to capture and preserve sound? Scott did not anticipate or intend audio playback. Instead, the machine was meant as a form of transcription device, one that would make visible, and "read-able," the soundwaves of human speech. To achieve this, he invented a device he called the *phonautograph*. As described by Alec Wilkinson in *The New Yorker*, Scott

> fastened a sheet of paper around the cylinder, then blackened the paper in the smoke of a burning lamp. Pressed to the cylinder was a stylus made from pig's bristle. The stylus was connected to a diaphragm stretched across a narrow opening at the bottom of a small barrel. Turning the cylinder with the handle, Scott stood at the open end of the barrel and talked or sang.

In 2008, according to news reports, one of Scott's *phonautographs* (created on April 9, 1860) was discovered in a Paris archive and brought to the attention of physicist Carl Haber at the Lawrence Berkeley Laboratory in California. An expert in early audio (among other things), Haber and colleagues reverse-engineered the process, extracting sound from the patterns Scott had made 148 years earlier. In the recording, someone, presumably Scott, is singing "Au Clair De la Lune."

Thomas Edison's Phonograph

Nearly two decades after Scott recorded into his *phonautograph*, inventor Thomas Edison created a machine that could not only record but also play back sound. Edison brought his "talking phonograph" to *Scientific American* in 1877, which reported:

> Mr. Thomas A. Edison recently came into this office, placed a little machine on our desk, turned a crank, and the machine inquired as to our health, asked how we liked the phonograph, informed us that it was very well, and bid us a cordial good night. These remarks were not only perfectly audible to ourselves, but to a dozen or more persons gathered around, and they were produced by the aid of no other mechanism than the simple little contrivance explained and illustrated below.

44

Thomas Edison with phonograph, ca. 1878. U.S. Library of Congress.

As Edison demonstrated, a person would speak into a horn. The resulting sound waves would affect air pressure, causing an attached diaphragm to vibrate. In turn, the vibrations would move a stylus (a sort of needle), which would make correspondingly shallow or deep indentations on tin foil (depending on the air pressure) as the cylinder rotated. "These indentations are necessarily an exact record of the sounds which produced them," *Scientific American* reported. The journal cited work conducted two years earlier, in 1875, by Alexander Graham Bell and Tom Watson, in which sound vibrations were transmitted between two receivers, leading to the telephone. Edison's device reversed the process, so that the sound waves encoded in the recording medium (tin foil) could be retraced through the stylus, resulting in vibrations that were translated to sound waves and amplified for listeners. In Edison's earliest surviving recording, from 1878, he can be heard reciting "Mary Had a Little Lamb."

The Early Recording Industry

Tin foil soon gave way to various formulations of wax as a recording medium, and a range of inventors continued to improve cylinder recording technology while also developing disk recording technology. Content of recordings runs the gamut from classical music (such as Enrico Caruso singing opera, recorded in 1902), to jazz (the Original Dixieland Jass Band, recorded in 1917), to recorded sermons and eventually, radio broadcasts. Anthropologists, ethnographers, and musicologists brought this bulky technology into the field to document not only music but also speech, wildlife, and more, often working in rural areas in search of natural and cultural artifacts that were deemed to be at risk in an age of rapid urbanization and industrialization. Some of this field work, especially initially, was for research purposes only; the recordings would be transcribed for print publication, rather than disseminated as sound. But as technology advanced, audio itself began to be archived. Soon, a commercial market developed for recordings that could be played at home.

The Early Music Industry
Prior to World War I, the music industry was built around the publication and distribution of *sheet music*—musical scores on paper—in part to satisfy demand created by the availability of relatively affordable, factory-produced pianos. But by the end of the war, in 1918, musical *recordings* had begun to supplant sheet music as the

most popular means of music distribution. In the form of 10- and 12-inch disks, these recordings spun at 78 *revolutions per minute* (rpm) and were played on hand-wound turntables. Over time, as electricity was brought to growing numbers of homes, turntables operated mechanically.

Acoustical vs. Electrical Recording

The "acoustical era" ran from the 1890s to 1925, according to the Library of Congress's "National Jukebox" site. What that means is that "all sound recordings were made by mechanical means without the use of microphones or electrical amplification." Groups of performers would cluster in front of large recording horns, and "mixing" was done primarily by positioning people at varied distances from the horn. This set-up, and the technology itself, limited the acoustical range of what could be recorded. In the mid-1920s, electronic microphones and amplifiers began to be used in recording studios. These converted *acoustical energy* (sound waves) into *electrical energy* (audio signals) and back again.

Vinyl

In the 1940s, record companies began to use polyvinyl chloride—or simply, "vinyl"—as the medium for duplicating records. With vinyl came other changes, including Columbia Records' introduction, in 1948, of long-playing records (*LPs*), which were 12 inches in diameter and played at a slower rate of 33–1/3 rpm, so that more playing time could fit on the disk. A year later, RCA Victor introduced a seven-inch vinyl *single*, which played at 45 rpm. Both became industry standards, replaced only in the late 1980s with the introduction of the digitally based compact disc (CD) and eventually, digitized streaming audio.

Home Recording

Home recording devices capable of "cutting" a record were available but expensive in the early part of the 20th century. Instead, people enjoyed public recording booths, usually found in arcades. Inside the booth, with the curtain drawn, the user would insert a coin, speak into a microphone, and a seven-inch disk of their voice would be immediately produced, along with a paper sleeve to protect the recording. For many people, from the 1920s through the 1940s (and continuing to some degree to the 1960s), this was the only way they could actually record their own voice. But another technology, under development since the turn of the century, was emerging.

In the late 19th century, Danish inventor Valdemar Poulsen began investigating the possibility of using magnetism to record sound onto wires. In 1898, he built a wire recorder, the *telegraphone*, and in 1900 he proved its effectiveness by recording the voice of Emperor Franz Joseph of Austria at the World Exposition in Paris. (According to the website of the Lemelson-MIT Program, this device made today's voicemail possible.) By the 1920s, other inventors had replaced wire technology with magnetically-coated ribbon (magnetic *tape*), although wire recording continued through World War II. As seen in the previous chapter, magnetic recording provided the basis for analog audio and video technology. Audio tape remained popular in various forms through the second half of the 20th century, including reel-to-reel tapes (which were used both in professional recording studios and at home), 8-track tapes (for playing back music that had been commercially released), and finally audiocassette tapes.

Motion Picture Sound Technology

When evaluating archival footage that has an accompanying audio track, it's important to consider the two as separate components. Sound and images, even when they seem aligned, may not be authentically paired; instead, the pairing may be constructed. There are a number of ways in which sound and motion picture footage are combined.

- *Synchronized* sound: This is sometimes referred to as *natural* or *diegetic* sound. When you use your smart phone to shoot something, you capture the sound at the same time. It's the audio that was actually being made, both within and beyond the frame of what you're filming. If you're filming with a system that records picture and sound separately (for example, shooting 16mm film and recording audio on magnetic tape), synchronized sound can also be achieved by aligning the separately recorded tracks.
- The *illusion* of sync: If a film is shot silently (or *MOS*), or if a combination of camera footage is used, filmmakers may align non-sync sound and footage in short enough segments that sync is approximated.
- *Enhanced* sound: This can mean a couple of things. In some cases, as above, audio that might have accompanied visuals is absent or needs to be "sweetened" to be heard better, such as with the addition of sound effects. But it can also mean *non-diegetic* sound,

which is audio not directly tied to visuals but added for reasons such as emotional resonance or informational value. Films may have many layers of non-diegetic sound, such as narration or voiceover commentary, added sound effects, and music.

- *Ambience* or *room tone*: This is a recording made of a location as it naturally sounds, without dialogue or additional sound effects, music, or extraneous noise. Motion picture sound recordists may record street noises, the sound of the ventilation system in a room, or the natural sounds of a forest, for example, for a variety of uses, including as a *bed*—sound that is mixed underneath dialogue, music, added sound effects, or other tracks to establish a sense of place and to smooth over other sound edits.

When fact checking archival materials, consider the sound carefully, especially if the soundtrack you are working with is not the *raw* track (the audio that was picked up by microphones simultaneous with shooting), but the track that was produced through the course of editing and sound mixing. You may be hearing sounds that don't correspond with the picture and that might, in some cases, misrepresent the scope, import, or tone of the event portrayed on screen.

Dickson Experimental Sound Film (1894)

At Internet Archive, you can find a short clip, "The Dickson Experimental Sound Film," dating from about 1894 or 1895, in which a man plays a violin into a large receiver while two men dance. The sound appears to be *synchronous*. We see the bow against the violin and hear the notes at the same time, just as if we were present during the actual recording. But this is not the case. In the 1890s, there was no way to record audio and film at the same rate of speed. In 2000, the U.S. Library of Congress asked noted film and sound editor Walter Murch if he could synchronize them. "The soundtrack ... had lain in a bin of broken Edison cylinders," Murch wrote in a discussion thread of the Cinema Audio Society. Somehow, someone had realized that this particular cylinder, with about two minutes of audio, was connected to the 17-second fragment of film. The problem, Murch notes, "was the film was shot at 40 fps, not 24, and the sound was running wild on a cracked 1890s cylinder." Working with a VHS tape of the footage and a cassette of the audio, he got to work. The synchronization "was easy enough given the time-stretching and compressing powers of the Avid," Murch wrote, referring to his computer-based digital editing system. "Sean Cullen, my assistant, digitally crunched the film to 30 fps (video) and I then

48

found various possible synch points and adjusted the length of the track accordingly." Much also noted that if you listen carefully, before the film begins you can hear someone say "The rest of you fellows ready? Go ahead!"

Talkies

Some early films did add orchestral sounds. Between 1902 and 1906, for example, French director Alice Guy directed over 100 *phonoscènes*. These are short films created on the *chronophone*, a synchronized sound system invented in 1902 by her mentor, Léon Gaumont, according to her biographer, Alison McMahan. A surprising number of these films, by Guy and others, can now be found on YouTube. (In 1907, Alice Guy-Blaché left Paris with her new husband, Herbert Blaché, to continue as a pioneering filmmaker in the United States.)

Alice Guy (center frame) directing a *phonoscène* (ca. 1906, Gaumont). Note the two audio horns to her right, and above, an exterior backdrop. Image courtesy Anthony Slide.

50   Closer look at same image of Alice Guy directing; the record says they're filming the opening ballet of *Romeo and Juliet*. Image courtesy Anthony Slide.

Vitaphone and Movietone

Even with these advances in film audio, the equipment to show films with accompanying sound was expensive and the results remained unsatisfactory. Until the late 1920s, theater owners continued to hire musicians to accompany the silent films that played on their screens. Scene-setting and dialogue were handled with onscreen title cards called *intertitles*, and actors pantomimed emotions they could not express in words. But by the mid-1920s, engineers from the Bell Telephone Laboratories and Western Electric in the United States had developed a system that would become known as the *Vitaphone* process.

The system used a recording disk that was 16 inches in diameter and rotated at 33–1/3 rpm (the standard at the time in the phonograph industry was still 78 rpm). This meant that audio could play long enough to accompany one reel (about 1,000 feet) of 35mm motion picture, projected at 24 frames per second—a running time of about 11 minutes. In 1926, Warner Brothers used the Vitaphone system to add a symphonic score and some limited synchronized sound effects to *Don Juan*, a feature film starring John Barrymore (Drew's grandfather). Preceding this film, moreover, was a selection of short films (under 10 minutes) promoting the Vitaphone system. These included a four-minute introduction by Will Hays, the first chairperson of the Motion Picture Producers and Distributors of America, and musical performances including *La Fiesta*, featuring singer Anna Case and the Metropolitan Opera Chorus. Clips from these short films can be seen in Warner Brothers' 1946 documentary short, "Okay for Sound."

Warner Brothers and the Vitaphone Corporation followed the success of these shorts with *The Jazz Singer* (1927), an 89-minute, black-and-white film. As with the shorter sound films, the primary use of the audio track is music, and like most silent films of its era, much of the dialogue is handled with intertitles. Al Jolson, a popular Lithuanian-born performer of the 1920s "jazz age," plays Jackie, a Jewish singer who performs against his religious father's wishes. When he sings, and later when he speaks, the sound is synchronized. While *The Jazz Singer* is often credited as the first talking picture, the first *all*-talking picture came a year later, with the gangster drama, *Lights of New York*, directed by Brian Foy.

Optical Sound on Film

Synchronized disks weren't the only technology used for "talking pictures." The idea for an *optical track* was in development in Germany as early as 1918. The technology would allow audio waves to be recorded directly onto film as pulses of light. This idea was advanced by American inventor Lee de Forest, an early pioneer of radio. In 1922, he opened a company in New York City to create short sound films, using a system he called *Phonofilm*. At the Internet Archive, viewers can hear and see short films such as *A Few Moments with Eddie Cantor* (1923) and *President Coolidge, Taken on the White House Ground* (1924). For various reasons, the technology didn't catch on with the major studios, and the company was out of business by the end of the 1920s.

In the meantime, another company—the William Fox Corporation, a forerunner of 20th Century Fox—introduced its own system, *Movietone*, with the 1927 release of *Sunrise*, directed by F.W. Murnau. The film itself was silent, but its music track was fully synchronized through the use of technology almost identical to the Phonofilm, involving an optical representation of the sound that was printed alongside image frames, from which the sound could be decoded—akin to the squiggly lines seen on film prints still in use today.

In 1929, the Western Electric Company debuted a short film, *Finding His Voice: An Animated Cartoon Synchronized to Voice & Sound*. Directed by F. Lyle Goldman and Max Fleischer, the 11-minute film demonstrated Western Electric's own system, which used essentially the same technology as both Movietone and the Phonofilm used. Today, multi-track digital sound continues to be optically reproduced on motion picture projection prints, using enhancements to this original technology.

Synchronous Field Recording

The technology for recording synchronous sound in studio settings improved rapidly after the 1920s, but there were still limits on what could be achieved in the field. Many of the government films of the 1930s and 1940s, for example, created in the United States, Canada, and elsewhere, relied on diverse audio tracks that included music, sound effects, voiceover, and narration, with minimal—if any—actual synchronous field recording. Classics such as *The Plow that Broke the Plains* (Pare Lorentz, 1936), *Night Mail* (Basil Wright, Harry Watt, 1936), and *London Can Take It!* (Humphrey Jennings, Harry Watt, 1940) are examples of this. In contrast, government propaganda films shot in the studio were more likely to have synchronous tracks, such as the 1944 U.S. Office of Education training film, *Supervising Women Workers*.

Crystal Sync

As noted in the previous chapter, in the late 1950s and early 1960s an important change occurred when 16mm film cameras light enough to be shoulder-mounted, coupled with *crystal sync*, allowed picture and sound to be recorded synchronously and also wirelessly—giving new freedom to filmmakers and news reporters.

The Motion Picture Soundtrack

A film's completed soundtrack is the end result of a complex process in which multiple audio components are combined. A 16mm documentary team in the 1980s, for example, might have gone into a sound mix with 16 or more checker-boarded tracks of audio—separate 16mm magnetic tracks (or *mag tracks*) that may have included music, sync sound, sound effects, room tone, narration, and interviews. Each track ran the full length of the edited picture; spaces between were filled with blank material called *filler*. These tracks were carefully blended, or mixed, to create a master audio track, which might then be converted into the negative of an optical soundtrack. This negative and the picture negative were then *married* (printed together) onto a third piece of film to create the final release print.

Nowadays, digital tracks (called *stems*) are computer files, and sound is both edited and mixed on a computer using software such as Avid's Pro Tools.

Audio Transmission: Radio

By the 1840s, American inventor Samuel Morse and others had developed the *telegraph*, a system by which electrical signals could be transmitted over long distances on land via a wired system of relay stations. The telegraph required physical lines through which the signals could pass, however, and was therefore not useful to those needing to send a message far out to sea, or between vessels at sea; that would require being able to transmit signals through the air. This problem was not solved until 1901, when Italian inventor Guglielmo Marconi sent the first radio signal across 2,000 miles of ocean, from the United Kingdom to Newfoundland. Marconi's work built on that of Germany's Heinrich Hertz (who discovered electromagnetic waves in 1880, and radio waves in 1887), and Nikola Tesla, who immigrated to the United States from what is now Croatia (and determined that radio waves might be used to transmit sound and even images.) Within a few years of Marconi's work, wireless telegraphy (also known as *radiotelegraphy*, because of its reliance on radio waves) gave way to *radiotelephony*, the ability to transmit actual sounds—and not simply signals—over the air.

Radio broadcasting as we think of it today emerged in the 1920s. On Thanksgiving Day, 1921, students broadcast live play-by-play of a football game between Texas A&M and the University of Texas. A Texas A&M website notes, "It took six radio operators, special abbreviations, lots of equipment and Morse code, but amateur radio operators throughout the state of Texas could keep up with the gridiron action." The game ended in a frustrating 0-0 tie. As broadcast offerings expanded, customers clamored for receivers, which they could buy in stores or build at home from kits. Early radio content was diverse, from sermons and Bible readings to music, news, and entertainment, including radio dramas, comedies, and quiz shows. Later, as television began to eclipse radio in popularity, many radio stars and programs began to migrate there. Comedian Jack Benny, featured in radio shows including *The Jell-O Program Starring Jack Benny* (premiering in 1934), debuted *The Jack Benny Program* on CBS-TV in 1950 and, for a time, continued to enjoy popularity in both media. A radio quiz show that was launched on CBS radio as *Take It or Leave It* eventually debuted on CBS-TV in 1955 as *The $64,000 Question*. The 30-minute weekly radio drama *Dragnet* (1949), featuring Jack Webb, became a television series in 1951, where it enjoyed a two-decade run.

What does this history mean for scholars and media makers hoping to hear radio broadcasts from the past? In fact, a surprising number

Family in New Bedford, Ma., listening to radio, Spring 1942. Photo by John Collier, Jr.; U.S. Farm Security Administration/OWI, from the U.S. Library of Congress.

of them have been preserved. By around 1930, important broadcasts were recorded onto *transcription disks*, shellacked aluminum disks of various sizes. Wire recorders were also used, until they were replaced in the 1950s by reel-to-reel magnetic audio tape. Both wire and magnetic recordings could be edited by physically cutting and re-connecting segments, but the magnetic recording devices were easier to use. As discussed in upcoming chapters, acquiring these *air checks* is generally not difficult, and some of it is in the public domain. Many of the most important news and entertainment shows are even available re-mastered on home CDs and DVDs or via digital and streaming formats.

Sources and Notes

Physicist Carl Haber's work is described in detail in Alec Wilkinson's "A Voice from the Past: How a Physicist Resurrected the Earliest Recordings," *The New Yorker*, May 19, 2014. To hear the recording, go to Becky Ferreira's "Listen to the Eerie Warbles of the Oldest Sound Recording in History," *Vice*, April 9, 2017, online: www.vice.com/en_us/

article/9a7x48/listen-to-the-eerie-warbles-of-the-oldest-sound-recording-in-history. The *Scientific American* article can be viewed online, http://edison.rutgers.edu/yearofinno/TAEBdocs/Doc1150_PhonoSciAm.pdf?DocId=PA084.

More information about Edison's early work can be found at www.nps.gov/edis/learn/historyculture/origins-of-sound-recording-thomas-edison.htm. See also the Library of Congress site, www.loc.gov/collections/edison-company-motion-pictures-and-sound-recordings/articles-and-essays/history-of-edison-sound-recordings/history-of-the-cylinder-phonograph/. To hear other examples of early recording, visit the website of the University of California Santa Barbara Cylinder Audio Archive, http://cylinders.library.ucsb.edu/history.php. The LC's "National Jukebox" site is www.loc.gov/jukebox/about/acoustical-recording. For more information on voice recording booths, see Kate Ida, "The History of Those Recording Studio Booths," *Vinyl Me, Please*, at www.vinylmeplease.com/magazine/history-those-recording-studio-booths/. The Lemelson-MIT site is https://lemelson.mit.edu/resources/valdemar-poulsen. The Dickson Experimental Sound Film (1894–1895) can be found here, https://archive.org/details/dicksonfilmtwo/DicksonFilm_High.mov. The discussion with Walter Murch can be found in a thread at the Cinema Audio Society, www.filmsound.org/murch/dickson.htm. Among available information about Alice Guy Blaché, see the biography by Alison McMahan (Continuum, 2003) as well as Pamela B. Green's biographical documentary, *Be Natural: The Untold Story of Alice Guy-Blaché* (2018; see https://zeitgeistfilms.com/film/benaturaltheuntoldstoryofaliceguyblache). Film footage of Guy directing the scene is available through log in (professionals only) at the Gaumont Pathé Archive, www.gaumontpathearchives.com/index.php?urlaction=doc&id_doc=275441&rang=2, which notes that this may be the first filmed record of a film shoot. (A bit of this footage is currently on YouTube, https://www.youtube.com/watch?v=xKg_ovr8aS0.) For a humorous look at the early days of talkies, see *Singin' in the Rain* (1952), written by Betty Comden and Adolph Green and directed by Gene Kelly and Stanley Donen. Will Hays's onscreen spoken introduction to the Vitaphone can be viewed on YouTube in a clip posted by Warner Brothers www.youtube.com/watch?v=FbIWXbLQw4o. *La Fiesta* and other Vitaphone examples can also be found online. The 1946 Warner Brothers short, "Okay For Sound" includes clips from each novelty short shown at the premiere of *Don Juan*; it can be found on the Internet. For more information on the Phonofilm, see the Engineering and Technology History Wiki, https://ethw.org/Phonofilm. De Forest's papers are archived at the Library of Congress. *Finding His Voice* can

55

be found on the Internet Archive, and at www.filmpreservation.org/pre served-films/screening-room/finding-his-voice-1929#. Max Fleischer's name may be familiar due to popular characters of his, including Popeye and Betty Boop. *Supervising Women Workers* (1944, 10:36 minutes) can be viewed at https://archive.org/details/Supervis1944. For an excellent commentary on the use of these propaganda films as they affected women in the workforce before, during, and after the war, see Connie Field's *The Life and Times of Rosie the Riveter* (1980, 65 minutes). Texas A&M information about the 1921 broadcast is at https://today. tamu.edu/2011/11/21/a-look-back-memorable-games-and-historical-moments-that-shaped-the-texas-am-university-of-texas-rivalry/.

56

CHAPTER 4

User Beware: Evaluating the Archival Record

The extraordinary power and appeal of the audiovisual record and works derived from it stem in part from the fact that we are seeing and hearing it for ourselves, and therefore believe it to be real. But as filmmaker and scholar Bill Nichols notes, documentary films do not *reproduce* reality, they *represent* it. In arguing about why ethical issues are central to documentary filmmaking, Nichols notes that the photographic image "is subject to qualification because:

- An image cannot tell everything we want to know about what happened.
- Images can be altered both during and after the fact by both conventional and digital techniques.
- A verifiable, authentic image does not necessarily guarantee the validity of larger claims made about what the image represents or means."

The need to interrogate the origin of third-party materials applies equally to still photographs, motion picture footage, and audio, whether in combination or alone. You should find out who created the materials and when, for what purpose, and to reach what audience(s). Who funded their creation? What was included and what was left out, both at the point of original recording and through the process of editing and distribution? What more can you learn about the events these materials purport to document, and can you verify the accuracy—drawing upon other reference sources—of that documentation?

Fake News

Despite how it may seem, charges that an oral or written account is false or fake are not new to this era. Political opponents, business competitors, and personal rivals have long planted seeds of falsehood for their own gain, often at significant cost to others. False and defamatory assertions, including content spread through government propaganda—posters, radio and television broadcasts, newsreels, and online—have fueled mass violence. "Fake news" is also a phrase used to discredit opposition or criticism, even when it's factually based.

Altered Still and Motion Picture Images

The history of altered still and motion picture photography—often focusing on works intended to have journalistic or documentary value—may be as old as the technologies themselves. Documentary work has long resided on a contested spectrum between journalism and art. Some photographers may argue that alterations can strengthen the power and overall "truth" of an image, for example, by removing distraction. But where is the line between "enhancing" reality and altering our perception of it?

When and how works are altered varies, as manipulation may occur before, during, or after an image is captured. In their 2019 online exhibition "Altered Images," the Bronx Documentary Center (BDC) offers a range of examples that demonstrate alterations, placing them into three categories: staging, post-production, and captions. Their examples include "Spanish Wake," an iconic 1951 photograph by W. Eugene Smith, in which six women are assembled around the bed of a dead (or dying) man. The BDC reports that the photographer altered the original image in the darkroom, darkening the image and redirecting the gaze of two of the women down, rather than toward the photographer. Smith did not agree that he'd violated any ethical standards, according to an interview on the site that was originally conducted in 1956 and published in *The New York Times*: "I don't object to staging if and only if I feel that it is an intensification of something that is absolutely authentic to this place," Smith said. Asked why he breaks "this basic rule of candid photography," Smith answered, "I didn't write the rules—why should I follow them? ... I ask and arrange if I feel it is legitimate." He said he printed his own pictures for "the same reason a great writer doesn't turn his draft over to a secretary ... I will retouch."

Let's look more closely at the BDC's three categories of image alteration: staging, post-production, and captions.

Staging

There are many reasons that still and motion picture photographers might stage scenes, although, in some cases, we may never know why. For example, filmmaker Errol Morris spent considerable time trying to determine the sequence of events in two Crimean War photographs taken in 1855 by British photographer Roger Fenton. In his 2011 book, *Believing is Seeing (Observations on the Mysteries of Photography)*, Morris considers writer Susan Sontag's assertion that the two images, taken from the same tripod position, *first* showed numerous cannonballs to the left of the road, and then showed the same cannonballs after they had been scattered—presumably by the photographer—onto the road.

After: In this image, some cannonballs are scattered on a previously clear road. *The Valley of the Shadow of Death* (1855). Photo by Roger Fenton. U.S. Library of Congress; Roger Fenton Crimean War photograph collection.

Morris conducted his own investigation by interviewing experts, visiting the site, and exploring primary sources as he set out to determine the time of day, light, and shadows in each image. In the end, he concludes that Sontag is likely right—but possibly not.

Staging "Photo Ops"

Staging may be done not only by photographers, but also by those being photographed. In its code of ethics, the National Press Photographers Association cautions "visual journalists and those who manage visual news production" that they should "[r]esist being manipulated by staged photo opportunities." These include government or public relations set-ups, some of which are relatively innocuous, such as the "photo opportunities" in which politicians are seen eating corn dogs at state fairs or doing "ordinary" things such as bicycling or clearing brush at a ranch. Sometimes the effort is more calculated, and the visuals may be designed to heighten or distract from the actual content or policies of the people portrayed.

Staging Documentary Films (or Elements of Them)

In the December 19, 1970 issue of *The New Yorker*, film critic Pauline Kael took Albert and David Maysles and Charlotte Zwerin to task for their documentary *Gimme Shelter*, charging that the events depicted were entirely set up by the filmmakers. "If events are created to be photographed, is the movie that records them a documentary, or does it function in a twilight zone?" Kael asked. "Is it the cinema of fact when the facts are manufactured for the cinema?" The film focuses on a free concert given by the Rolling Stones in December 1969 at the Altamont Speedway in northern California, northeast of San Francisco—a last minute change of venue. Chaos erupted, and a man in the audience was fatally stabbed.

In a letter to *The New Yorker* that was not published, the filmmakers defended their work's authenticity. "The facts are: We were involved in producing a film of the Rolling Stones' tour of the United States, not in producing concerts," they wrote. "We did not produce the event … In fact, the filmmakers were not consulted and had no control over the staging or the lighting at Altamont. All of the cameramen will verify that the lighting was poor and totally unpredictable."

It's interesting that in 2006, Martin Scorsese directed another film about the Stones, *Shine a Light*, in which the he *did* set up much of the production, and yet few critics described it as anything other than documentary. Scorsese chose the venue (New York's Beacon Theatre, much smaller than was typical for the Stones at that time), had the stage redesigned, brought in massive amounts of film lighting, and helped to select the song list. All of this is depicted in the film, and is therefore not dishonest or disqualifying: it becomes a film about Martin Scorsese making a film about the Stones at the Beacon Theatre. But what's not apparent to viewers, as reported in *The New Yorker* by contributor Shauna Lyon, is that Scorsese and his team also "cast" the audience. They required photos from potential audience members, who would be paid $75 to attend. "You should be dressed trendy, sexy, hip," they posted. "Do not come looking sloppy or disheveled. Women really glam it up, but not trashy … Again, you are not just attending a concert, you are working. MOST IMPORTANT NOTE: You guys will be in the very front of the stage and will be the only people on camera for the documentary. We really need high energy." As a result, many of those filmed closest to the performers are likely significantly younger than the actual fan base of the Rolling Stones, who were then in their sixties.

Fifty years from now, *Gimme Shelter* will remain useful as a source for scholars or media makers in search of footage that shows the Stones as they were in 1969, at the time of the concert at Altamont. *Shine a Light*, on the other hand, offers a valid look at the band and at Scorsese. But the array of excited young people in the front rows, like the theater itself, do not accurately depict the Stones' usual milieu as it was in 2006.

Washington, D.C.-based researcher David Thaxton encountered evidence of a more serious example of staging, this time by the U.S. government. In the 1980s, he was looking for footage related to a 1964 incident in Vietnam's Gulf of Tonkin. (The Navy of North Vietnam had allegedly fired on two U.S. ships near the Gulf while they were in international waters. The administration of U.S. President Lyndon Johnson cited these attacks to obtain Congressional approval for expanding the war. It was later revealed that the first attack may have been provoked by one of the U.S. ships and that the second incident never happened.) The subject index to the U.S. Navy collection had been discarded, so Thaxton began to go through all of the cards chronologically. "I came across this group of 11 or 12 reels, and it was written on the card, 'shot day for night,'" he said, meaning that they were filmed in the daylight, but filtered to appear as night. "I asked the Archives to make viewing prints of them. And when I looked at them, I thought, 'My gosh, they have gone back and restaged the entire Tonkin Gulf incident to provide a record of which ship was where and when they started firing.' Was it the truth? No, of course not. It was shot days later."

Staging vs. Re-enactment
Staging is the creation of an event or image that would not have existed without prior intervention. Perhaps emboldened by so-called "reality"

television, in which artificial situations are set up so that they can play out before the cameras, some nonfiction filmmakers are adopting the same approach, sending people into situations and filming what happens. The resulting footage, as third-party material for a future project, needs to be carefully considered to determine what, exactly, it represents. Similarly, staging may involve the "re-enactment" of an event based on facts insufficiently grounded in evidence-based research.

There is sometimes a fine line between staging and re-enactment, and the challenge to determine which is which is as old as documentary itself. Consider the 1920s films of Robert and Frances Flaherty. At a time when few people were world travelers but growing numbers enjoyed going to see "picture plays," most of which were scripted drama, the Flahertys' work presented views of life in faraway places, including the Canadian Arctic (*Nanook of the North*, 1922) and Savai'i, an island in the South Pacific (*Moana*, 1926). These were viewed as authentic accounts by contemporary audiences, and an uncredited review of *Moana*, written by John Grierson, introduced the use of the word "documentary" to apply to motion pictures. In *The New York Sun*'s regular column, "Picture Plays and Players," Grierson wrote, "Of course, 'Moana,' being a visual account of events in the daily life of a Polynesian youth and his family, has documentary value."

However, as we understand "documentary" today, both *Moana* and *Nanook* fall short. They present outdated, romanticized, and Westernized stories about their subjects. But the filmmakers themselves don't seem to have claimed the work was nonfiction. The title card for *Moana* reads: "Adolph Zukor and Jesse L. Lasky present MOANA, a romance of the golden age." Likewise, the title card for *Nanook* reads: "Revillon Freres present NANOOK OF THE NORTH, A story of life and love in the actual arctic." These were *stories*, filmed in remote locations with local people, but meant to play alongside "picture plays." Nanook was played by a man named Allakariallak; his "family," his way of life, and even the igloo in which he lived were all contrived by the filmmakers. Likewise, the "cast" of *Moana* worked with the Flahertys to re-enact practices that they no longer performed. This information is critical to those seeking to use this footage as if it were strictly ethnographic, and enhances overall scholarship about the Flahertys. In making *Nanook of the North*, for example, Flaherty enlisted the cooperation of the Inuit people, and *they* re-created for him a traditional walrus hunt, dressing in traditional clothing and hunting with harpoons, rather than guns.

As noted in Chapter 2, the venerable newsreel series *The March of Time* also relied on a combination of re-enactment and the real thing.

Nanook of the North (1922).

Their depiction of *Kristallnacht*, the night when Nazis raided Jewish shops, for example, was mostly filmed with actors and props in a studio in New Jersey; a story about music collector John Lomax recording Huddie Ledbetter (Lead Belly) at the Louisiana State Penitentiary and later meeting up with him in Texas was actually re-enacted months later in Connecticut. (One key way to know if something was filmed as it happened or was created—or re-created—for the camera is the presence of a slate, marking multiple *takes*. This is why digging deeper and going through outtakes—and hoping they have not been discarded—can make a difference.)

Creative Visualization vs. Fake Archival

At times, filmmakers may create the *appearance* of archival footage, which is sometimes but not always deceptive. An example of a film that audiences understood to be a creative construct is Canadian actor and filmmaker Sarah Polley's *Stories We Tell* (2013), an intimate look at her family's history. The filmmaker's press materials describe it as "genre-twisting"; she also described it as a "hybrid film, between documentary and experimental film." In order to visualize a story for which the visual record was limited, Polley used old Super 8 cameras to create what appear to be home movies, in which she portrays her mother, who died when Polley was eleven. The film's press, and Polley's own fame as an actress, meant that the audience understood that this was a creative choice, and not an attempt to pass off "fake" home movies as if they were real.

Another, older example is English filmmaker Peter Watkins's *Culloden* (1964, known in the United States as *The Battle of Culloden*), which takes the form of a live 1960s-style BBC television news broadcast, including an on-air reporter, as it covers the famous British battle of 1746. It's difficult to imagine that anyone thinks a television crew was present to cover the actual event.

Along these same lines, the stylized visualization and re-enactments in Errol Morris's *The Thin Blue Line* (1988) are not deceptive. Morris used high-end professional gear to film multiple versions of the same event—the shooting of a Dallas police officer during a routine traffic stop in 1976—in order to demonstrate the unreliability of eyewitnesses. (Had Morris been present at the actual event, there would have been a single version.) Yet when the film was released, a reporter asked Morris how he happened to be on the road that night. "Was this reporter suggesting that I had been out on the roadway with a 35-millimeter film crew *the night of the murder*, and *just happened* to be at the right place, at the right time to film the crime—over a decade earlier?" Morris wrote in a blog for *The New York Times*. (Additional stylized imagery of the interrogation of Randall Adams, likewise, is clearly re-enacted.)

In contrast, *faking* involves deception, whether well-intended or not. In 2005, *Mighty Times: The Children's March*, a 40-minute film co-produced by HBO and the Southern Poverty Law Center (SPLC), received the Academy Award for Best Documentary Short. Produced and directed by Robert Hudson and Bobby Houston for SPLC's "Teaching Tolerance" initiative, *The Children's March* documented the involvement of students in a campaign for civil rights in Birmingham, Alabama in 1963. While the film included a significant amount of what appeared to be archival footage and stills, much of that material was original. As reported by *The New York Times*, the filmmakers used "vintage cameras and distressed film stock to shoot more than 700 extras, trained dogs and period automobiles and fire engines on various locations in Southern California." When the Academy Award nominations were first announced, some filmmakers complained about what they called "faux" documentary, and the Academy asked filmmaker Jon Else for advice. As Else later told NPR reporter Robert Siegel, the issue was not the use of re-enactments *per se*, which even then were fairly standard in the industry and often used effectively and honestly. "The question with this film comes from the fact that the archive footage—the real archive footage—and the very skillfully dramatized archive footage are seamlessly woven together," Else said, "so that the audience really has no way of knowing whether a particular shot, say, of police commissioner Bull Connor, is the real Bull Connor or an actor." The issue was resolved when the filmmakers agreed to modify the film. The material they created themselves was set apart with a graphic border that resembled sprocket holes. In addition, the film added an up-front disclaimer: "Portions of this film were reenacted using vintage cameras and film stocks."

Another issue with *The Children's March* and, frankly, many documentary films, is the use of footage to represent something that it is not. In seeking to make a case about the virulence of racism in Birmingham, Alabama, up to and including the year 1963, the filmmakers "spliced in shots of particularly ferocious white attacks on blacks from other cities in other years," Else reported in his 2017 memoir. These included "the Little Rock school crisis in 1957, shots of the Watts Riot in 1965 and arch-segregationist Lester Maddox confronting blacks at his Atlanta restaurant in 1964." As discussed elsewhere, the *generic* use of archival materials is not inherently bad, but it needs to be positioned in a way that acknowledges its lack of specificity. For those seeking to draw upon completed media projects for their own archival research, the use of generic or misused footage, stills, and even audio underscores the need for your own, independent fact checking.

Captions

As the Bronx Documentary Center site makes clear, the problem of false captioning is not limited to broadcast or print publication, but also images and video shared on social media. An example they give is a FOX13 Memphis posting in April 2015 that showed an urban area engulfed in flames. The caption read, "BALTIMORE IN FLAMES," but the image was actually the city of Valencia, in Venezuela, in a photo taken more than a year earlier. (The station removed the image a couple of days later, acknowledging that it should have been fact checked.)

False captioning is not a problem of one news source; it is a global problem that can have deadly consequences. Consider what happened in India in 2018, when disturbing video of children killed in a 2013 chemical attack in Syria was used as the visual for a baseless story that children in India were being kidnapped and killed. The false rumor and horrifying but completely unrelated video went viral in India, and in the ensuing panic, five innocent men were killed.

Post-production

Falsification in the processing of images has always existed. Sometimes its use was fanciful. Consider the "Cottingley Fairies," allegedly captured in photographs taken by 16-year-old Elsie Wright in 1917. Some viewers believed they were real; others were skeptical. In fact, skepticism has also been one—but by no means the only—response to photographs of unidentified flying objects, as well as the Loch Ness Monster, Bigfoot, Yeti, and other creatures of legend.

When it comes to journalistic integrity however, even minor falsification is prohibited, as documented in the guidelines of major news organizations including the Associated Press. The World Press Photo Foundation, which "believes in the power of showing and the importance of seeing high-quality visual stories," holds an annual visual journalism contest that specifically prohibits altered entries. Yet in 2015, according to a report in *The New York Times*, a full 20 percent of the photos that made their way to the final round were disqualified after judges compared the final image with the original digital file, "often because of significant addition or subtraction to the image content."

Using Technology to Deceive

The use of technology to alter or enhance visual imagery is not, itself, a bad thing. Creators of the television series *Game of Thrones* (2011–2019), filmed on location in Croatia and Iceland, used CGI to manipulate existing landscapes to suit the series fantasy setting. For the television documentary *Alexander Hamilton* (2007), director Muffie Meyer used CGI to turn 21st century Alexandria, Virginia into 18th century New York City. She also used slide projections behind actors in a studio to give the impression of interviews filmed on location throughout the U.S. Northeast. Neither of these examples is a violation of ethics. *Game of Thrones* is a fictional series, and Alexander Hamilton (1757–1805) lived long before motion picture photography existed; no one thinks the actors speaking words from the documents of the past are *actually* those people, any more than they believe that they are seeing an actual New York street in the 1780s.

Challenges emerge, however, when increasingly sophisticated technology is used to distort what is then presented as the factual audiovisual record. How are people to know what can or cannot be trusted? To this end, in 2019, Glenn Kessler of *The Washington Post* published a report, "Seeing Isn't Believing: The Fact Checker's Guide to Manipulated Video."

"These videos—spread by politicians, advocacy groups and everyday users—are viewed by millions," Kessler wrote. "The Fact Checker set out to develop a universal language to label manipulated video and hold creators and sharers of this misinformation accountable." He identified three main ways that video was being altered:

- "Missing context," which includes both misrepresentation of real media by saying it's something it isn't, and isolation, that is, taking a real piece of media out of its original context to subvert its meaning;
- "Deceptive editing," which includes omission or removing parts of the item that would reveal its true meaning, and *splicing*, or removing sections or juxtaposing pieces of media that don't belong together; and
- "Malicious transformation," which includes doctoring the image or sound in order to provide a manipulated artifact of the event, and fabrication, using artificial intelligence (AI) to create what have become known as deepfakes.

Missing Context

Context, as defined by Merriam-Webster, describes "the parts of a discourse that surround a word or passage and can throw light on its meaning" and "the interrelated conditions in which something exists or occurs." Kessler describes two ways in which context can be removed. The first is *misrepresentation*, which is the same thing as false captioning. For example, someone intending to mislead viewers (and generally, to outrage or excite them) posts a picture and represents it as something entirely different than what it actually is. The other is *isolation*: "Sharing a brief clip from a longer version [which] creates a false narrative that does not reflect the event as it occurred." Unfortunately, examples of this kind of distortion are plentiful, including those used by members of one political party or religious group to falsely attack others.

Responsible editing of material, whether print or audiovisual, demands adherence to the meaning of the original work as it was recorded. For readers and viewers, an awareness of editing is important. Unless you are watching raw footage or a live interview or event in which there are no abrupt visual changes or audio changes, you are likely seeing an *edited* version. If you are using this edited material as a third-party source for a new work, go as far back to the original as you can to be sure the context and meaning have not been distorted, whether inadvertently or not.

In case anyone thinks these kinds of dirty tricks are new, look into the political campaigns throughout U.S. history (or world history, for that matter). Then, thinking about audio, film, and video recordings from the past 130 years, consider how many ways what you are seeing or hearing may have been edited. It's incumbent on the user to fact check what people say, what happens on screen, and what the news reports say, in their original context. People make mistakes. People get only part of the story. And sometimes, people intentionally deceive or mislead.

Deceptive Editing

In deceptive editing, Kessler says, a "video has been edited and re-arranged." The result is that key information necessary to fully understand context and meaning has been deliberately left out (*omission*), and/or that unrelated material has been combined to create a new, false narrative (*splicing*).

Malicious Transformation

Kessler defines *malicious transformation* as meaning that "part or all of the video has been manipulated to transform the footage itself." As discussed elsewhere in the book, not all transformations of footage are malicious. People may choose to *colorize* black-and-white images, or enhance (or add) sound effects; they may slow down or speed up footage, freeze frames, and find other ways to alter the material. Provided they adhere to ethical standards pertaining to the form of work they're creating, this isn't generally a problem—although those who later use this material in a new work (in other words, who will be relying on this work as supposedly accurate historical evidence) should do everything they can to understand how the material was transformed.

Malicious transformation, however, is generally intended to create a false and/or negative impression of a person, place, or event. This is achieved in two ways, Kessler writes: through *doctoring* and through *fabrication*. Doctoring is more straightforward. In 2018 for example, someone altered a video featuring Emma González, a survivor of a high school shooting that year in Parkland, Florida. In the original footage, she is seen ripping up a large paper shooting target. In the digitally-doctored video, intended to stir outrage against her political views, the target was replaced with a large copy of the U.S. Constitution. In another example, from 2019, opponents shared video of Nancy Pelosi, Speaker of the U.S. House of Representatives, in which she appeared to be drunk or disoriented. Analysis revealed that the video had been deliberately slowed to achieve this effect.

Deepfakes

The deepfake (or deep fake) is the newest, and perhaps most dangerous form of manipulated audiovisual media. Using artificial intelligence (AI), real people may be portrayed doing and saying things they neither did nor said. In 2018, actor and director Jordan Peele teamed up with *BuzzFeed* to create a convincing PSA featuring Barack Obama. The image is of the former president, speaking words that appear to be his. But as Peele reveals, the tools of artificial intelligence (AI) are allowing Peele to imitate Obama's voice, saying things Obama never said—and if you didn't know it was fake, you might never detect it. Other deepfakes superimpose people's images onto the bodies of strangers, a problem especially prevalent in both "celebrity porn" and "revenge porn."

In a 2018 article for the *Oklahoma Law Review*, Professor Marc Jonathan Blitz noted that technologies for altering video and audio material "will likely allow individuals to create convincingly realistic footage of events that never occurred." The article explores the global dangers this presents, should individuals begin to engage in "a kind of informational Hobbesian war of all against all—with people constantly falsifying one another's sense of what is real." What powers does government have against informational attack? And how does the need to protect the truth weigh against the First Amendment protections of speech?

Playing with the Documentary Form

Mockumentaries are a form of entertainment that uses a documentary format for fictional purposes. On April 1, 1957, for example—April Fool's Day—the BBC's *Panorama*, a current affairs series, featured a family in southern Switzerland harvesting spaghetti. Director Rob Reiner's *This is Spinal Tap* (1984), a fake documentary about a hapless fictional heavy metal band from Britain, with Reiner playing the documentary filmmaker, was enormously popular with mainstream audiences, who understood the film was a satire. In 2001, Ricky Gervais and Stephen Merchant launched *The Office*, a mockumentary sitcom. Other mockumentary television comedies include *Arrested Development*, which premiered in 2003; *Parks and Recreation*, which premiered in 2009; and *Modern Family*, which also premiered in 2009.

Trouble emerges, however, when the documentary form is used to convey content that is invented, intending the work to be entertainment without making it clear to audiences that what they're seeing and hearing is not actual documentary evidence. An example of this is Animal

Planet's *Mermaids: The Body Found* (2012) and its follow-up the next year, *Mermaids: The New Evidence*—the "most-watched telecast in Animal Planet's history," according to *Entertainment* magazine. Even today, the IMDb listing for the sequel describes it as a "startling documentary" with "never-before-seen evidence"—even as they list the names of the actors who play the scientific experts. (A fast disclaimer in the closing credits acknowledged the work as fiction.)

Another faux-documentary form might be called *speculative* documentary. These use documentary styles—and, often, real-life interviews and archival materials—to explore alternative histories or invented scenarios. An example is *The Visit: An Alien Encounter* (2016), written and directed by Danish filmmaker Michael Madsen. The film is billed as a documentary about "an event that has never taken place—man's first encounter with intelligent life from space." Another example is the Discovery Channel's *What If?* (1996) series, which pursues alternate histories, such as one in which the Reverend Dr. Martin Luther King survives an assassination attempt in 1968 and assumes the U.S. presidency a year later.

Bias

In considering any audiovisual materials, whether created yesterday or in the 1890s, it's important to consider the issue of *bias*. It's commonplace today to decry "media bias," although the term is widely misused. As Merriam-Webster defines it, bias as a noun is: "unreasoned judgment" or "prejudice." Bias may be positive or negative; one can be biased "toward" or "against" something. But many people also confuse bias with perspective or point of view, and in that sense, bias is an unavoidable aspect of being human. We all see the world through the lens of our experiences, upbringing, professional training, nationality, religion, ethnicity, education, the times in which we live, and more—whether we are conscious of it or not.

Bias can creep into how we frame stories, and even the choice of which stories to tell or not, and responsible storytellers are on guard to be sure that the argument they're making is based on solid evidence. It's important to protect against "confirmation bias" or the temptation to cherry pick, seeking out only material that supports a point of view. A solid argument should withstand contradiction. Along these lines, a savvy examiner of the audiovisual record must look for, recognize, and try to understand the bias of its creators and, as necessary, seek out information that will enable the materials to present/represent a more accurate, honest, and inclusive record—or be presented for what it is, in the proper context.

In their book, *After the Fact: The Art of Historical Detection,* historians James West Davidson and Mark Hamilton Lytle offer an excellent example of how bias can affect the credibility of archival sources. In the 1930s, the administration of President Franklin D. Roosevelt launched the Federal Writers' Project (FWP). Among its tasks was a project to interview previously-enslaved people whose freedom had come with Emancipation, in 1863, and the end of the U.S. Civil War two years later. More than 2,300 interviews were conducted, with the interviewers writing notes and then later reconstructing the interviews on paper. For their 2009 book, Davidson and Lytle posed a series of questions to be considered in relying on such interviews as historical evidence. For example, they wondered how these 2,300 individuals were selected and how representative their experiences might have been, considering that there had been more than four million people enslaved in the United States prior to 1865. By the 1930s, when the interviews took place, those who were interviewed were invariably elderly; how sharp were their memories? Or, given the good health that had allowed them longevity, how representative were the conditions they had faced as children, compared to those who did not survive past middle age, as was more common?

Additionally, Davidson and Lytle noted that interviewers, "simply by choosing their questions, define the kinds of information a subject will volunteer." These questions offered cues as to the kinds of answers they were seeking. But with these "slave narratives," as they're known, the authors wondered if there was one over-riding factor influencing the information gathered:

> If such interviewing cues influence routine conversations, they prove even more crucial when a subject as controversial as slavery is involved, and where relations between black and whites continue to be strained. In fact, the most important cue an interviewer was likely to have given was one presented before any conversation took place: Was the interviewer white or black?

In their book, Davidson and Lytle present as evidence their discovery of a narrative conducted by a young white FWP interviewer with an elderly black woman she calls "Susan Hamlin." Hamlin is led to believe that the interviewer is from the welfare office, and her answers about slavery paint a generally positive, even stereotypical view of life under enslavement. Authors Davidson and Lytle were curious about a statement that Hamlin made to the interviewer, that someone else had interviewed her

71

about slavery the previous month. They found another FWP interview with a "Susan Hamilton," who is almost certainly the same woman, and her memories are starkly different. She describes seeing enslaved women hung from the ceiling and whipped until they were near death; of couples marrying one day and being separated and sold the next; of women giving birth in the morning and being forced back into the fields by noon. Based on how the woman spoke to the interviewer, Davidson and Lytle make a case that the first interviewer was a young black man, and that the elderly woman had been less guarded around him, and more truthful.

Sources and Notes

Bill Nichols, *Introduction to Documentary*, 3rd edition, was published in 2017 by Indiana University Press and is strongly recommended. The Bronx (NY) Documentary Center site is www.alteredimagesbdc.org. A transcript of W. Eugene Smith's interview in 1956 was published by *The New York Times* (January 3, 2013). Errol Morris's *Believing is Seeing (Observations on the Mysteries of Photography)* was published by Penguin Press in 2011. The pictures discussed here, "The Valley of the Shadow of Death," can be viewed online at the Library of Congress, www.loc. gov/pictures/collection/ftncnw/item/2001698869/. The National Press Photographers Association code of ethics are online, https://nppa.org/code-ethics, as are those of the Associated Press, www.ap.org/about/news-values-and-principles/. According to authors Kevin Macdonald and Mark Cousins (*Imagining Reality: The Faber Book of Documentary*, Faber & Faber, 2006), the filmmakers' response to Pauline Kael was written as an open letter to *The New Yorker*, but not published. It appears in print as an appendix in their book. Shauna Lyon's "Wanted: S.W.F., Loves Keef" appeared in *The New Yorker* (November 13, 2006). The interview with David Thaxton comes from the first edition of *Archival Storytelling*. John Grierson's uncredited review of *Moana*, "Flaherty's 'Moana,' A Poetic South Sea Film, Comes to the Rialto" appeared in *The New York Sun* (February 8, 1926). Information about the two *March of Time* stories comes from research conducted by the authors. Press material for Sarah Polley's *Stories We Tell* (2012, 108 minutes) can be found online, http://onf-nfb.gc.ca/medias/mediakit/STORIES%20WE%20TELL%20press%20kit.pdf. The quote is from Steve Erickson, "Sarah Polley on Secrets, Super 8, and Stories We Tell," *Studio Daily* (May 8, 2013). Morris's discussion of the reporter's reaction to his film can be found in "Play It Again, Sam (Re-enactments, Part One)" and "Play It Again,

Sam (Re-enactments, Part Two)," *The New York Times* (April 4 and April 10, 2008). *Mighty Times* is discussed in Irene Lacher's "Documentary Criticized for Re-enacted Scenes," *The New York Times* (March 29, 2005); Jon Else's interview with NPR's Robert Siegel (March 29, 2005) is at www.npr.org/templates/story/story.php?storyId=4566421; Else's book, *True South*, was published in 2017 by Penguin Random House. For more on Contreras, see "AP Severs Ties with Photographer who Altered Work" (*AP in the News*, January 22, 2014, www.ap.org/ap-in-the-news/2014/ap-severs-ties-with-photographer-who-altered-work). The website of the World Press Photo Foundation is at www.worldpressphoto.org/About-us/37373. For information about changes to their ethical guidelines, see James Estrin, "World Press Photo Introduces New Ethics Guidelines for Contest," *The New York Times* (November 25, 2015). A "making of" reel about *Game of Thrones* is on Vimeo, https://vimeo.com/133433110. A video about the making of PBS's *Alexander Hamilton* is at the film-maker's website, www.middlemarch.com/filmography/alexander-hamilton/. Journalist Glenn Kessler's *Seeing Isn't Believing* is online, www.washingtonpost.com/graphics/2019/politics/fact-checker/manipulated-video-guide/?utm_term=.0f5432820e09. The *BuzzFeed* information comes from Todd Spangler's "Jordan Peele Teams with Buzzfeed for Obama Fake-News Awareness Video," in *Variety* (April 17, 2018). An episode ("Fake Believe") of the *New York Times*'s television essay show, *The Weekly* goes behind the scenes with some deepfake technicians in their Toronto office. Marc Jonathan Blitz's "Lies, Line Drawing, and (Deep) Fake News" is in *Oklahoma Law Review*, vol. 71, no. 1, 2018. A BBC report on the 1957 spaghetti harvest, and a link to the film, can be found at http://news.bbc.co.uk/onthisday/hi/dates/stories/april/1/newsid_2819000/2819261.stm. Andrew David Thaler wrote in *Slate* about the faux mermaid documentary controversy, "The Politics of Fake Documentaries: *Mermaids: The Body Found* and its Ilk Have Done Long Term Damage" (August 31, 2016). See also James Hibberd, "Mermaid Hoax Drowns Animal Planet's Ratings Record" in *Entertainment* (May 28, 2013). James West Davidson and Mark H. Lytle's *After the Fact* was published by Alfred A. Knopf in 1982; thank you to University at Albany colleague Susan McCormick for bringing it to our attention.

CHAPTER 5

Evidence on Film: A Conversation with Rick Prelinger

Rick Prelinger is an archivist, filmmaker, writer, and educator based in the San Francisco Bay area. In 1983 he founded Prelinger Archives and spent the next two decades collecting over 60,000 "ephemeral" films—his term for amateur, advertising, educational, and industrial films. In 2002, the collection was acquired by the U.S. Library of Congress's Motion Picture, Broadcasting and Recorded Sound Division, even as it continued to grow. For the past several years, his primary interest, both as a collector and as an academic, has been home movies and amateur films, with approximately 17,000 items currently held. Throughout his career, he's been an activist regarding issues of copyright, and a fervent evangelist for the importance of the public domain.

In 2000, Rick formed a partnership with Internet Archive (archive.org), and he still serves on its board. This is a major online resource for research of all kinds, including searchable databases of television news broadcasts, a lending library, a repository for public domain films and books, the official access point for older NASA films, and—as its name implies—an archive of the internet itself, caching and making available for research thousands of web pages that are no longer active. On the site, he's posted a subset of his collection for free download and reuse by media makers and researchers, much of it under the provisions of a Creative Commons license. For commercial purposes requiring formal licensing, the collection is represented by Getty Images. In 2004,

Rick and his wife, Megan, a cultural historian and archivist, co-founded the Prelinger Library in San Francisco as "primarily a collection of 19th and 20th century historical ephemera, periodicals, maps, and books, most published in the United States. Much of the collection is image-rich, and in the public domain. The library specializes in material that is not commonly found in other public libraries."

A professor of film and digital media at the University of California, Santa Cruz, Rick is also a filmmaker and writer. In 2004, he created *Panorama Ephemera*, a 90-minute archival feature that "focuses on familiar and mythical American images (1626–1978)," according to the Vimeo site where it can be viewed. In 2013, he released *No More Road Trips?*, a 79-minute "dream ride through 20th-century America made entirely from home movies," also on Vimeo.

Most recently, he's returned to *Lost Landscapes*, a project that was launched in 1991, in which he brings forgotten films back to the places in which they were filmed. "I found three hours of home movies shot in 1938–39 by Ivan Besse, manager of the Strand Theater [in Britton, South Dakota], and took them back to Britton for a screening," he told *The Essay Review* in 2017. "As the audience sat in the Strand watching Ivan narrate 53-year-old scenes of themselves and their kin, the room stirred with excitement and conversation, and I realized that moviegoing and silence weren't necessarily intertwined." In 2007, he returned to Britton and discovered a packed audience. Since then, he and Megan have gathered local audiences to watch home movies, outtakes from feature films and industrials, promotional films and other types of footage about their communities in Detroit, Oakland, San Francisco, Los Angeles, and New York.

Kenn spoke with Rick in San Francisco on September 10, 2019.

I haven't seen No More Road Trips?—*is it only shown to live audiences?*

It's an 80-minute feature, and it's a dream journey across the country through other peoples' home movies. And like most of my films now, it's made to be shown before an audience that talks their way through it. So it's a participatory film. [But] I've open-sourced them all; you can download almost everything I've made. Prelinger.com points to them.

Has your approach to understanding what you call "ephemeral films" changed over time?

In the old days, the point that I used to make about the old industrial and educational films, which I used to call "ephemeral films"—now

I like Charles Acland's and Haidee Wasson's term a lot better, "useful cinema"—films that have a job to do; I used to value these films as pointers to histories that weren't well understood or that had been forgotten. I think now we have to look at them as more than just pointers; they were *weaponized*. They're films that don't just depict persuasions, but were weaponized as part of those persuasions.

This past summer in New York City, some of your works were screened as part of a retrospective honoring the late media artist Gretchen Bender. Your event was titled, "Nineteen-Eighties: The Archives Explode," and it included seven films you'd collected that were created in the 1940s and 1950s, with titles like "Are You Popular," "Live and Learn," and "In the Suburbs." What was that like, in 2019?

It became very clear to me that we've got to look at these films now through the prism of *whiteness*. They were weapons to not simply document, but also to sustain and strengthen white supremacy. And it gets really interesting when you broaden your horizons a little bit, and I think they're much more relevant to audiences now, in a different way. You've read about the controversy around the murals here in San Francisco.

The Depression-era mural at George Washington High School, yes. [According to The New York Times, *"'The Life of Washington' frescoes were painted in the mid-1930s and funded by the Works Progress Administration. (Victor) Arnautoff, who was a Communist, depicted George Washington in a critical light, showing him as a slave owner and a leader of the nation that annihilated Native Americans."]*

I went to see them about a month ago, and it was all old white lefties who were there to defend the murals. And it made me really think about: my whole life, and my life with Megan to a great extent, has been about collecting and preserving outdated, or simply bad, ideas. We've got a library filled with historical mistakes and false consciousness. And we've collected films that, in many cases, are about bad ideas. And it makes me wonder. I think the question at hand right now is *How can we use bad ideas? What roles do bad ideas play?*

We've always had these platitudes about archives, like "the past is prologue." That's not a very deep insight. We have to ask more of our material, and we have to ask more of our practice as archivists and as people who use archival material. And so this next quarter, I'm teaching a course in sponsored and educational film, called "Made to Persuade"—I stole the title from Dan Streible. I've taught it once before,

78 Rick Prelinger. Photo: Megan Prelinger.

and this time I want to foreground it as: *What good are these films? How can we leverage them?*

In *No More Road Trips?*, there were two things that I didn't want to [include]. One of them was footage of Native people engaged in ceremonies, because, first off, we don't know if they're Native people or white people dressed in regalia, and we don't know if these ceremonies were really performed with consent; maybe it was the Depression and people needed money. So I didn't put that in the film. The other thing I didn't put in the film was a scene where an elderly white couple, traveling around the country, stop in Oklahoma at the house of a very, very poor African-American family. And the [white] man makes a big show out of giving nickels to the kids. I thought there's no purpose in showing this, because white people will think, "Oh well, that's patronizing and gross, but we've moved beyond that." And I don't know that we really *have* moved beyond that. I don't think it serves a purpose to lull people into a certain kind of complacency.

The same thing is true with a lot of these really amazing industrial and educational films and with a lot of home movies. What does it mean to show them? How can we leverage them to really make some change?

One of the films I like to quote is the industrial you have about the "wonders" of asbestos siding.

Right. *According to Plan.*

They're the shingles on the house I grew up in; they were lauded as this gorgeous design element.

We had them too. And I think we as makers and archivists, we haven't done enough to squeeze meaning out of these films; to see what they can tell us. We use them as b-roll. Or we use them as sound bites that are quite superficial. I still don't see much work that really questions archival material, and that uses it in a critical and interesting way.

You've talked a lot about finding new ways to tell stories.

There are many things that are good about traditional storytelling. It can be done well; it can be done with style. *Listen to Britain* – beautifully made. I was at the Traverse City Film Festival a few years ago and I ran into Jim DeVinney, and told him I always remember what he did with *The Kennedys*, where Bobby Kennedy is shot. [Rather than] show the Ambassador Hotel, he found a clip showing volunteers for McCarthy in Wisconsin who see [the assassination] on TV. And so he records the event as it's broadcast, and the reaction, and it's so much more powerful.

Let's talk specifically about home movies, vs. the industrial and educational ones. What first attracted you to home movies, and when did you start collecting them?

The first home movies I collected, I think, were in 1985, when [fellow archivist and collector] Bob Summers and I drove out to Long Island to buy a collection from a guy; he said his father had been the elevator operator in an apartment building in New York where the family from Levy's Rye Bread lived. According to Madeline Mitchell, an intern at the Library of Congress [fellow], it's not the same Levy family. But it was a beautiful home movie collection of Europe in the thirties and so on, and it's in the collection that went to the Library of Congress in 2002; there were a fair number of home movies.

I really began to get seriously interested in the mid-2000s. Megan and I began to look at home movies; we would project them and take notes. Home movies really aren't cinema, they aren't film, they fall into a tradition of personal recordkeeping. They're very direct, concrete evidence of all sorts of stuff that didn't otherwise get photographed—or they're extremely enigmatic. They're loose and playful, but they're also really structured, and they sometimes show some of the most rigid and intransigent aspects of our society. They're pleasant, but they're also filled with interpersonal violence. They show happy ceremonies, because usually home movies are shot out of love; people don't usually shoot home movies of things they don't want to remember. But they also show injustice, and power imbalance, and they show problems. And it's so undiscovered.

In terms of being used in other works?

You first see home movies in *Brother, Can You Spare a Dime?*, [a feature-length archival documentary about the Great Depression, by Australian director Philippe Mora and released in 1975], where they have home movies from the [Franklin D. Roosevelt] collection. So there's a long history of working with home movies. But that said, we're just at the beginning of understanding what they might mean. For one thing, home movies solve this storytelling problem, because they already imply a narrative. You have a shooter and a subject; you have some kind of relationship between whoever is structuring the gaze and whoever is being gazed at. And we empathize a great deal with home movies, in a process that's kind of mysterious to me, just as mysterious as how we empathize with line-drawing, with cartoon characters.

I like the sheer overwhelming evidence, and I love the way it slips away. The family stops by the road, and then there's a pan beyond the car, and you just see the beginning of the gas station, and you want to see more: *Who's there? What's the headline on the newspaper sitting on the rack?* In recent years, some historians and some people who do archival theory have started to talk as much about absence as presence; that archival absences speak as loudly as archival presences. We're seeing this now in terms of queer and trans histories. A lot of archives are referring explicitly to silences that need to be addressed.

Tell me a bit more about Lost Landscapes, *the project you are doing, that uses home movies to tell stories of American cities over the past century.*

I've had really positive experiences doing the *Lost Landscapes* thing. I wish I could get away from the title (but it's sort of burned in), because I don't like talking about loss. Amazing things happen when people deal with history in a public and a shared way. And the idea that perhaps some topics are better served by that kind of treatment than they might be by documentaries that go through the standard distribution channels. I don't regard "filmmaking *qua* filmmaking" as inevitable or even necessary in many cases; we can do so much more in performance or in sharing. That's part of the big experiment of Internet Archive: *if footage is ubiquitous and it's free, what will people do with it?*

It sounds kind of grandiose, but at the base of our project has been an attempt to build a fairly complete ethnographic record of North Americans in the 20th century—or at least, from the mid-twenties through the eighties. *What were we doing? What did things look like?* We have about 17,000 home movies; that's largely what I work with. We've got about 6,000 scanned. Not all scanned well; about 5,000 of them are scanned pretty well. And constantly more. A lot of my life is going to be focused on trying to come to terms with them.

I think that's a great service. I've used home movies also as a reference for things, like when I was working on the Steven Soderbergh film, The Good German (2006), *and we were looking at home movies from Berlin after the war, and using them as a reference for costumes, set design, etc.*

I'm going to jump on a word that you used, which is "service." Although archives should be a lot better at addressing people's needs for historical material, it's more than that, and you can talk about archival filmmaking in the same way. It's a social practice. History, doing history in whatever way one may do it, is actually rearranging the pieces of the puzzle. It's

Frame grab from *The Good German*. The Hollywood set recreates 1945 Berlin as documented in old footage and photographs.

part of a long effort that involves millions of people. It happens all over the place, and it's been happening for a long time, to kind of reconfigure the world. Collecting and making material available, making work with it, is about changing the world.

I've come to reject the [service] model. It isn't just fulfilling an expressed need, it isn't answering an email or making it possible for somebody to download something. History should be infrastructure. You should be able to walk by that house and understand who lived there. *Did someone get evicted? Was there a murder there?* History should be infrastructure, and in cities that are intensively historicized, like London and Paris and Berlin, you see that. You see plaques, and you see a lot of augmented reality [works]. In Montreal, you can hold up your phone and see *vieux Montréal* at the same time as you can see Montreal in the present day. So the idea of "service," while necessary, narrows the conception of what archives really can be.

Media technology has gone from 16mm to 8mm to Super-8mm film, and then to video and digital formats, which means people are making more and more of what we would call "home movies." In terms of quality, is this newer work necessarily better, and how will archives keep up with the quantity?

The great thing about personal media is that it stands outside considerations of value, of quality. If you go to home movie-based conferences, you realize that a lot of people are more interested in structured work, like amateur films, which generally have a storyline of some sort. But I like the anarchy and the unpredictability and the randomness of [raw] home movies, and [think that] the reason home movies are valuable to us today is because they were saved *despite* their value. We love the errancy. We love the fact that the tremors of the photographer translate into the shaking of the camera, especially in 8mm. And I think the same thing is true for what people are doing today with their phones.

What about quantity, and guarding against loss?

I'm not concerned about loss; I'm *so* not concerned about loss. We should be careful to keep what we've got, and we shouldn't intentionally destroy material. Whenever this happens, this is an act of aggression. It's *been* an act of aggression: Afghan Film Archives; TV Palestine; Sarajevo National Library—these are cases of intentional destruction. But loss is formative. When I was starting to collect in the eighties, people would call up and say, "Do you have any African-American home movies?" And I would say, "Not really." We all thought they were really scarce, and that was just because we weren't stepping outside our own community and talking with people. The *sense* that there's a loss—or an absence—is formative; it makes us look harder.

A lot of stuff won't get saved, especially after the digital turn, but it's fine. And especially now, there's a whole emerging discourse about archives and climate change. Because there's a real ethical issue: should you collect something you might not be able to take care of, either because it takes a lot of juice to keep drives spinning, or because you're low against the ocean, or because you're not sure that you can collect sustainably? *Huge* moral self-questioning going on. Ethical self-questioning.

Where do you come down on that?

The idea of the big repository, I just don't think we're socially or economically going to support that; certainly not right now. I think we all have to figure out ways to work together and achieve the best practices we can. You have your Ransom Centers, Libraries of Congress, and Wisconsin State Historical Societies, which fulfill an institutional model; and then you have your Freedom Archives and your Western Neighborhood Project collecting local material [in San Francisco]; and then you have individuals. The post-custodial archives model is huge in different parts of the world now.

83

Can you give an example of that?

Caroline Frick is a post-custodial archivist at the Texas Archive of the Moving Image, [which has what they call the] Texas Film Round-Up. They'll go to—I don't know, Wichita Falls—and they'll digitize material, and then they return it. They're a digital collection. And this comes out of the model, like in post-revolutionary Cuba. There were all these films, and people [said], "We don't have a way to keep them safely because we can't afford air conditioning, so let's just show them and think of the archives as memory. If people see them and talk about them, the films *live.*" We have to take a lot of this more seriously, because there's not going to be money. National Archives has announced that by 2022, agencies need to submit digital records; they won't accept physical records. I don't know how that translates over to physical moving image material. So, we're trying to do our bit with home movies.

In the past, you've talked about what you called an "Intellectual Property Preserve," which was an idea to treat archival material as a national resource, along the model of our national parks. It was about collecting copyrights, as opposed to collecting physical materials.

I wrote a piece about this in 1997, and as it turned out, almost in the same month, Eric Eldred was sitting down with Larry Lessig and talking about the same thing, and they moved toward Creative Commons. My idea was that people would be given incentives to donate copyrights, in the same way that people had donated land to the National Parks system. If Mr. Murdoch could get a hundred-million-dollar tax deduction for putting Fox News on film into the public domain, I think that would be really interesting. I don't think you can do that right now, even if you wanted to. You can't really donate copyrights and take a deduction, but it would be a great idea.

I guess the last thing I want to ask you about—and it's a big thing—is this idea of other forms of storytelling. Using archival as texture, hybrids.

Right now, there's tons of interesting work going on with archival material, but it's in the independent space, or the experimental or *avant-garde* space, and people won't see it. There's still a kind of conservativism. I mean, a lot of people who are documentary filmmakers who've been noticed, or who have a commission and distribution, they really get conservative, and they're not being positively reinforced to try different things. And precious few people seem to want to just let the footage speak. A lot of times, the footage speaks louder than anything that might go with it.

I'm really interested in documentaries that have a spatial, rather than a temporal, structure. To me, it seems incredibly reductive and limiting that we only have the marching forward of temporality in a documentary, where you say something, and then I counter it, and then you say something back. What if it's organized spatially? There are all sorts of other ways to think about how these things can happen, and there's not much incentive to do it.

Like I say, I think we're just at the beginning of thinking about how to work with home movies, and for that matter, all archival material. The question is much more, "Are we going to keep people interested in the first hundred years of moving image making?" What's the audience now for the 17th century—all the historical documentation and record that exists from then? To a certain extent it's generational, and as you say, we don't have an archival hold on post-'95 material. I'm not terribly worried about it. I think some strategies will gel to make that heritage a little more accessible.

Sources and Notes

For more information on Rick Prelinger, visit his website, at www. prelinger.com. The U.S. Library of Congress's Motion Picture, Broadcasting and Recorded Sound Division is at http://www.loc.gov/rr/ mopic/. The Prelinger Archive can be found at the website of the nonprofit Internet Archive, https://archive.org/about/. The 2004 film, *Panorama Ephemera*, can be viewed online, https://vimeo.com/277208141. The 2013 *No More Road Trips?* is also online, https://vimeo.com/69781280. Some information about the Besse screenings is from Lucy Schiller's "Essayist Interventions: Taking the City into the Theater," *The Essay Review*, 2017, http://theessayreview.org/essayistic-interventions-taking-the-city-into-the-theater/. The quote about "Viewing lost landscapes" is from *inquiry@UC Santa Cruz Research Magazine*, accessed online, https:// inquiry.ucsc.edu/2018-19/viewing-lost-landscapes/. The book edited by Charles R. Acland and Haidee Wasson is *Useful Cinema* (Duke University Press, 2011). Information about the 2019 Gretchen Bender retrospective can be found online, http://redbullarts.com/newyork/news/gretchen-bender-so-much-deathless/. *The New York Times* quote about the San Francisco mural controversy is from an August 10, 2019 article by Carol Pogash, "San Francisco School Board May Save Controversial George Washington Mural." "Made to Persuade: The Moving Pictures in Our Head" is the title of an essay by Dan Streible, part of a booklet written to accompany the DVD, *Made to Persuade: Films from the 8th Orphan Film Symposium* (NYU Orphan Film Project, 2012, produced by Streible and others). It can be found at Internet Archive. The 1952 film, *According to Plan: The Story of Modern Sidewalls for the Homes of America*, can be found at Internet Archive. *Listen to Britain* (1942, 20 minutes, b/w) was created by Humphrey Jennings and Stewart McAllister for the British Government's Ministry of Information. *The Kennedys* was a two-episode, four-hour PBS series that premiered in 2003. The 1968 assassination of U.S. presidential candidate Robert F. Kennedy appears in the second hour of episode two, "The Sons." That hour was produced and directed by James A. DeVinney, and written by DeVinney and Geoffrey C. Ward. Information about the series can be found online, www.shoppbs.pbs. org/wgbh/amex/kennedys/. For more information about identification of the "Jack Levy Family Collection" at the U.S. Library of Congress, see https://blogs.loc.gov/now-see-hear/2019/07/investigating-home-m ovies-from-the-prelinger-collection/. Information about the Franklin D. Roosevelt home movies can be found via his presidential library and museum, www.fdrlibrary.org/collections-list. The phone app for Montreal is called *"Montréal en Histoires,"* and is available free, www.

montrealenhistoires.com/en/mobileapplication/. The archive references are to the Harry Ransom Center, University of Texas at Austin; the Freedom Archives (https://freedomarchives.org) in San Francisco; and the Western Neighborhoods Project in San Francisco, www.outside lands.org/. Information about the Texas Film Round up can be found at the website of the Texas Archive of the Moving Image, www.texas archive.org/library/index.php/Texas_Film_Round-Up. A discussion of the Cinemateca de Cuba preservation issues can be found in a journal article by Janet Ceja Alcalá, "Imperfect Archives and the Principle of Social Praxis in the History of Film Preservation in Latin America," *The Moving Image*, Vol. 13, No. 1 (Spring 2013), pp. 66–97. In August 2018, the U.S. National Archives shared a plan that included not taking paper records after December 31, 2022, www.archives.gov/news/articles/lead ers-share-national-archives-vision-for-a-digital-future.

86

WORKING WITH ARCHIVAL MATERIALS

CHAPTER 6

Finding What You Need

How do you make your way through the labyrinth of commercial archives, online images, and databases of stills and motion picture footage? How do you take advantage of known search strategies and techniques, and at the same time discover fresh material that can make your project unique? In this chapter we offer some basic information about how and where to start looking, either as a first step in doing your own research or in preparation for your work with a professional. While this chapter is primarily geared toward media makers, we hope it may also prove useful to those searching for material for research purposes.

Look for Existing Films on Your Subject

For many, if not most, filmmakers, a first step in archival research is to ask, "What other media projects exist on this or a closely related topic, and what materials did they use?" This information can be useful for a number of reasons. First, it prepares you to "pitch" your film to funding sources, distributors, and broadcasters. They are going to want to know what other projects on your topic exist, and how yours will be different—why it's needed. It's also an excellent way to determine what footage from the past may exist that would enrich your project—and by digging even deeper into the source of that footage, you may find additional material that informs both your research and storytelling. Looking at existing works includes looking at works created during the period you're exploring (i.e., *contemporaneous* material), and later works that *draw* on that material.

For example, if you're doing a documentary film about the Black Panther Party in Chicago, director Howard Alk's 1971 film *The Murder of Fred Hampton*, which was filmed before and after Hampton's killing in 1969, would be a contemporaneous source and would serve as primary source material. That footage then became a source of archival material for later projects, including "A Nation of Law?," an episode of the second season of PBS's *Eyes on the Prize* (1990), and the feature documentary *The Black Panthers: Vanguard of the Revolution* (2015). The creators of these two latter works both drew on footage of Hampton, not only from Alk's work but from a range of independent and news sources; they were not present to film Hampton themselves, so they acquired footage from others.

If you're now (in 2020 or after) proposing a film about Fred Hampton and/or the Chicago Black Panthers, it's important to be aware of all of these projects, both for their research and the arguments put forth by the filmmakers, and—as per the focus of this chapter—as a potential source of audiovisual material upon which you can draw.

Note that when contemporaneous source footage, whether from a single source or from a range of sources, has been edited into a new work, such as *The Black Panthers*, you *may not* simply lift the edited archival sequence for use in your own film. This is true even if you track down and license every piece of archival material within that sequence from its original source, because the edited sequence is the copyrighted creative work of this new set of filmmakers.

Follow Up On Material That Interests You

In either case, if you find third-party materials that you think will advance your own project, follow up on them as soon as possible. If you wait too long to determine the *provenance* (history of creation and ownership) of the material, you may not leave sufficient time to locate and contact rights holders, obtain screeners and clean masters, and license those materials. It's frustrating to become dependent on material only to discover late in the process that you can't find people, access the footage, or perhaps afford to license it.

Use Credits as a Research Starting Point

In the case of films that have incorporated third-party footage, you may be able to determine the source of material from the credits. Most archives require onscreen credit as part of their license agreement. You generally won't be able to tell which shots came from which archive, but you'll get a good sense of the pool of archives used by the filmmaker. Pay attention to when the film was released, because material available then may not be available now, or perhaps the archive credited no longer controls the rights or has been bought by another, usually larger, archive. But the onscreen credits are often a good place to start.

Can You Hire a Researcher Named In the Credits?
If you see the name of an archival (or music) researcher in the credits of a film you admire and it's relatively recent, don't hesitate to see if you might be able to hire that researcher for your own project. As discussed in Chapter 7, it's not unusual for researchers to reuse their notes and logs from one project to benefit another, especially if the projects are separated by time or are not so identical in subject matter as to be competitors. A professional researcher's notes from a career's worth of projects are a tremendous asset to any producer. Do *not* hire researchers and expect them to readily identify and locate archival material used in projects on which they *weren't* involved; this can actually be more work than starting from scratch.

Finding the Rights Holder To an Older Film
Suppose that you're developing a documentary about the history of a California firefighting unit, and you discover that an independent film was made about the same unit 40 years earlier. That film played at some festivals and on the local television station, and you've found a copy in a library. In that case, by going through the credits and searching online, you may be able to locate the filmmakers or their distributor, or find out whether the film and, ideally, outtakes have been bought, donated to an archive, or are otherwise available.

Search the General Topic Online

It usually makes sense to do a general search, using any good search engine, to see what you can discover about your subject and what relevant images, audio, or completed projects you might find. However, grabbing this material off the web and editing it into your film, trusting that you can figure out later where it came from, is often a mistake. Of course, if the rights holder is clearly identified and you can confirm that the material will be available to you in the future—maybe someone has posted their own footage of a recent event online, for example, or you find something on the website of the news agency that shot it—you might incorporate the material into your film as you edit. Otherwise, a search of leading databases can give you a sense early on whether or not you can access the material you find that you're interested in, how much it may cost you, and whether or not there are lower-cost alternatives.

Online Databases

One place to begin is the Internet Movie Database (www.IMDb.com). Be sure to double check information before relying fully on it, as the site allows user-generated content, after vetting it. IMDb is most useful for searching out film titles and names of cast and crew, but it also has a useful "subject" search mechanism. Think of every possible key word that might apply and try them one at a time. You'll get a lot of results that are irrelevant, but you may also discover unexpected works that relate to your subject matter.

Sometimes, but not often, archival credits are listed on IMDb along with all the other credits in the film, or you may find archival credits under "companies," along with production companies, distributors, and sometimes even equipment rental companies. Usually, you will find names of credited archival researchers under "other" or "miscellaneous" crew. Sometimes the credit is under the "producer" category, as "archival producer" is a title often given to researchers who also handle everything to do with archival budget, clearances, and technical issues. Otherwise, an internet search should lead you to more information about how to screen the film (online, a library, a streaming service, etc.), so that you can watch the credits. As noted above, if the film is relatively obscure, it may only be distributed by the filmmakers or their families, or by the distribution company, if there is one.

Other useful online sources include:

- The online catalogs of organizations such as the National Library of Medicine, the U.S. Library of Congress, the U.S. National Archives, and the Imperial War Museum in the United Kingdom.
- National archives of different countries, such as Germany (www.bundesarchiv.de/EN/Navigation/Home/home.html), Russia (https://cinema.mosfilm.ru and http://gosfilmofond.ru/) and Japan (www.nfaj.go.jp/english/). While these sites may be in that country's native language, you can use translation programs built into most web browsers to get a rough translation.
- Subject databases, such as Art on Film Online (www.ArtFilm.org). These are created not for a specific archive but for a specific subject; in this case, "fine arts, architecture, photography, decorative arts, and related topics."
- The British Universities Film & Video Council (http://bufvc.ac.uk); this site offers links to a number of U.K. collections, including those with film, television, and radio holdings.

It's important to remember that virtually no online catalog represents the complete holdings of an archive—or even *close* to the complete holdings—and most catalog, whether online or printed, offer only brief descriptions at best. If you see something intriguing online or in a publication, but need to know more, contact the archive directly.

Explore Professional Organizations and Associations

Another way to find challenging visuals (or films about obscure subjects) is to contact professional groups whose members specialize in imagery, whether present-day or archival. There are several large international member organizations specifically concerned with the preservation and restoration of archival audiovisual materials. Most of these organizations have listservs, many of which are available for posting by non-members (which means you can post queries). Generally, members of these organizations are eager to help:

- Association of Moving Image Archivists (AMIA, at amianet.org);
- Focal International (focalint.org, a U.K.-based organization of international archives and film researchers),
- International Association for Media and History (IAMHIST, at iamhist.net);
- International Federation of Film Archives, (FIAF, at fiafnet.org).

A Note About FIAF

FIAF's website is one of the best ways to find archives from all over the world, from the State Film Fund of Azerbaijan to the Ingmar Bergman Archives in Sweden. Under the "community" heading and the "organization" subheading, click on the links for both "members" and "affiliates." Under "publications," you can buy a copy of the complete list of members and associate members of the organization with all their contact information. You can also become a member or affiliate, as appropriate, and access the list of member archives.

Explore Networks and Production Houses

Search through the websites of the venues that produce archival programming. These include not only the programmers themselves—broadcast and cable networks worldwide—but also the production companies to whom they increasingly outsource production. You can find their names on the Internet Movie Database; follow the trail to these companies, see what else they've done, and explore credits on their programs.

Distributors

It can be useful to spend time exploring the websites or catalogs of distributors known for films in your general subject area. For example, California Newsreel, Direct Cinema Ltd., New Day Films, PBS Home Video, and Women Make Movies are examples of U.S. distributors that specialize in independently produced documentaries. Some distributors specialize by subject area or genre, such as health or anthropological films.

Explore Print Reference Materials

Book and article research may lead you to information about media coverage. In addition, be sure to spend time looking through references *about* archival collections, such as finding aids.

94

Researching Visuals: Some Organizational Strategies

Whether working on your own or with a researcher, and whether looking for completed films or shots and stills, there are a few basic steps that will make finding third-party materials more efficient and effective.

Be Organized

Production can be a messy, complicated, and often long and drawn-out process. It's far better to take the time and care at the outset to set up some records management systems than to suffer the consequences of having been sloppy in documenting information, dates, and more.

Make a Chronology

For any work that has a historical component, it's a good idea to make a chronology chart of the important events in your film. If, for example, you are making a documentary project about your father, you might have a column with all the major events in his life, being as exact as possible with dates. Then expand it to include columns for major events in his community, the nation, and the world. Add to that a reference column for popular culture—hit songs and movies, for example.

Take the time to include details and citations. Too often, media makers shortcut this important step, offering only vague entries ("1940s, World War II; 1950s, Korea") that are less than helpful when you return to this chronology after time has passed. Further, the chronology will likely be a basis for much of your archival as well as content research. Also note: the fact that two events happened around the same time does not necessarily indicate cause and effect. Your awareness of both, however, enriches your possibilities for "setting the stage" for your story. An excellent example of a television series that ran its own fictional narrative parallel to real historical events was the AMC series, *Mad Men*, which is set primarily in New York in the decade between 1960 and 1970. Over seven seasons, series creator Matthew Weiner and his writers engaged their characters in events of the day, as seen and heard in archival material on period television sets and radios and incorporated into the characters' lives.

Make a Wish List

As you develop your chronology and the project overall—shaping it from idea to outline to treatment—you should begin to form a *wish list*; that is, a comprehensive list of archival material you hope to find. If you have specific, fact-checked dates as well as the correctly spelled names of places and individuals, it's *always* easier for you, an archive, or a researcher to find coverage of that event. In producing a historical biography, don't settle for a photo of your main character that was taken 40 years after your story takes place, when a bit more research could turn up images from the appropriate time. If you search the proper dates and places and discover that, in fact, there *is* only one photograph of your main character, then you know what your limitations are and can take creative steps to address them. Be careful of this as well when using archival materials to inspire costume or set design for period fiction films.

As explained in Chapter 8, the initial ordering process is designed to bring a variety of possible materials into the editing room in order to give you and your editors choices as you shape the story. Don't make your wish list so specific that you close the door to creative options. In other words, your wish list might include something like this:

1999, January 19: Bill Clinton's State of the Union Address
  Specific quote needed:
- "For the first time in three decades, the budget is balanced. From a deficit of $290 billion in 1992, we had a surplus of $70 billion last year and now we are on course for budget surpluses for the next 25 years."

But if you're looking for context and additional coverage, a broader search would be more effective. You might request:

- Everything showing Congressional statements about balancing the budget, especially during the Clinton administration (1993–2001), but also from Congress in the last 50 years.

Using Search Engines

Once you know what you need, you're ready to tackle the big archives. A growing number (but still not all) of the major archives worldwide have online search engines. Knowing how to use these effectively—and understanding that most archives have additional holdings that are not online—can make a big difference in whether you find what you need or wind up empty-handed. If you search by key word, remember to try synonyms and alternate forms of words, in case the search engine doesn't automatically find them. For example, entering *forest* into a search engine may also bring up *forests, forestation, deforesting*, etc., or it may not; you may need to enter some of these terms in a separate pass. You might also want to search for *woods*, and maybe even *trees* and *grove(s)*.

Searching By Date

Most databases will allow you to put in a specific date or a range of dates along with your key word(s). In general, do not search a specific date, but instead create a *date range*, starting a few days before you think the event took place and ending a few days after. You may have gotten the date slightly wrong in your timeline, or a news story might have been logged in on the day *after* an event actually happened. Also, by searching a bit more broadly you may discover a useful item that illustrates the "lead up" to an event or its aftermath.

Searching: Commercial Still and Footage Archives

In 2010, FOCAL International reported that the "customer base for archived media content has grown rapidly in the past few years," adding that "the global trade in audio-visual archive content generates some $450 million dollars (U.S.D.) in revenue a year." This creates both opportunity and tension, as FOCAL reports: "Preservation of content stored on an array of formats, many of which are near-obsolete, is … an

Jackson Lake in Foreground, with Teton Range in
Background, Grand Teton National Park, Wyoming
(1941–1942). Photo by Ansel Adams. U.S. Department
of the Interior, National Park Service.

on-going challenge, with the demands of commercial value constantly weighed against cultural and heritage preservation."

The list of commercial archives is lengthy, and currently includes such companies as Alamy, Getty Images, Agence France-Presse, AP Images, Pond5, Shutterstock, Critical Past, and others. Most have online databases. While this may seem like a tremendous boon to producers and researchers, it can also be problematic, because the option for a producer or researcher to work on location at these archives has all but disappeared. This may suit the needs of commercial clients, such as advertisers, who often need little more than the short clips they can order, pay for, and download immediately. The system works against the interests of many filmmakers, however, who may want to review as much material as they can get on a particular subject in order to construct scenes that can tell a story visually. Additionally, media makers (and scholars) are often searching these archives for materials that will serve as evidence. Supplying key words to a technician who doesn't know the history and is simply filling an order limits that possibility. As an example, a key word search may result in a five-second clip of French president Emmanuel Macron walking with American president Donald Trump in Colleville-sur-Mer in June 2019. A chance to screen reels of footage would allow the researcher to go through full statements both men made in speeches later that day, along with related material such as cutaways of the gathered crowd and press.

If you're only finding the tip of the iceberg, take heart. When an online clip offers a hint as to what's in the archive's holdings, you *can* contact the archive to see about getting the rest of the story digitized. Most archives do not have the resources to digitize their entire collections, but they encourage these requests. You may be asked to pay a fee to help cover these costs, but it can be worth it.

Royalty-free vs. Rights-managed

Note that while some archives offer both *royalty-free* and *rights-managed* licenses, some specialize in one or the other. Rights-managed material tends to be more expensive to use, in part because the licensing is more complex, as discussed in Chapter 11. Royalty-free images are licensed with a flat fee. These distinctions are important even during your initial search, because different types of material tend to be available with these two kinds of licenses. Rights-managed licenses tend to cover more specific or rare footage, including historical and news footage.

Royalty-free images may be somewhat generic and illustrative: for example, a time-lapse beauty shot of a sunset, ocean waves crashing on a beach, a non-specific shot of schoolchildren in a playground, or storm and weather footage. You can save money and time if what you need can be found in this type of material. Additionally, most royalty-free images can be easily located and purchased online. You may never need to interact personally with the archive; you simply pay with a credit card and download the image(s). Some commonly used websites that license material on a royalty-free basis include Pond5, Periscope, Critical Past, and Shutterstock. Increasingly, royalty-free images are being created in 4K, so they can be appropriate for almost any use, including theatrical features.

Searching: Networks and News Agencies

Like the all-purpose giant, Getty Images, many television networks and news agencies, such as Reuters and Associated Press, sell their footage on a commercial basis. Some groups represent only their own collections. Others offer a basket of holdings that they've acquired or represent for sale on behalf of the rights-holders.

U.S. Television Networks: News

Until 1970, there were only three major television networks in the United States: ABC, NBC, and CBS. PBS, which is not a network but a consortium of member stations, was launched in 1970. Fox News followed in 1996. CNN, a cable network that launched in 1980, should also be added to this list, as should other cable news stations such as MSNBC. While ABC's television news collection does not have significant holdings before 1963, the collections of CBS and NBC do.

- ABC News footage is currently handled by ABC News VideoSource (abcnewsvsource.com) in New York, a news licensing organization within the Disney-ABC Television Group.
- CBS News, also based in New York City, is currently represented by Veritone, in Costa Mesa, California (which was previously Wazee Digital in Colorado). The representation of CBS News material has bounced around from company to company over the last 15 years, and in general, CBS News material is the most difficult to obtain for that and other reasons. The collection is still important; CBS News was considered the leader in television news throughout the 1950s and 1960s and into the 1970s.
- NBC News Archives sells its own footage, and recently established a brand new online presence, the NBC News Archives Xpress (nbcnewsarchivesxpress.com). The Archives Xpress offers relatively short clips, however, so you might be better off searching the site and then contacting the NBC News Archives staff in Rockefeller Center, New York, for additional guidance. The staff are extremely familiar with their holdings and the history of their news division.
- Fox News also licenses clips of its own programming. To find out more, start with your local Fox affiliate station. Normally, they'll vet the request first, and then send it to corporate for additional vetting. Note that Fox will *not* license any footage that contains any of their talent, which is actually most of their footage. Depending on the circumstances, and partly because of this, producers who want to use clips from Fox News and can claim that their use is a "fair use" (see Chapter 13) may seek to obtain the clips through other means, such as Internet Archive.
- CNN (Cable News Network) can be an important source of footage. As with Fox, CNN makes it difficult and expensive to use a clip from one of their "branded shows," such as *Anderson 360* or *Larry King Live*. After a 2019 merger between Time Warner and AT&T, CNN is owned by WarnerMedia. The online collection and information about licensing can currently be found at collection.cnn.com.

Searching: Internet Archive

Filmmakers often rely on Internet Archive (archive.org) for public domain recordings, texts, and even music (they have over 35,000 live concert recordings, for instance, including a whole collection on The Grateful Dead). Note that in the case of concert recordings, you will probably have some third-party underlying rights to clear, so review our licensing chapters to make sure you're covered. They also have feature films that have fallen into the public domain, along with old radio shows, patent office documents, and a 13,000-volume audiobook library.

Some key offerings of Internet Archive:

- The Wayback Machine. When Internet Archive was founded in 1996, its goal was to archive the internet itself. Part of the site, https://archive.org/web/, includes nearly 25 years of searchable web history—currently more than 384 billion archived web pages to explore.

- The Prelinger Collection. Filmmaker and archivist Rick Prelinger (see Chapter 5) is a long-time supporter and contributor to Internet Archive. He has placed thousands of items from his personal collection of "ephemeral films" on that site. These include industrial, social, educational and corporate films that have fallen into the public domain, as well as home movies and other film artifacts. They can be downloaded and used by filmmakers for free under certain conditions, posted on the site.

- The NASA Collection. While the National Aeronautics and Space Administration remains the place to go for still images and animations created by this independent agency of the U.S. federal government, Internet Archive (https://archive.org/search.php?query=nasa%20collection) has become the semi-official repository of older NASA footage of the Mercury, Gemini, and Apollo space missions; Skylab and other weather and communications satellites; the Voyager space missions; and other past NASA-related events.

- The Television Archive News Search Service. The Television Archive News Search Service (https://archive.org/details/tvnews) is one of the newer parts of Internet Archive. It is a collection of video recordings of virtually every national news-related broadcast and cablecast since 2010 (with a few from 2009 and earlier, including the events of September 11, 2001). It can be filtered by year, topic, source, language, and more. For each entry, it has a clip (usually in standard definition DVD quality, in 30–60 second segments)

Apollo 11 liftoff, July 19, 1969. Collection of the U.S. National
Aeronautics and Space Administration.

that's married to a written transcript. The collection is searchable
by any word anyone says. This means that if you want to know on
what date the president made a particular comment, if a major
news entity broadcast it, you can locate it. You can also find a
video copy of that clip and either license it from the copyright
holder or, if your use is a fair use, simply use it. Internet Archive's
searchable Television News Archive, which can also provide you
with a physical copy, is the resource fair use advocates have long
been waiting for.

Searching: The Vanderbilt Television News Archive

Since August 1968, Vanderbilt University in Tennessee has been assembling its Vanderbilt Television News Archive (https://tvnews.vanderbilt.edu/), recording and cataloging every network evening news broadcast on all three major American networks. In 1995, they added some CNN programming, and in 2004 added content from Fox News. Among other things, this allows people to research news programming that pre-dates material in Internet Archive's holdings.

Vanderbilt makes screener tapes of these broadcasts available *for research use only*. The tapes include a burn-in of the network name and the date and time of the broadcast. They are a tremendous resource, allowing you to see whether and how a story was covered, as a step toward acquiring materials directly from the copyright owner. However, when you then go to the network itself to clear a clip you've obtained from Vanderbilt, you may run into difficulties. This is because Vanderbilt's archive consists of *air checks*, which are copies of a show exactly as it aired, often taped off air. The network that initially aired that segment may have since recycled or destroyed the original. (This was especially true in the earlier days of videotape.) In addition, networks usually index programs differently than Vanderbilt does: by individual story subject matter and/or event date, for example, rather than by program name or air date. If they *are* able to locate the material, you may encounter an additional complication, because using a clip that features a news anchorperson or reporter often involves special permission, whether for the use of their voice or likeness or both. Most networks will charge you up to double the normal license fee for any seconds you use of their personnel, because they'll need to pay guild fees to SAG-AFTRA, the union to which reporters and anchors belong. Clips from branded shows like *60 Minutes, Dateline NBC, ABC 20/20*, and long-form documentary specials like *CBS Reports* will always require special permission and longer turn-around times to get approval.

Searching: Public Archives in the United States

Materials held in U.S. government collections are often in the public domain, in which case no use licenses are needed. Some of the most important sources of this material are located in or near Washington, D.C. These include the U.S. National Archives and Records Administration

(NARA), the U.S. Library of Congress (LC), and the Smithsonian Institution.

U.S. National Archives and Records Administration

"Of all documents and materials created in the course of business conducted by the United States Federal government, only 1%–3% are so important for legal or historical reasons that they are kept by us forever," reports the website for the National Archives (nara.gov). Yet this small fraction of the total materials represents millions of print and audiovisual materials. Established by President Franklin D. Roosevelt in 1934, NARA's materials currently include: "approximately 10 billion pages of textual records; 12 million maps, charts, and architectural and engineering drawings; 25 million still photographs and graphics; 24 million aerial photographs; 300,000 reels of motion picture film; 400,000 video and sound recordings; and 133 terabytes of electronic data."

NARA's primary repository for audiovisual materials is in College Park, Maryland, but there are branches around the country, including at the American presidential libraries. If you are researching long distance, you can take advantage of the National Archives Catalog, which "currently contains archival descriptions for 85% of the holdings of the National Archives, authority files, and over 2 million digitized copies of records," according to the site (www.archives.gov/research/catalog/help/using.html).

Viewing NARA Materials

NARA's 2018–2022 strategic plan calls for significantly increased digitization of its holdings (including documents) to expand public access, a core part of the agency's mission. By 2024, their goal is to have digitized "500 millions of pages of records and make them available online to the public through the National Archives Catalog." Even this ambitious goal, however, represents just some of their holdings, and only a small percentage of their audiovisual collection is actually online and downloadable. For these reasons, and because of how complex and specialized the sub-collections are, it often makes sense to hire a professional researcher who knows the archive well. For information on obtaining copies of material found at the National Archives, see Chapter 7.

NARA Highlights: Moving Image Collections

The National Archives is *not* a stock footage house. Rather, it's a place where the government stores its records, and for that reason, preservation is its primary concern. Collections are broken down by *Record Group*. For

103

example, Record Group 85 (RG 85) contains the audiovisual collection of the Immigration and Naturalization Service, while RG 225 contains material from the National Aeronautics and Space Administration (NASA). Materials donated to the Archives by nonfederal agencies are placed in Record Group 200 (the so-called "gift collection") and then broken down by sub-collection. The following collections are part of RG 200, except where indicated:

- The Universal News Collection. While every Hollywood studio had its newsreel, only Universal gave its entire run (1929–1967) and outtakes to the American people; all other newsreels must be obtained from commercial sources. The Universal News collection includes some 150,000 titles, and each complete newsreel presents roughly seven or eight stories that last about a minute each. NARA holds nearly the entire Universal News collection, with the exception of some issues from the World War II years and some early soundtracks that were destroyed in a fire. The outtakes are often even more useful than the newsreels themselves.
- *The March of Time* outtakes. The newsreels themselves (1935–1951) have been digitally restored and are under copyright, but *most* of the outtakes are in the public domain and available from the National Archives. While *The March of Time* provides interesting social and political history, these newsreels also include content that was manipulated and even faked. Often, the outtakes illustrate this.
- The Ford Film Collection. About 5,000 films, mostly short, produced by automaker Henry Ford between 1915 and 1956. This collection of 35mm and 16mm films documents his family life, the inner workings of his factories, and his travel, especially through Central and South America. It also depicts other industries, such as textiles, milling, and agriculture, especially in the 1910s and 1920s.
- The Harmon Foundation Collection. This nonprofit personal foundation was in existence between 1922 and 1967, created to recognize and document African-American achievement in the arts, business, education, and other ventures.
- Military collections. An extensive range of materials from the various branches of the U.S. military. Major collections include: *U.S. Signal Corps* material (RG 111), which covered the U.S. Army's activities; the *Navy* collection (RG 428); the *U.S. Air Force* material (RG 342); and the *Marine Corps* material (RG 127), which includes paperwork dating back to their founding in 1775.

104

NARA Highlights: Stills Collections

The National Archives maintains approximately six million photographs, negatives, transparencies, posters, other fine art, political cartoons, portraits, contemporary slides, and aerial photographs from over 170 departments of the government.

- The Army Air Force record groups include photographs taken by famed photographer Edward Steichen; also images of the African-American pilots from Tuskegee University (the Tuskegee Airmen).
- The Civilian Conservation Corps Collection photographs show the work of the CCC, a Depression-era program that put people to work between 1933 and 1942 doing rural reclamation, reforesting, and restoring historic buildings and sites.
- The Works Project/Progress Administration collection includes photographs and artifacts collected between 1922 and 1944 from the WPA and related organizations pertaining to construction projects, conservation activities, health and sanitation efforts; art (including the Federal Art Project), music, theater (including Federal Theatre Project posters and other visuals); infrastructure work, such as the construction of airports, bridges, and roads; and photographs collected for use in the state guidebooks created by the Federal Writers Project. The WPA record group, 69, is one of the most accessed sections of the National Archives.

NARA Highlights: Sound Collections

The National Archives sound collections include radio broadcasts, speeches, interviews, actuality sound, documentaries, oral histories, and public information programs from a range of sources, both public and private. The earliest recording is from 1896; most recordings were made between 1935 and the present, with a strong emphasis on the World War II era. Highlights include:

- National Public Radio Catalog. Includes NPR news and public affairs broadcasts, 1971–1978.
- Milo Ryan Phonoarchive Collection. Includes approximately 5,000 donated recordings, primarily of CBS-KIRO (Seattle) radio broadcasts from 1931 to 1977, with a focus on news and public affairs.
- World War II War Crimes Records. Provides thousands of recordings from the International Military Tribunal at Nuremberg, Germany; the most prominent are the testimonies of Nazi defendants and witnesses to the Holocaust. Another record group, 226, relates to the Office of Strategic Services (OSS), the predecessor to the Central

Intelligence Agency. This includes radio recordings designed for broadcast in Germany, Japan, and the United States, as well as American songs sung in German by Marlene Dietrich and a speech that was to be broadcast in Germany if an attempt to assassinate Hitler succeeded.

- The ABC News Radio Collection. Includes 27,000 broadcasts from ABC News Radio consisting of programs from 1943 to 1971. Note that these items may not be in the public domain.
- NASA Audio Collection Catalog. Includes some 1,400 NASA sound recordings (1952–1975), including live communications between astronauts and mission control, public affairs programs, press conferences, speeches, and mission highlights.
- Supreme Court Oral Argument Collection. Includes about 5,000 sound recordings of oral arguments presented before the U.S. Supreme Court (1955–1978). Copies of these are available to the public.

NARA is arguably the best and most accessible source of moving images, still pictures, and sound recordings in the world. As mentioned, much of it is in the public domain, either because it was created by the U.S. government with tax dollars or because it was donated to the American people without restrictions. Not everything at the Archives (especially in the gift Record Group 200) is rights free, but a vast majority of the most important materials are.

U.S. Library of Congress
Founded in 1800, the U.S. Library of Congress (www.loc.gov) "is the largest library in the world with more than 168 million items." These include "more than 39 million cataloged books and other print materials in 470 languages; more than 72 million manuscripts; the largest rare book collection in North America; and the world's largest collection of legal materials, films, maps, sheet music and sound recordings." In fact, the collections include everything ever created in the United States that is or was registered for copyright protection, and the collection is added to each day. Unlike the holdings of the National Archives, much of what's housed at the Library of Congress is protected by copyright, and the Library of Congress is not authorized to grant rights to these materials. However, its collections are invaluable for research, and some important items are in the public domain.

As was the case with our description of the National Archives, any attempt to represent the vast holdings of the Library of Congress within a single chapter is impossible, but we'll list some highlights.

LC Highlights: Motion Picture Collection
Moving image collections particularly accessible to filmmakers include:

- The Paper Print Collection. Between 1894 and 1915, about 3,000 films were submitted for U.S. copyright protection by filmmakers including Thomas Edison and D.W. Griffith (in the United States) and Georges Méliès (in France). Because there was no established format on which to submit films for copyright registration prior to 1912, filmmakers used long, photo-sensitive rolls; each film frame printed through to this "paper print" roll. In the 1950s, archivist Kemp Niver directed a project that put these rolls on an animation stand and re-photographed them, frame by frame, onto modern motion picture film. The paper print collection is rich with reality images (about 1,300), such as troops leaving for the Spanish-American War, images of the aftermath of the 1906 San Francisco earthquake, and footage of various celebrities and political figures. The other 1,700 or so films in the collection are among the earliest fiction films. All of this material has, in the last decade or so, been digitally transferred and restored.

- The *Meet the Press* Collection. Includes almost 2,000 episodes of this influential Sunday morning news show, which has aired on NBC since 1949 (they are housed with the papers of the show's creator, Lawrence Spivak). Additional, more recent episodes are available directly from NBC News.

- The George Kleine Collection. This is the private collection (including films and papers) of Kleine (1864–1931), a film industry pioneer. The collection includes a variety of fiction and nonfiction films, including some of the earliest foreign films, produced before 1926, to make their way to the United States.

- Confiscated Enemy Films. This is a collection of works confiscated from Germany, Italy, and Japan during WWII. The German collection includes the newsreel *Die Deutsche Wochenschau*; missing issues in the run can be found in other archives in Germany and the United Kingdom. The Italian collection includes *Istituto Luce* newsreels (1938–1943). The Japanese collection includes three newsreels: *Asahi News* (1935–1939), *Nippon News* (1940–1945), and *Yomiura News* (1936–1940). Several decades ago, this material was considered to be in the public domain and free to use, but copyright to all captured material has been returned to the originating countries. Many prints remain on deposit at the Library.

LC Highlights: Stills Collections

Many of the millions of still photographs and artwork at the Library of Congress are in the public domain. Increasingly, low- and high-resolution digital images of these can be found through the Library's Print & Photographs Online Catalog (www.loc.gov/pictures/). Because digitization of stills is far from complete, you or a researcher should visit the Library in person to complete your research. Highlights include:

- The Farm Security Administration/Office of War Information Collection (FSA/OWI). This is probably the most famous photographic collection at the LC. The FSA's holdings represent roughly 250,000 photographs made between 1935 and 1942; the Office of War Information covers the 1940s. The FSA and OWI had an overlap of subject matter. The photographers represented in the two collections include Walker Evans, Dorothea Lange, Marion Post Wolcott, Ben Shahn, Russell Lee, and Jack Delano, whose Kodachrome photograph of World War II roundhouse workers in Iowa is on the cover of this book.
- The Detroit Publishing Company Collection. This features roughly 40,000 scenic postcards and photographs created between 1880 and 1924, mostly in the United States but also in Mexico, Europe, and Asia.
- The Arnold Genthe Collection. Genthe (1869–1942) emigrated to the United States from Germany in 1895, settling in San Francisco. The collection is extensive (some 19,000 images) and includes photographs of the residents of San Francisco's Chinatown before the 1906 earthquake, and of the quake's aftermath.
- The Civil War Photograph Collection. Includes photographs taken by or on behalf of Matthew Brady, or acquired by him, as discussed in Chapter 2.
- The African-American History Collection. This includes material (1909–1940) from the National Association for the Advancement of Colored People (NAACP), such as the NAACP campaigns against lynching, and portraits of famous African-Americans. A sub-collection, the W.E.B. DuBois albums, offer a glimpse of African-American life around 1900.
- The Edward S. Curtis Collection. Includes materials from Curtis's 20-volume *The North American Indian*, issued between 1907 and 1930, in which life among some 80 Native American tribes was documented. The collection includes over 1,600 prints.
- The Frances Benjamin Johnston Collection. A pioneering American photographer, Johnston (1864–1952) photographed

108

American social, political, and educational life, including classes at the Hampton Institute and the Tuskegee Institute. The collection includes about 20,000 prints and 3,700 glass and film negatives. It's been extremely useful to numerous documentaries needing illustrations of early 20th century southern rural life and has been consulted by art directors and costume designers on narrative features.

The Library of Congress also houses the collections of various news agencies, newspapers, and magazines. These include some five million photographs from the collection of *Look* magazine (1937–1951), including photographs by Stanley Kubrick and Gordon Parks. This collection is in the public domain, although images may not be used for "advertising or trade purposes." The Library also has collections from various newspaper morgues, wire services, and other news agencies, dating between the 1890s and the late 1960s.

LC Highlights: Sound Collections

The sound collections of the Library can be broken down into two distinct categories: radio broadcasts and everything else. The *radio broadcast division* includes donated and deposited material from a wide variety of sources, including:

- Armed Forces Radio, with a third of a million recordings covering Armed Forces Radio and Television Service (AFRTS) *domestic* broadcasts from the mid-1940s to the present. These include music and talk but are generally not news oriented.
- Donated broadcasts from radio stations WOR (New York), CBS Radio, WRC (Washington), as well as from the BBC (from about 1900 to the 1980s), and National Public Radio (NPR) from 1973, two years after it began.
- Broadcasts from Germany during the Third Reich, a companion to the captured German footage collection. Speeches and other audio are included.

The collections of *general sound recordings* include:

- Speeches by prominent politicians, entertainers, scientists, and others who've appeared before the National Press Club, beginning in 1952.
- The Archive of Recorded Poetry and Literature, from a series of readings given at the Library, beginning in the 1940s.

- An oral history project conducted by the Marine Corps with soldiers returning from the Pacific in the latter days of the Second World War.
- A collection donated by anthropologist Margaret Mead, which includes field recordings and lectures.
- The Vitaphone (and other synchronous disks) collection, which includes soundtrack disks from some of the earliest American "talkies," as described in Chapter 3.

LC Highlights: Newspaper and Magazine Collections

The Library of Congress carries an important collection of newspapers and news magazines (including some foreign publications). The collection starts in 1760 and continues to the present. For historical filmmakers, among the most useful publications are *Harper's Weekly* and *Frank Leslie's Illustrated Newspaper*, both of which offered cartoons as well as illustrations of news and features—sometimes factual, sometimes fanciful—in the years before 1880.

LC Highlights: The American Folklife Center

The American Folklife Center at the Library of Congress (www.loc.gov/folklife/) has been tapped by filmmakers and researchers since its inception in 1976. (It should not be confused with the Smithsonian Institution's Center for Folklife Programs and Cultural Heritage, which includes the Folkways Recordings.) This LC collection is thin on moving image holdings—these mainly include concert performances and ethnographic films—but it holds roughly 250,000 *still* images from fieldwork in rural areas of the United States.

The crown jewel of the American Folklife collection is its recorded sound material: more than 49,000 hours of audio recordings, from the first ethnographic cylinder recording in 1890 to recordings created this year. It includes spoken word (in various dialects and languages), recorded music, oral histories, and what has come to be known as "roots music." It's here that you'll find the field recordings of John and Alan Lomax and other collectors. There are also recordings of slave narratives and music performance collections, including those featuring Jelly Roll Morton and Woody Guthrie.

Other Routes to NARA and LC Materials

Commercial Archives

Finding and ordering materials from NARA and LC, which are both large government institutions, can take time, making it worthwhile to employ the expertise of film researchers who specialize in these collections. For clients with more money than time, it's possible to find some of the public domain material held at NARA and LC at commercial archives, and ordering from these commercial venues may make sense. In addition, if you just need a shot or two, the commercial route may prove to be less expensive because the government archives require that you duplicate entire rolls of their masters. In other words, what you spend in licensing costs paying for public domain material at commercial archives may be offset by what you save in duplication costs at government archives.

"Royalty-free" Intermediaries

Filmmakers who don't have the budget to go through commercial archives but are also concerned about working directly at NARA or LC—because of location, budget, time, or other constraints—often have a third option. Some companies serve as "intermediaries" between the government institutions and independents who need quicker, easier access to some of the more popular collections. They offer a limited amount of public domain government material to which they hold reproduction masters. Items can be ordered directly through them, often for a relatively low usage fee. This is entirely legal; the only drawback is that these companies hold only a fraction of everything that's available at the big institutions, and a thorough search through these institutions is always preferable unless you need something very specific.

While it's always better to go to the original source if you can, here are just two particularly useful intermediary companies:

- Footage Farm (www.footagefarm.com), which has masters of both NARA and LC footage, in addition to some unique Soviet films, old Christian films, and public domain educational films from the 1930s to the 1970s.
- North Wind Picture Archives (www.northwindpictures.com), which offers a collection of more than 500,000 public domain (still) images drawn from the Library of Congress's collection of 19th and early 20th century images of life in Europe and the United States, primarily pre-photographic illustrations from magazines and newspapers. Many of their images can be ordered with hand-coloring as an option.

Diverse Other Collections

One of the more challenging and enjoyable parts of film research is the sleuthing, as you try, with or without a professional guiding you, to uncover new and underutilized sources for material. These finds, in turn, often take your research and project in unexpected directions.

NARA and LC Source and Permission Contact Lists

Since not everything held at NARA and LC is in the public domain, and as a help to producers and film researchers, both institutions have posted lists that consist of a large number of commercial archives, stock footage houses, and even other government archives, along with contact information. These lists can serve as an excellent jumping-off point for producers as they explore the world outside these two major collections. The NARA list, for example, delineates the following categories of sources: newsreels, international sources, U.S. government sources, motion pictures sources, broadcasting sources, stock footage sources, presidential libraries, and miscellaneous sources. Unfortunately, these lists aren't always kept up to date—an issue that is most significant when it comes to commercial collections (which are more likely to shift ownership), but is less so for university collections, government collections, and places like the BBC and the Museum of Modern Art in New York.

Personal and Local Collections

Throughout your project's development and production, ask the experts or consultants you're working with about any personal collections of artifacts, photos, amateur films, and memorabilia they may have, or if they know of such collections. Scour books for photographs and graphics, remembering to make note of the credit line on any items you find. This is important if you need to go back to the originals in order to make higher-quality reproductions and/or license the materials for use.

Home Movies

Home movies are available from many individuals and from a variety of archives, including commercial collections such as Getty Images, online archives such as Internet Archive, and regional collections such as Northeast Historic Film in Maine, which also holds the collections of many New England television stations.

Ask at libraries or historical societies about home movies, and you may be referred to local collectors or others who've made or have access to footage. You might also consider placing an ad or using social media to seek material. If your project attracts press interest, consider including a pitch that you're seeking home movies, snapshots, and other materials.

Local Television News

It has always been very difficult to obtain news footage directly from local television stations. Stations are not set up to provide footage to outsiders and rarely have the time or personnel to conduct research, provide screeners or masters, or develop license agreements. Still, it's worth a try. Always work with the news director, rather than the station manager, because that person has a closer link to the archive. If the station has not kept its older footage, ask if their material was donated to an organization. (Sometimes you'll be referred to a collection of their older news film at a local public library, university, or historical society). If they are an official network affiliate, the footage may have been sent to the network.

Even when stations do have footage, their lawyers will often intervene and prohibit third-party sales because of potential lawsuits. But don't give up. Remind them that any license agreement they or you draw up is likely to indemnify them and put the onus for any legal actions on you. If you think there may be legal concerns, you and your lawyer should review your project's *errors and omissions* liability policy as well, to make sure you're covered for anything that may come up.

113

Historical Societies, Universities, and Public Libraries

Most cities and even many small towns have a historical society, museum, and/or library that may prove to be a source of valuable material. Most universities have special collections, housed not only in libraries but also sometimes within departments or programs. Just about all universities and their libraries have websites, often with online finding aids.

In these places, as in others, you are likely to find that someone must ultimately conduct research on site. If you or a team member can't do this work, ask the university library or historical society personnel if they would do the research for you and what they would charge. If they don't have the time (many don't), see if you might hire a student to be your proxy for an hourly rate. For example, on the documentary film, *Song for Cesar* (2020), about the music and art that grew out of the United Farmworkers Movement in California, an important collection of photographs taken by a movement insider was at the Beinecke Library at Yale University. Kenn hired and coordinated the work of a Yale undergraduate who, with guidance from the collection curator, did a great job finding the 30 or so photographs Kenn and the producers needed, out of a collection of over 9,000.

Depending on the copyright status of the material, some archivists at these sites may allow you to create your own reference images in person (using a portable scanner, camera, or smart phone, for example), as long as you come back to them for master copies (if needed) and licensing. It's a good idea to include a slate in the shot, or in a shot immediately before the picture of the item, that indicates the library accession number or other identifier. This can be as simple as a scrap of paper with the information handwritten on it.

As an added note, individuals and organizations, both well-known and obscure, will often donate their papers (and, increasingly, audiovisual materials) to these types of archives. Reviewing obituaries can prove surprisingly useful in steering you to specific collections, which may include letters, diaries, documents, and even images that can inform your film. Journalist Edward R. Murrow's papers and audiovisual materials, for example, were donated to the Fletcher School of Law and Diplomacy at Tufts University. Obituaries can also help you locate surviving family members who might have the individual's personal materials, or perhaps could tell you where they were donated.

A sampling of other important local collections in the United States includes:

- Bay Area Television Archive (part of San Francisco State University)
- Chicago Historical Society
- Harry Ransom Center at the University of Texas/Austin
- Newberry Library in Chicago (which holds the nation's best collection of antique maps)
- Wolfson Archives at the Miami-Dade College

Political Commercials

One of the best sources of historical political commercials is Internet Archive. Another important source is the Julian Kanter Political Commercial Archive at the University of Oklahoma; see https://pcc.ou.edu/ for details, and follow links to search the catalog. One advantage to the Kanter Collection is that many of their holdings are from high-quality original film prints. A disadvantage is that they tend to charge high usage fees, and you may need to get other clearances before using some of their holdings.

Lastly, look at the "living room candidate" site at the Museum of the Moving Image (www.livingroomcandidate.org/). There, you can watch entire television commercial packages for U.S. presidential campaigns from 1952 to the present. Again, some of these may require permission if you are not using them in a way that qualifies as fair use.

Photojournalism: Agencies and Newspapers

Good photojournalism can be history-changing and iconic, and some-times the line blurs between photojournalism and museum-quality art, as evidenced by the work of photographers such as Henri Cartier Bresson, Helen Levitt, W. Eugene Smith, Ruth Orkin, and Sebastião Salgado. Even Ansel Adams, thought of as a landscape photographer, was sometimes a photojournalist; his images and text about the Manzanar War Relocation Center in California, a Japanese internment camp, were published in 1944 as a government booklet, *Born Free and Equal* (1944).

Many filmmakers have discovered that the use of powerful still images, alone or in a sequence, can be extraordinarily effective even when moving image also exists. Filmmakers can run audio over such a sequence or combine motion and stills, as was done to great effect in the Oscar-winning *If Beale Street Could Talk* (2018), written and directed by Barry Jenkins, based on James Baldwin's 1974 novel of the same title.

Many photojournalists are (or were) members of agencies such as Magnum or Black Star, or worked for wire services like the Associated Press or what was formerly UPI (now owned by Getty), Gamma-Liaison (also represented by Getty), Agence France-Presse (the world's oldest continuing photo agency), and others. Consult these photographic agencies and their websites for stills; also be sure to check the photo morgues (or archives) of newspapers and magazines. In some cases, newspapers have consigned their photo archives to commercial agencies to represent for commercial use.

Newspapers as Archival Visuals

Obtaining images of actual newspaper pages has become easier in the digital age. Most libraries in large cities subscribe to online newspaper databases, even while they may still have bound volumes (or microfilm/microfiche) of these same publications. There are commercial sources of old newspapers as well, including Newspapers.com, a subscription service run by Ancestry. As of this writing, their collection includes a searchable database of facsimiles of over 12,000 newspapers from the 1700s and after. Newspapers.com tends to favor local and state papers from the United States, which is very useful for local stories, and they also have some nation-wide domestic and foreign publications.

ProQuest (proquest.com) is a database of all kinds of written materials, subscribed to by many public and university libraries and accessible through them. Of course, for more targeted searches, check the database of a particular newspaper. Several universities have mounted efforts to digitize local area newspapers, so try that as well.

Corporate and Industrial Collections

Corporate collections relevant to your subject can be a source not only for content research but also audiovisual materials, from public relations to advertising. Generally your first contact would be with the company's publicity department. (Note that television commercials produced after the 1950s may be subject to additional clearances.)

Depending on your project's needs, you should also explore the archives of national or international *industry groups* related to your subject, as well as specialized magazines and other publications that cater to the industry you are exploring. One extraordinary source of industry publications, going back decades, is the Prelinger Library in San Francisco.

Sources and Notes

"A Nation of Law?" was directed by Terry Kay Rockefeller, Thomas Ott, and Louis Massiah for the second season of *Eyes on the Prize*. *The Black Panthers* was directed by Stanley Nelson. The 2010 FOCAL report can be found at www.focalint.org/industry-news/news/243/audio-visual-archives-see-opportunities-for-growth. Information about the U.S. National Archives is available from their website, www.archives.gov/publications/general-info-leaflets/1-about-archives.html. Information about the U.S. Library of Congress is available from their website, September 2019: www.loc.gov/about/general-information/#year-at-a-glance. NARA's list of archival resources can be found at www.archives.gov/research/order/film-sources-contact-list, while the Library of Congress's list can be found here: www.loc.gov/rr/mopic/onlinesources.html. Information about Ansel Adams's *Born Free and Equal* can be found at http://anseladams.com/born-free-and-equal/ and at the Library of Congress, www.loc.gov/pictures/collection/manz/book.html.

CHAPTER 7

Should You Hire a Professional?

As many of you already know, finding, using, and negotiating archival materials can be very complicated. Depending on how much material you need to use, what the source of that material is, and what use you plan to make of it, you may want to seek professional assistance. In fact, a quick scan of the credits of recent award-winning films will reveal that many filmmakers use archival specialists. There is a range of experts available whose knowledge of stills, footage, archival sound, and music can enrich your film and streamline the research and licensing process. Drawing on conversations with researchers in the United States, Canada, Australia, Italy, and Russia, this chapter offers advice for how to get the most out of your work with professionals, especially visuals researchers, and strategies that should prove to be useful even if you take on some or all of this work yourself.

Do You Need Help?

Even if your budget is low to nonexistent, don't be too quick to dismiss the idea of using a professional research consultant, either for music or visuals. Depending on how much of these materials you're hoping to use, professionals can often save you the cost of their fees and much more. They can:

- Help you accurately budget for archival materials;
- Warn you away from materials that are unavailable or likely to be budget-busters and steer you toward appropriate substitutions;

- Alert you if you're being quoted commercial rates for material that is in the public domain and may be available for significantly less elsewhere;
- Help you discover new or unusual materials that make your film stand out from others on similar topics;
- Be your eyes and ears at distant archives, thus saving you travel expenses;
- Help you explore creative ways to use archival materials more effectively.

If you're doing a film that relies heavily on archival materials and/or depends on the use of commercially-recorded music, and/or depends on access to feature film or television material owned by a major studio, chances are you *should* hire a professional. It's more than likely that the costs involved, provided you find someone with relevant experience, will be offset by the quality and even affordability of what's found, not least because they are likely to be more effective than you in negotiations with rights-holders. "You're benefiting not only from the speed factor, because we cut through and get callbacks and emails returned, [but] also we just know where the good stuff is," explains Canadian researcher Elizabeth Klinck, who received the 2019 Academy of Canadian Cinema and Television's Board of Directors' Tribute for her career as a visual researcher and her volunteerism in Canada and beyond. "Furthermore," Klinck adds, "a researcher is likely to know when a company is charging as much as $150 per second for material that is available rights-free elsewhere, such as at the U.S. National Archives."

Italian researcher Mauro Tonini agrees. "A researcher knows archives, collections, institutions, experts," he said. "Sometimes they know about different footage, something that will allow you to tell the story from an unexpected angle." Furthermore, he adds, "Not every producer knows how to judge the quality of archival footage. And sometimes they don't know how to handle it and correctly use it; I've seen format distortions that are unacceptable, horrific color corrections."

Australian archival researcher and archival producer Lisa Savage, too, stresses that contacting a researcher earlier can lead to cost savings later. "I had one director say to me, 'I wish we'd put you on at the beginning, because you've already saved us thousands of dollars in license fees, because you found alternatives, and you've had deals.'"

It's very important to accurately budget for archival use, even as you're writing your first project proposals and seeking funding support. An archival researcher can discuss your needs and look over your budget,

118

which might give you a competitive edge when you're fundraising. (Proposal reviewers *will* notice if you're promising material you likely can't deliver within your budget or time frame.) Too often, though, a project is at the rough cut stage or farther before a professional researcher is consulted. Producers learn the hard way that their anticipated costs to license the music and visuals that they already built their project around are impossibly high, and at times the project itself needs to be reconceived. The discrepancy can be huge—a budget of $5,000 for license fees that should more accurately be at least $80,000, for example. Too late, a director hoping for theatrical release and Oscar contention may find that they can only afford to clear rights for film festivals, as discussed in later chapters.

In other words, don't *not* contact a researcher simply because your budget is limited.

Can *You Do It Alone?*

If you're seeking material from local or familiar sources (people you know, historical societies, a local corporation), you don't necessarily need a researcher. Likewise, if most of what you want is held by a handful of archives and you have the budget to license from them, you probably don't need help finding and obtaining those materials, and you may not need help negotiating license fees—although you should have a lawyer review the final agreements. Plenty of filmmakers have successfully negotiated permission to use material from radio and news programs, feature films, commercial advertising, and more.

On the other hand, it still may be worth hiring a professional for a day or even a half day of consulting early on. The rate for visuals research and research consulting varies, but at present in the United States it hovers between about $300 and $600 per day, with $350 to $400 per day being the norm for someone with experience.

Working Internationally

If your research involves archives outside your home country, a researcher may be essential. Mauro Tonini says that for the past few years, he's "worked more for international producers than for Italian ones, providing footage and other material from Italian archives and collections." There is a wide variety of repositories in Italy, he notes, each with its own specialty. "There are some larger archives here, like Istituto Luce, Cinecittá, or Alinari (for still photographs), where you can pretty much do research online," Tonini says. "Alinari is the oldest photographic museum in the world, founded in 1854 in Florence. And then there's RAI television; you can't do research online with them, you have to go in and screen. Many smaller archives have very interesting materials. Some are quick and efficient, like the municipal film archives in Milan and Bologna. With others, like the Friuli Venezia-Giulia Regional Film Archive, you need to [be on-site] to do specific research."

Tonini also conducts information research for international clients. "I like both," he says, explaining that he's currently doing research for a nature/anthropology series about the north Italian lakes. "I had to find out personal stories that could get the public [to watch] and at the same time make them curious about the lake environment," he says. "I came home from the lake some days ago and I'm writing my final report now, with all of the information they'll need to decide which stories they prefer, when and how they can be told, what they can shoot and what the interviews could show. I'll also tell them about locations, possible scheduling and contacts. I had to find out also where and how they could film wild animals." Noting the challenge—the October shoot coincides with hibernation and migration—he adds that he'll accompany the crew to the region when they film, and serve as translator.

Alexander Kandaurov was a researcher in Moscow when we first spoke with him in 2008. Now retired, he recalls the relative centralization of collections in Russia, dating back to the days of the Soviet Union: "When it comes to audiovisual libraries, the two largest collections in Russia are the Russian State Archives of Film and Photo Documents, in Krasnogorsk, and the Russian State Archives of Scientific and Technical Documents, in Moscow." Gosfilmofond, the state film archive in Russia that was founded in 1948, is another important source of material. "This treasure trove stores all Soviet feature films and foreign newsreels and documentaries captured by the Soviet Army in World War II, including German, Chinese, Japanese, and many others," he says.

Music Consultants

When it comes to clearing music, a specialist who works with licensors every day can mean the difference between a "yes" (or a disappointing but still useful "no") and weeks, if not months, of unanswered emails and voicemails. As in the film industry, busy music executives are notorious for ignoring calls from filmmakers they don't know.

While some visuals researchers are also familiar with music clearance issues, most are not, because music clearances are uniquely complex.

A music specialist can help you license commercially-recorded music (from music publishing companies and labels, big and small) or guide you to stock music libraries, which offer less expensive options. *Music supervisors* can significantly enrich your film by helping you to create a musical soundtrack that serves as an additional story element, or that immediately immerses your audience in a bygone time and place. The Internet Movie Database (IMDb.com) describes a music supervisor as "A person who coordinates the work of the composer, the editor, and sound mixers. Alternately, a person who researches, obtains rights to, and supplies songs for a production." For example, for *Abraham and Mary Lincoln: A House Divided* (2011), New York-based music supervisor Rena Kosersky provided recordings of music played on 19th century brass instruments and recommended a brass ensemble for on-camera performances. In addition, she says, "I discovered specific songs that the Lincolns loved, including the manuscript parts of a long forgotten 'Mary Lincoln Polka,' which was originally performed by the Marine Band at her White House reception." By searching public and private collections, Kosersky is able to provide music that is historically authentic as well as unusual. "I don't go for the icons," she explains. "There is so much marvelous music that isn't heard anymore that was famous at one time."

The cost to work with a music specialist varies greatly, depending on the services needed and the experience of the consultant. Some may charge by the hour; others, if they're primarily being asked to clear licenses, may charge per license. The actual cost per project will also vary depending on the amount of music needed and the complexity of the rights needed.

Finding A Music or Visuals Consultant

One of the most effective ways to find a skilled consultant is to look at the credits on films that are comparable in scope to the film you anticipate making. If an online search doesn't lead you to the person directly, try to make contact through the film's production company. Be aware that there is no licensing or accreditation for this kind of work, which means that anybody can claim an ability to do it. Always get references from people with whom the individual has worked, and watch films they've worked on to see if they might be a good match for your subject matter.

Houdini and the Water Torture Cell, ca. 1913. From the
U.S. Library of Congress/McManus-Young Collection.

When to Contact a Consultant

As noted, both music and visuals experts agree that they're often
contacted too late in the process to be as effective as they might be.
Producers will reach out to them when they need last-minute help in
finding or negotiating for materials after a member of the production
staff—often the most junior member—has hit a dead end. Not only
does this make the consultant's job more difficult, because it means
starting by untangling someone else's work (or smoothing over strained
relations between the staff member and rights holders), it also means
that opportunities for archival content may have been missed. "In the
perfect world, I would love to be in the beginning of a project, at least
have a treatment of it, and understand what some of the music concepts
might be," Rena Kosersky says.

122

How Much Time Will You Need?

It's often difficult, at the outset, for researchers to fully estimate the amount of time needed to find, preview, order, and clear footage or music. Those we spoke with say they do their best to offer a preliminary estimate and are willing to communicate with the filmmakers as interests and needs expand and contract. "Little things you can guess, but if it's anything broader, I always say, 'You tell me how many days, or maybe what I should do is spend three days, find what I can, make you viewing copies and then send [them] to you,'" says Washington, D.C.-based researcher Bonnie Rowan, an expert in navigating the collections at the U.S. National Archives and Library of Congress. "And then I'll make notes and I'll say, 'I didn't get to this, I didn't get to this, I think there's a lot more here;' that kind of thing." This is often the best way to work with a researcher.

Also as noted, most visuals researchers charge a day rate while they're researching on-site, but they may instead charge a per-hour rate if they are doing little bits and pieces of work, waiting for a phone call back from an archive or juggling online research for a variety of projects on the same day.

Remember That What You See Online is the Tip of the Iceberg

Given the ever-increasing wealth of online collections, media makers can get lulled into thinking that an archival search can be done from the home office, which is a big mistake. Professionals *do* use the web, of course, especially for jobs that involve a quick turnaround, and for high-budget commercial clients in need of the kind of material that's easily available through stock house portals. But "we are of the breed of 'just because it's not online doesn't mean it doesn't exist,'" says Savage, about herself and other archival researchers and producers.

In fact, only ten percent of the Library of Congress's over sixteen million images can be seen online (and only ten percent of those can be downloaded), Bonnie Rowan reminded us recently. Only 365 of their motion picture holdings are online, out of more than a million. Likewise, only about eight percent of the National Archives's motion pictures can be viewed online.

Also based in Washington, D.C. is Polly Pettit, who worked on Ken Burns's *The Vietnam War* (1990) and Stanley Nelson's *Freedom Riders* (2010) for PBS. She notes that while digitization at the National Archives is moving forward, it's still primarily for access via their *on-site* computer, rather than the web. "Their preservation lab has been doing a phenomenal job of digitizing reference copies from every prior format, so there are many mp4 [moving image] files," she says. "They've been able to convert whole collections much faster than we expected." At the same time, she adds, while these digital files "may not have been uploaded to their online catalog, there still may be a digital file in the reference room." For most of the collections in Washington, including the various Smithsonian archives and the National Library of Medicine, on-site research is best. Often producers will sit with the researcher for part of the time they are on site, in order to get a sense of what's being found. Particularly at the archives in Washington, this is a great idea, if your budget allows for it.

Additionally, the in-person involvement of a researcher can lead to discoveries that result from vague or missing labeling. A researcher may find people in footage who are not identified in the logs, for example. Along the same lines, they may help to correct the record and prevent you from misusing material inadvertently. While working as a film researcher on the final episode of the 1983 archival series *Vietnam: A Television History*, for example, Kenn found a reel of 16mm ABC News film marked "Vietnam Evac." It seemed to be exactly what he was looking for, footage of the panic that ensued at the U.S. embassy in Saigon as the last Americans left the country in 1975. Better yet, these scenes of the evacuation, with civilians clamoring over the embassy fence and grabbing at helicopters as they took off from the roof—iconic images of the war—were in better condition than other coverage he'd been finding of the event. The footage had no sound, which wasn't unusual. But something seemed off: every so often, the panic seemed to suddenly stop. People relaxed, climbed down from the fences, and came down from the roof. Finally, a slate on screen revealed the truth: this wasn't news footage of the evacuation of Saigon; it was news footage shot in Thailand about Hollywood director Michael Cimino's re-creation of the evacuation of Saigon for his film, *The Deer Hunter*.

Quality Research Often Demands More Time

Media makers who turn out "product" on impossible schedules and budgets may have to settle for whatever archival material is quickly available. When this happens, archival visuals (sometimes chosen by price and easy access) are used generally to cover edits or give viewers something to watch over narration, a technique often referred to as *wall-papering*. You can usually tell if a film was constructed in this way, not least because the archival visuals may have a generic quality to them. This technique can be found across the entire spectrum of filmmaking, from low budget to blockbuster and from documentary to drama. Budgeting sufficient time and money for research can mean the difference between using material that's barely relevant or that everyone's already used, and finding something groundbreaking and using it in a way that makes your project stand out.

Incorporating the Researcher into the Creative Team

When asked back in 2008 what makes someone a good archival researcher, whether for a documentary or a narrative film, Washington, D.C. researcher David Thaxton replied, "Curiosity, a knowledge of history, perseverance, and patience." A good researcher wants to pursue something to the bitter end; when it seems that every stone has been turned over, that researcher will wake in the middle of the night thinking of something else to try. Researchers are attracted to the passion and commitment of the filmmakers for whom they work. They, too, want to become passionate about your subject and film and to know that their contribution will be valued; that they are true colleagues. A skilled archival researcher can be far more than your eyes and ears at an archive; instead, they can serve as an essential part of your creative team. There are some ways in which you can help to make this possible, including the following:

Share the Treatment, Screenplay, or Manuscript

Unless you're only looking for a few shots or clips, send the researcher a copy of your film's treatment, or in the case of a fiction film, its screenplay or shooting script. If you are writing a book and using a researcher to help you obtain and clear photographs or other graphic materials, share the manuscript, or at least the relevant parts. Engage them in the subject matter. It's one thing to ask for "images of the victorious first weeks of the Nazi invasion into Russia in World War II," explains Russian researcher Alexander Kandaurov. "It's quite another if the producer says, 'I want you to find images showing the frustration of Russians, the bitterness, the grief, the will for revenge at any cost.'" The latter, he says, "is a challenge. I feel intrigued. My role is important. I feel I am a co-author and not merely a collector of images everybody knows from dozens of films."

By sharing the treatment, the producer is inviting the researcher or archive producer to bring their own expertise and the memory of years of previous research and countless hours spent in archives to bear. Archive producers have file cabinets full of notes from all the projects they've worked on. They also have extraordinary memories. They can bring all that to the table—*your* table. And as filmmakers themselves, by seeing the script or treatment, they can suggest alternatives that may work even better than what's called for.

Delegate Responsibility

When you've hired a researcher, don't independently cover the same territory. This may seem obvious, but it's a problem many researchers face. When producers "double up"—doing their own digging or, sometimes worse, their own negotiating while a consultant is doing the same thing on their behalf, it can hurt the project, says archival producer Lisa Savage. "Our main job is to build up a relationship with the footage providers; get them on your side. You can't do that if you've got 10 different cooks in the kitchen trying to do it as well."

Know Your Subject Well

The better you know not only the specifics of your story but also the context in which it takes place, and the better you communicate these details to your researcher(s), the more likely it is that you'll find a range of materials that are useful. The specifics you provide can make a tremendous difference when archival content is not cataloged thoroughly or accurately.

Be Flexible and Open to Alternatives

With both visuals and music, be aware that your odds of saving money go up when you know your subject well enough to recognize viable alternatives. It's not unusual for a researcher to know that the cost to license *this* footage of a World War II event is expensive but *that* comparable footage of the same event is available rights-free because it is in the U.S. public domain. Or, if your subject has already been well-covered and audiences are more than familiar with the same few moving image clips that every project uses, an archival producer may know of stills that have rarely been seen, giving you an opportunity to combine them into a powerful and unexpected photo montage. If you have your heart set on a song recorded by a specific artist but the record label is difficult to deal with, a music researcher or music supervisor may know a *workaround*—an alternative route to get what you need. Sometimes another artist has done a cover of the song on another label. Sometimes there may be "outtakes" or alternative performances of the same recording that are owned by the artist instead of the label.

Trucks loaded with potatoes line up in front of starch factory in Caribou, Maine (Oct. 1940). Photo by Jack Delano; from U.S. Library of Congress.

The Thrill of the Hunt

Archive researchers and producers often compare themselves to detectives, and while they may also be expert at handling clearances, that's rarely the most interesting part of their job. It's the thrill of the hunt that really inspires them. Here are a few examples of researchers' favorite discoveries:

- "One of the most amazing things about the Krasnogorsk Archives is that you may work there for years and yet run into something you never saw before," Alexander Kandaurov says. "Once I was doing research for a 'Stalin and Hitler' story by a British company. I was looking through a familiar and much-overused box of Stalin catalog cards when I ran into a card describing several reels of 'color rushes re Stalin funeral.' The rushes contained unedited raw color images of a variety of mourners at the coffin, starting with his children, Vasily and Svetlana."
- Mauro Tonini discovered the thrill of research as an art history student. "I had worked on some paintings by the Italian painter

Mario Schifano (1934–1998), compared with three films he made at the end of the 1960s," he says. "Schifano had been in New York and met [Andy] Warhol in 1964. Then he came back to Rome and started filming—well, he started in New York … I found the unpublished script for the most famous film made by Schifano, the documentary *Umano non Umano* (*Human not Human*, 1969), which he wrote himself, with a typewriter. A gold-miner having found a nugget would not have been so delighted."

More recently, Tonini was asked to work on a documentary for the History Channel and RAI, entitled *Viminale: Mussolini's Last Ship*, about an Italian merchant vessel that was sunk in the Mediterranean during World War II. "It previously had been used to carry Italian immigrants to Australia," he says. "A producer asked me to find any kind of photograph, document—anything that could help tell the story of this vessel. And, by the way, could I possibly find anyone who made their way to Australia on it in the 1920s?" Tonini had doubts: "After 80 years, was I really going to find anyone who was still living, and would they have any photographs or mementos?" The National Archives in Australia helped him to find passenger lists in their archive, which was not yet digitized. "Two sisters who traveled on that ship when they were just children were on the list—and they were still alive," he says. Again, through the archives, he found an old address and phone number for them, in Melbourne. "They answered the phone. Eighty years in Australia and they only spoke a southern Italian dialect. Can you imagine them living that way, so far from home, for their entire lives? You can make a wonderful film from a story like that."

■ Channel Seven had all these Sinatra films, 16mm news stories, and they were just labeled "Sinatra," Australian Lisa Savage remembers. "I got them all transferred, and I'm sitting there watching them, and one of them was gold. It was of Sinatra's bodyguards when he came out here [in 1974, on tour] and he made that big comment about journalists are prostitutes. And it's all on film, all with sound." Another find at Channel 7, she reports, "was Johnny Cash … It was him doing a concert, not in Sydney, not in Melbourne, but in an Aboriginal mission out in the Outback. And he's with his wife, and his son is probably about four. And he's … eating kangaroo tail; with June and Johnny on stage, singing; and he goes down a mine, with all the miners. It's amazing stuff. And it's color."

A Tradition of Advocacy

An unsung role of archival researchers, for which filmmakers really owe them a debt, is that of advocating for access and usability at the archives. To explain: There is an inherent tension in many archives, particularly those that are not commercial, between the demands of preservation and those of access and use. Organizations that house historic collections are focused on protecting materials for the long term, and some view outside access as a threat. Media makers, on the other hand, need access. They have archivists to thank for changes in some archives that have allowed them, for example, to carefully bring in equipment to make dubs to use in editing (prior to ordering higher-quality masters). Researchers have also fought for archives to remain open for longer hours and to keep their viewing equipment in good repair, and they continue to advocate for keeping public archives out of private hands.

Years ago, Bonnie Rowan was among those who fought for the right to make dubs of public domain material at the National Archives and Records Administration. "We screamed and yelled and went to Congress and went all over, and then they changed and said, 'Yes, you're right. We'll let you do it.' Then they took it away and we got it back. All of those things we do as freelancers in our unpaid time. We've discovered things that no one would ever know about, we have lobbied and spent a lot of time fighting to make the facility the way it is today," she says.

Notes and Sources

To contact those interviewed, visit their websites: Elizabeth Klinck (www.elizabethklinck.com), Mauro Tonini (www.maurotonini.com), Bonnie Rowan (www.linkedin.com/in/bonnie-rowan-8263a18), and Lisa Savage (http://savagearchive.tv). *Vietnam: A Television History* was originally broadcast in 1983 in 13 episodes but condensed in 1997 when it was re-licensed for rebroadcast on *The American Experience*. At that time, the final episode was dropped. *Viminale: Mussolini's Last Ship* was directed by Victoria Hughes.

CHAPTER 8

Organizing and Ordering Materials

This chapter is primarily for media makers planning to obtain third-party visual and aural material to incorporate into their work-in-progress as they edit. It may also prove useful to those who want to digitize their own archival collections, or those who need to access archival materials in a useable format for research purposes. It's organized in steps that include obtaining and formatting visuals for the editing process, and then obtaining and formatting *masters* for the final product.

For editors incorporating third-party material, the general assumption is that you're working on a computer-based nonlinear system, such as Adobe Premiere Pro, Avid Media Composer, or Final Cut Pro, which means working with a *timeline*. While this editing technology has come to be called *nonlinear*, the project (as it's constructed) moves in a single, linear direction—from the start of the work through to the middle and the end. This is visualized in graphic form with horizontal bars or tracks below the monitor(s); this "timeline" is what's referred to in the information that follows.

A Standard Workflow

Film and video projects, whether documentary or drama, tend to follow a straightforward production path described in the following sections.

Preproduction

- Outlines, treatments, and/or scripts are drafted as makers decide which story or stories they want to tell, how they want to tell them, and what the delivery format(s) are, taking into consideration schedules, budgets, and contractual requirements.
- Preliminary research of original shooting needs and third-party elements is conducted.
- Depending on the third-party materials producers may hope to use, an archivist or researcher may be hired to conduct and/or coordinate research and begin to plan for the clearance process. These individuals often work with production managers, assistant editors, post-production supervisors, and/or associate producers.

Production

- Location filming gets underway, as scenes, sequences, B-roll, interviews, and other original materials (created by the filmmakers themselves) are recorded. In the case of fiction films, the shooting script is followed. (Most documentaries are not generally scripted in advance, although they may follow a general *shooting treatment*.)
- Archival research also gets underway as needed, whether the film is fiction or nonfiction. Third-party materials are identified and usually rough copies, called *screeners* or *comps*, are acquired by staff and/or professional researchers. Experienced production teams know that a lot will change, for the better, as this process moves forward. When producing nonfiction, never force interview and archival material into a predetermined storyline or argument when your ongoing research and evidence is steering you in a different direction.

Editing

The editing process often begins while shooting is still underway, and it will continue as additional material is filmed, archival material brought into the edit room, and music is identified. This way, an assembly of the film is in progress and the emerging story and structure can be clarified, while the rough archival materials can still inform some of the shooting.

In general, the editing process (also sometimes called "post-production") of projects that incorporate third-party materials moves along the path explained below.

Getting to the Assembly

- Production and editing teams screen the *rushes* or *dailies*, the raw footage that's been shot, along with any archival material that's been gathered.
- *Selects* are made and a rough *assembly* of the film is created, which often mirrors the film's intended structure (or in the case of fiction, follows the shooting script) but may run three or more times the length of the final film. With documentary work, *an editing script* will evolve as work moves forward.
- Obtaining screener copies of third-party materials continues, and at this stage generally also involves the editor and assistant editors.
- Graphic designers may begin to work on an opening title sequence, original maps, or other graphics if necessary, and on any planned animation of still photos or artwork.
- A post-production supervisor will usually also be hired at this stage, in anticipation of the steps necessary to usher the final edited film through the process of creating a technically polished master for release.

Rough Cut

- A rough cut is longer than the final film, but the story, structure, major characters, and most significant archival materials should be in place. In general, the rough cut may be ready about halfway through the editing process. Filmmakers often invite outsiders to screen rough cuts to see if the story and film are working. (Note: If you are hoping to use commercially-recorded music, the complexity of rights clearance means that you *must* make music selections by rough cut and have backup choices for all your music.)
- Lessons learned from the rough cut screening(s) are incorporated as the film continues to be revised and cut down to time.

Fine Cut

By fine cut, the film is close to time, but may be a bit longer than the final edited length. Even this close to the end of the editing schedule, filmmakers may decide to make structural changes, and they often identify holes in the project that need to be closed with additional "pick up" filming or a new look at archival materials. Entire scenes or sequences may be discarded if they aren't needed now that the film has taken shape. Any third-party material that's been drafted into the film, if research has shown it cannot be acquired or licensed, will need to be replaced.

Picture and Sound Lock

As the name implies, a film is *locked* when it's at its finished length and no additional changes to the visuals will be made. At this point, *final archival masters* should be obtained and, if necessary, *up-res'd*, which means using a Teranex or similar device to bring the visuals up to the format and resolution required for the final deliverable. The up-res'd version of each shot will need to replace the screeners in the timeline, usually the work of an assistant or apprentice editor. You should also finalize all necessary clearances and paperwork. The sound lock generally comes slightly later, as music, effects, and dialogue tracks are created by the sound editors. They will provide *stems*; these are computer files that represent each individual audio track to be taken into the final sound mix.

At this point in the project, you should also be gathering up all of the paperwork you've collected along the way, such as releases, personnel contracts, licensing agreements, and fair use and due diligence letters from your production lawyer. All of these together comprise what's known as your *rights bible*.

Interrupting the Workflow

No media project follows a straight trajectory, and interesting things can happen when the workflow is interrupted or changed. Some of the best moments occur when filmmakers find archival materials in advance of shooting and use them to shape their approach, spark subjects' memories, or inform film storytelling. For example, a producer for the 1983 PBS series *Vietnam: A Television History* set out to explore a controversial 1965 CBS News report about U.S. forces setting fires in the village of Cam Ne in South Vietnam. Prior to shooting, he obtained a copy of the televised report and printed out frame grabs. The production team brought these images to Vietnam, where local residents helped to identify and locate some of the people in the report. The team then interviewed these people, powerfully intercutting the new interviews with the CBS material shot 16 years earlier.

Practical Considerations

Finding, ordering, and clearing third-party materials takes time, whether you're thinking of using just one recorded Motown hit or you're building an entire series on archival materials, such as *O.J.: Made in America* (2016). In the following sections there are some tips for helping you and your team stay on track.

Ngo Thi Thiep in footage from the *CBS Evening News*, 1965 …

Ngo Thi Thiep

… and as filmed by WGBH in 1981 for the PBS series *Vietnam: A Television History.*

Getting Organized

Given the specificity you'll need when obtaining masters for and rights to the materials you end up using, organization is everything. From the start of the project, set up and maintain a tracking system. Nonlinear editing systems have shot-logging utilities and can create organized, virtual bins for digital clips as material is ingested. Organize these bins in a way that works for the editing team, but aim for clarity and consistency, perhaps putting archive information into the clip names.

Build a Gatekeeper Database

If you are using a significant amount of archival material, consider logging that material into a *gatekeeper database*, to be maintained by an in-house archivist, assistant editor, or associate producer. As new items arrive, crucial information about them should be entered into the database by that person *before the material is given to the editors*. This information will be more complete and organized differently than the shot log your editor uses. It's geared toward financial tracking, reporting to archives in order to acquire masters and license agreements, and it's a way to maintain detailed, searchable content information. A properly designed system will enable you to:

- Search through detailed content information to find specific items by key word or date;
- Know which digitized clips are from which source;
- Develop a final report to each archive about what you've used;
- Construct your archival list for your film's credits;
- Confirm that materials haven't been misplaced or have failed to arrive;
- Keep track of burned-in archival ID codes; and
- Confirm, as appropriate, that you are being accurate in your use of historical materials.

You can develop any kind of gatekeeper system that works for you, from simple to complex. Many producers use spreadsheets. Kenn uses a system he created, SHOWLOG, which he sometimes licenses to productions. It runs on the database software FileMaker Pro, which is *cross-platform* (that is, it runs on a Mac or a PC) and includes a few key elements that you'll want to incorporate even if you design your own system: *story numbers, titles, thumbnail images, sources,* and *source ID numbers*. It's also useful if the system you use can record additional data as needed, and if you can link it to your *edit decision list*.

Story Number

SHOWLOG is predicated on the idea, developed by the producers of *The World at War* (1973), that each item (database record) in the system, regardless of what type of material it is, gets a unique identification number (called a *story number*). FileMaker Pro has a function where a field can be designated to auto-generate a unique number for each new record. A *story* is one archival item from one source with one *source reference number*—an identifier necessary for the archive to know in order to retrieve its original material. It might be a film reel number, a news assignment number, or some other designation. Sometimes it's burned into your rough copy, if you received it from the archive that owns it. This is also the basic "unit of measure" for your report to archives, after your picture is locked and you need masters.

- If there is physical material accompanying the item (such as a photograph, videotape reel, or CD), the item should be tagged with the same story number the database has assigned to it. This makes original items much easier to find and identify as your shelves fill up. If all of your material is being obtained digitally, there won't be physical items to label and store. In that case, use the story number as part of the clip name as you import items into bins.
- Sometimes, a screener file from an archive will have multiple stories, from different original reels or tapes at the archive, strung together. In that case, you should separate them into different clips. Log the head and tail timecode cues for each story into the database, and note if there's an additional burned-in archival reel number or other archive ID.

Thumbnail Images

If you have the technology to scan stills and/or create frame grabs from moving image, it can be very useful to include thumbnail images in your gatekeeper database for quick visual reference. Suppose you have five different portraits of Charles Darwin; thumbnails will help you differentiate between them. Including thumbnails is easy in FileMaker Pro, and the software can similarly include or point to QuickTime clips and audio files, although the file size of the database will increase exponentially.

Titles

Make sure that each item entered into the editing system's shot logger has a clip name or column that includes the story number. Often, editors using SHOWLOG will prefix a title with the story number, such as: "155 *Detroit Riots Broken Window*." With the story number, you can easily match a digitized shot in the editing system bin with detailed information about that item from the database, and essentially follow that piece of the jigsaw puzzle through its journey from arrival in the edit room through to the last stages of post-production. The thumbnail image of the item in the database serves as a double check.

Additional Data

You want your database to work for you and to help minimize the amount of time you spend tracking back through information. You'll need:

- Contact information for each potential source you're using;
- Price quotes from each archive you may be licensing from (although quotes may be revised later, through negotiations);
- Details about music rights owners for each piece of archival music;
- Details about the various guilds you may need to contact regarding actors who appear in entertainment clips.

Link to Edit Decision List

A key benefit of a gatekeeper database is that you may be able to link it to your edit decision list (EDL), which conforms to your final picture and sound lock. Linking can facilitate the creation of financial tallies, reports to archives, and even a log of your entire finished show, if you also log your original footage and music. Often XML files created by your editing system can be the key to linking EDLs to your database.

Do You Need a Gatekeeper Database?

SHOWLOG or any such database can be overkill if you aren't expecting to use more than a couple of shots or sequences of archival material, if it's all coming from one place, or if it's in the public domain (which means that you don't have to report back to an archive). Usually, when obtaining material from public domain sources, it's best to simply order your master materials up front, unless it's prohibitively expensive. But if your project is heavily archival or the sources are complex, it can be very helpful to develop a database *before footage and stills start to arrive* in order to track them.

Ordering the Visuals You Need

Remember that there are two points in the production process at which you'll be ordering visual materials. The first is when you need lesser-quality images for research and editing, as you figure out what you want to include. The second is when you've made final selections and need high-quality masters.

As noted, motion picture footage has been created using many technical formats, both analog and, far more recently, digital. Most current media projects require that this material be available for use in digital form. If you're lucky, the archive or copyright holder has already done the digitization and can send you screeners and masters as files. Otherwise, you'll need to find a way to have the original digitized. With still photographs that are not yet digitized, you may be able to do this work yourself using a flatbed scanner. Scanners with sufficient resolution, even for a 4K project, have become so inexpensive that many filmmakers keep one in the edit room or office in order to convert stills.

Ordering Motion Picture Footage for Research and Editing

Identifying the Copyright Holder
Although you can pull material off the web or copy chunks of already-edited films and use them as "scratch" material in your early editing, we strongly discourage this practice. Getting attached to material without knowing who owns it or how you might obtain and license masters is likely to result in major problems. Better to identify the rights holders and legitimate sources of "scratch" material early on.

Identifying Places that Hold Originals (or Digital Masters) of the Material You Want
Sometimes, the footage or stills you want are available from only one source. But for events that were widely covered—for example, a presidential inaugural speech or some other event documented by numerous news agencies, all of which copyrighted their own material—then you have a choice of where to go for footage. Take advantage of this when you can. Without limiting your choices, the more items you can order and ultimately license from the least number of different sources, the better. It can streamline the entire process and reduce overall costs.

This is also a good time to remember your *royalty-free* (vs. *rights-managed*) options. If you're filming a dramatic feature and the storyline is taking your characters to major cities around the world but your budget is keeping you and the crew in one location, a royalty-free stock house can be the answer. For a flat fee, and often from a single source, you can buy establishing and aerial shots of cities worldwide, sometimes referred to as *beauty shots*, and your audience will never know that your cast and crew remained in Brooklyn.

Requesting Screeners and Comps for Editing

What you need during the research and editing of your project are *copies* of the original material to work with. If you are getting them directly from the copyright holder, there are two main ways in which you obtain these *screeners* (as they are called in the case of moving images), or *comps* (which usually refer to stills and graphics):

- Digital downloads. If you are looking for material that originated relatively recently, during the digital era, you or your editor may be able to simply download a digital file directly from the archive's website. You'll need to create a free account with a login, and then often you can look for stills or moving image, download a screener when you find something you want, or even set up a *lightbox*, a digital space on the website that allows you to stash images you find to show your editor and/or download later. You can also do this with any older, analog materials *if* the archive has already digitized and posted them.

- Materials that are not online. For most large archives, digitizing their older material is an enormous, expensive, and ongoing project. As they digitize something, they post it, so that you can access it as we just described. However, despite the vast quantity of images, both moving and still, that are online, the huge majority of material held by many archives—especially historical, government, and news archives—has *not* yet been digitized. Some websites have "place-holders" to at least tell you about material not yet digitized: NBC News's online database, for example, displays icons with text descriptions of items that are still awaiting digitization. For items like these, you will have to have the archive digitize specifically for you from their original.

Depending on the archive and the format of the original material, there might be a lab fee involved, as well as a time delay. If you know or suspect something exists because of other research you've done or something you've seen, you can ask the archive to try to find it for you in their collection. Provide them with all the information you can about the item, especially the date the event happened. You may or may not have to pay them a per-hour research fee. Alternately, some archives will allow you to send in your own film researcher to search in person, or to come in yourself. Unfortunately, in recent years, in-person visits have been discouraged by many archives.

Most of the time, screeners and comps will be both watermarked and of a lower quality, to prevent unauthorized use; for this reason, "slop" or "scratch" copies may be other terms used to describe this placeholding footage. The material you receive will likely have timecode or other ID information burned into the image area, which will be essential when it's time to order masters.

Sometimes, an archive will prefer to mail you a physical copy of material in their holdings, for example, a DVD, or photocopies of stills for you to review. This is more likely when you request materials from smaller, noncommercial archives such as museums, historical societies, libraries, and private collections, although it's also true even of some of the presidential libraries that are part of the U.S. National Archives.

Obviously, if the screener comes in a physical format, you'll need to find a way to digitize it for your use while editing. If you don't have the appropriate player for a particular video format, you may need to call around to find a lab that has maintained this *legacy* equipment and can digitize the material for you. Almost always, if the physical material you're sent is film footage (8mm, 16mm, etc.), you'll have to go to a lab or post-production house to have the film transferred to a digital format, which can be expensive (but yields the best quality).

Often you can download comps directly from the websites of the copyright holders (such as Getty or AP Images) or from licensing stock houses (such as Shutterstock). Some of these places may offer to do research for you and create a "lightbox" or folder with suggested items, but you or your researchers should also look through the collection yourselves. Not only is this likely to lead to unexpected discoveries or new ideas for your project, but as people who know your subject best, you're more likely to identify vaguely labeled or mislabeled materials, or find your characters in photographs even if they haven't been tagged.

Creating Your Own Slop Visuals

For visuals of physical materials, such as books or posters, media makers will scan or shoot their own slop visuals. As with any scans or photographs, keep track of where everything comes from, even if it means creating a digital or print file for reference, with images and source information. You are probably going to want to locate the copyright holder in order to clear some of these images later.

Working With Burned-in Timecode and Identifiers

As noted, copyright holders and/or the archives that represent them are likely to send you materials that are watermarked; moving image materials may also be marked with timecode and other identifiers to help you to track material while editing. Remember that the timecode your editing system creates or reads during import may or may not match the burned-in timecode, which is tied to the archive's master. Most screener files do not have *machine-readable* timecode, which means that your editing system will assign its own timecode as it ingests or imports this material. For reporting usage, paying license fees, and obtaining final masters, it's the timecode burned in to the actual image that's important.

Ordering Visual Masters for the Finished Project

Until you are nearing picture lock, rough materials like those described above are all you'll need to edit with. That they will be lower resolution, for the most part, is a positive, because it helps to prevent slowing down or overloading your system. Additionally, you almost never have to pay for screeners, unless a source charges you lab fees because they needed to create a digital file or dub from one medium to another on your behalf. Lastly, you don't yet have to commit to (or pay for) any licensing. However, you should be aware of which rights negotiations are likely to be complicated (which nearly always includes third-party music), and those rights should be locked down earlier rather than later—certainly by fine cut, if possible. You need time to make other choices if the material you want isn't available or affordable.

With some exceptions, you should wait to order masters until a) your picture is locked, and b) you're certain that you can access and afford all of the third-party materials you've included.

Ordering Masters Early

There are a few scenarios in which ordering your masters before picture lock makes sense:

- When the material is in the public domain or for other reasons does not have to licensed, or if there is no license fee;
- When your access to the materials is limited, or the materials might become unavailable (for example, they might change hands, be discarded or lost, or continue to deteriorate) before you finish your editing process;
- When you're dealing with a large government agency that is likely to have a significant backlog of orders and they're going to charge you for dubs as well as masters.

In the first two cases (and they often overlap), it's wise, if you can afford any archive or lab fees involved, to order masters even as you're ordering screeners of most other things. At a minimum, order masters of this material once you know you'll be using at least *some* of it in your final film, even if you're still between fine cut and picture lock.

An example of the third case would be ordering from the National Archives (NARA) or the Library of Congress. Given the potential of slow turnaround times and their cost for the duplication—even for screeners—it often makes more sense just to get masters right away.

Ordering Moving Image Masters

In most scenarios, ordering moving image masters goes hand-in-hand with licensing your use of them. Your post-production supervisor (who should be on board by this time) and your film researcher(s) can discuss with you which formats are ideal for master delivery, given the format in which your project is going to be finished. One of you will need to tell an archive or lab exactly what file format you want, so that the masters you receive will slide into the timeline of your final edit effortlessly, requiring the least amount of correction and fine-tuning later. Also, the format you order masters in can have a significant impact not only on your budget but also on the visual and technical quality of your finished film.

143

As discussed in Chapter 15, in most cases you'll be ordering masters in tandem with licensing their use, so you'll need to provide specific information on exactly what you're using, down to the frame. Often, the archive will provide you with a form to fill out, requesting detailed information on the burned-in timecode, your in and out cues for each shot, and a visual description of the shot (so the archive can double-check that they're giving you the right piece). It can be advantageous to provide the archive with a QuickTime of the shots you are licensing. If you do, make sure it contains just exactly the frames you are licensing and no more.

Get the Best Master From as Close to the Original as You Can

Most archives have already digitized and posted their most requested stories, originally shot on film or video, in order to make the process of ordering and fulfillment easier and less expensive for everyone. If they haven't yet done this, you may end up paying to have something digitized for the first time, but once you do, the archive then can post a copy of the digitized version to make it easier for the next researcher or producer who comes along.

Protocol dictates that even after they've made up-to-date masters, archives keep the original materials in their vaults, in case new technologies demand a new form of copy. Unfortunately, you can't assume that this is the case. All too often, original footage has been lost or dumped after "up to date" master copies are made. Why is this a problem? Think about a news story from the 1950s that was originally shot on 16mm film. Imagine that sometime in the late 1970s, that film was transferred to videotape, maybe even 3/4" U-matic. U-matic may have been considered broadcast quality in its time, but today it's considered low-quality and technically problematic.

For this reason, you want the lab to get as close to the original as possible. A 16mm original contains far more resolution and information than a 3/4" analog video dub. From the film original, you want the archive to make the highest quality master possible. If your film is headed for theatrical release, that likely means having a 4K scan performed (although with original 16mm or 8mm footage, a 2K scan is often enough, as these formats hold less information to begin with, compared to 35mm film footage). The idea is to work with the archive's technicians to get the material to look its best in the format you need for the medium in which your project will be distributed. Nowadays, 4K is standard for projects meant for theatrical release and generally required by commercial streaming services and traditional broadcast. Some film festivals also require 4K digital delivery, often with—at a minimum— Dolby 5.1 sound. If you're producing something for the web, where file size and resolution may not be critical, you may not need or even want a 4K master. On the web, loading time and smoothness of playback may well be as important as picture quality.

Of course, if all you've got is the U-matic tape, you and your post-production team must do your best to enhance it. Using a Teranex, which most post-production houses now have, you can often achieve a near-miraculous improvement in picture quality.

Deciding Which Delivery Format You Need for the Archival Masters

Because most media professionals use computer-based editing systems, the choice of delivery format is a lot easier than it used to be. The following information may change, but here are some of the current delivery formats available:

- *Final Cut Pro*: Many editors working with Final Cut Pro on an Apple computer prefer to receive masters as QuickTime Pro Res, QuickTime Animation, or QuickTime HD files. Note that QuickTime is no longer compatible or safe to use with Windows-based machines, even for simple playback, and Apple will no longer support the use of QuickTime in any form on Windows.

- *Avid Media Composer*: Avid Media Composer, which was the original nonlinear editing tool and has been continually updated, can take DNx and DNxHR, but can also use mxf, avi, mpeg and even 3-D and IMAX® materials.
- *Adobe's Premiere Pro* (which is cross-platform) can import a variety of formats and combine them seemingly effortlessly.

This list is by no means exhaustive. There is a veritable alphabet soup of both working and delivery formats, all of which are continually subject to change. The good news is that the price of hardware drops all the time, while computer processing speed and cheap storage increase, making working with Ultra High Definition (UHD) 4K projects much more feasible than it used to be, even for the independent filmmaker.

Ordering Motion Picture Masters from NARA and the Library of Congress

As noted, it can be a good idea to skip the screeners and order digital masters right away from agencies with large public domain holdings, such as the U.S. National Archives and the U.S. Library of Congress. This can be expensive, however. Both NARA and LC, out of concern for preservation, will only copy entire reels, not individual shots or sections. If you are requesting masters from archive originals that have already been digitized, this won't be very expensive, but of course most of their voluminous collections have never been digitized. If you need a digital master file from a film original, the result will be visually stunning, but the cost of having whole reels copied can be prohibitive. Weigh that cost against the fact that you have no licensing fees, and often you'll find the tradeoff worth it. If not, you can obtain most government public domain materials from private companies that broker them, as discussed in Chapter 6.

The following is the general process for ordering from these two important archives:

U.S. National Archives and Records Administration

To obtain moving image material from the National Archives, you or your researcher will fill out an *Item Approval Request Form* (*IARF*), which lists the items you want sent to the lab. This form is available on NARA's website. Within a day or two, you'll receive the IARF back from the Archives, filled in with the length and *preprint* (the source of your copy) format available for each item, along with information about whether the material is subject to copyright (in which case it cannot be released without further documentation that you've obtained permission).

Look at the preprint designation to determine if the quality will work for you; NARA has various preprint formats, and sometimes a different one than what they've assumed might be more suitable to your needs. For example, if the Archives returns your request form listing a 3/4-inch videocassette as the *intermediate* for footage you want (because it's cheaper), and you're planning to release your film theatrically, you might ask them if they also have a *film* intermediate from which they can do a 4K scan. It will be more expensive, but vastly superior in quality.

Also understand the important distinction between *intermediates* and *preservation copies*, noted on the returned IARF with an "I" or a "P."

- *Intermediates* are always used to make your copy; an "I" on the form means that the Archives already has one available; you don't need to pay to have one made. Intermediates are often stored on site at the Archive's facility in College Park, Maryland.
- *Preservation copies* are the Archives' originals and are never used to make your copy directly. They are often stored in a separate facility elsewhere, and it can take at least a few days for them to arrive in Maryland for your order. If the only thing the archive has is a preservation copy, you will need to pay for a suitable intermediate to be made, and then your copy will be made from that intermediate. The Archive keeps the intermediate for the next customer who needs it. Thus, each media maker "pays it forward" for the next one who comes along and requests that material.

If an intermediate is available for the materials you want, it will usually take the Archives one to three days to get the material to a lab, and you should get your digital file (or physical copy, if that's what you want) about 10 to 12 business days after that. If an intermediate is *not* available, the turnaround time will be longer (estimate at least 20 business days), and your lab costs higher, so you should hope for a maximum number of "I"s on your returned IARF.

When NARA returns your order form (IARF), they'll send (or you should request) a list of laboratories in the Washington area that are authorized to do work for them. It's up to you to choose one of these labs and then fax or email the completed IARF to the lab. At that point, the lab will provide you with a cost estimate. You *must pay this estimate up front, directly to the lab, before the lab will call the items in from the Archives.* It's a good idea to actually have a phone conversation with the lab at this point, to discuss the technical details of your order, so you get the best possible copy you need at the lowest cost, with no surprises. Once the job is done, the lab will bill you for any charges over the estimate, or reimburse you if the estimate turned out to be high.

U.S. Library of Congress
The moving image ordering procedure at the Library of Congress is similar to that of NARA. You fill out a form called the *Request to Copy Film and Videotape in LC Collections*, and return it to the Motion Picture, Broadcasting, and Recorded Sound (MBRS) division of the Library of Congress. Remember that a great deal more of the Library of Congress's material is under copyright than that held by the National Archives. Obtain any permissions necessary before attempting to order copyrighted material from the Library of Congress or it will just slow down your process. They won't process any orders for copyrighted material if you don't have written permission.

Unlike the National Archives, the Library of Congress has its own duplication facilities, so you prepay *them* for lab work and the process is handled internally. But the process is not necessarily faster, and it's still a good idea to obtain your master up front (as opposed to just a screener), unless there is a compelling financial reason not to.

Ordering Moving Image Masters from Commercial Sources

Ordering from the Web
Ordering moving images from commercial websites is sometimes as simple as returning to the page from which you downloaded the screener or comp of a clip (when the archive sells by the clip, rather than by the second). You indicate which rights you want, pay the license fee with a credit card, and then download the high-resolution file, in QuickTime or some other format. Otherwise, you can choose to order by phone and pay the fee by credit card over the phone. The clip or clips will then be unlocked for downloading. They may only be available in one format, such as QuickTime Pro Res, and you may need to convert to a different *codec* (a means of encoding or decoding the digital data) at your end. The archive may give you a choice, especially if you discuss it with them over the phone.

Also, talk to the archive on the phone if you are buying several clips and want to discuss some kind of quantity discount. You should also make sure the archive's boilerplate license agreement, usually found on their website, provides you with the rights you need. You may need to get a modification: for example, you may need a *film rider*, which gives you additional rights necessary for many theatrical features, or you may need a longer rights term, or in-context promotional rights. Some sources offer both "standard" and "enhanced" agreements (which are more expensive but encompass more rights).

Ordering Masters: Do You Need 4K?

There are many variables to consider when ordering a high-definition digital master, if and when an archive or lab gives you a choice. As with all of this, an experienced film researcher or post-production supervisor can be an essential liaison between you and any archive or lab that is digitizing your masters.

High Definition

Do you need a master that's HD, or do you need 2K, or 4K? These numbers refer to a program's *resolution*: how many pixels (single units of information) appear in a vertical and horizontal grid on the screen. Assuming an image was shot in focus, the more pixels there are, the sharper the image will be. With HD, it also matters if the recording is *progressive* or *interlaced*. Interlacing involves splitting each video frame into two parts, called *fields*, and all television broadcasts were interlaced before the days of HD; therefore any standard definition (SD) materials you obtain will of necessity be interlaced. High definition recordings, however, can be made either interlaced or progressive (denoted by a lower-case "i" or a "p"). There are reasons why interlacing is occasionally preferable, such as when you're transferring from SD video to HD, or when outputting to certain formats. All things being equal though, a progressive (or *non-interlaced*) signal is almost always preferable.

Other than interlacing (which is not a factor in resolutions higher than HD), what are the differences between these formats?

- HD, or full high definition, normally consists of a *raster* or grid of around 1920 pixels across the screen by 1080 pixels down the screen (all raster sizes are also dependent upon *aspect ratio*, which we'll explain in a bit). There is also a version of HD that has only 720 pixels down the length of the screen, but as HD technology has advanced over the last several years, 720 is no longer considered ideal.
- 2K is usually around 2048 pixels by 1080 pixels, so it has a higher resolution *across* the screen than HD, but not *down* the screen. (The

148

exact number of pixels often varies between consumer and professional formats, camera manufacturers, and television monitors.) 2K can be ideal for digitizing from 16mm film, 8mm and Super 8mm, and standard definition video formats;

- 4K, also known as ultra-high definition, or UHD, has a grid of around 3840 pixels by 2160; thus, it is sharper than HD and 2K in *both* horizontal and vertical resolution. This is an ideal resolution for archival that was created on 35mm film or digital videotape;

- 8K, or UHD-2, at the time of this writing, is gaining in popularity. With a grid of about 7680 pixels across and 4320 pixels down, it's four times the resolution of 4K. When it comes to transferring archival—or for almost anything except projection onto a very large screen in a huge auditorium, 8K is likely overkill. While 8K home televisions are currently being offered as a marketing gimmick, it's unlikely most people can see a difference between 4K and 8K on even the largest home sets (and there are other limiting factors that render the difference even less important). Also, remember that each increase in resolution means more disk space, because the file contains more information, and editing systems will struggle under the strain of larger file sizes. Finally, because 4K already has the approximate resolution of 35mm film, any archival you might need to digitize won't gain any more meaningful detail at 8K than it has at 4K. When might you want to go to 8K? Three exceptions come to mind:

- When you're working with wide-screen archival that was originally shot on 70mm film, such as Cinerama® and Super-Panavision®, which Stanley Kubrick used to shoot *2001: A Space Odyssey*;
- When you're working with IMAX® and other giant-screen films or copies designed to be projected in large arenas;
- When you're creating a three-dimensional film, because of the technology employed in today's 3-D glasses.

Aspect Ratio

Aspect ratio refers to the relationship of an image's height and width, whether it's more square or rectangular. It's very likely that the aspect ratio of the project you're creating will be different from the various aspect ratios of the archival visuals you're using, but this doesn't affect the process of ordering masters; you deal with this in your own post-production.

For that reason, when ordering your masters, *always* get the size that maintains the *correct original aspect ratio*. This is the only way that you'll be able to see and have access to all of the content information in the frame. As always, be careful of the nomenclature. If you ask the lab for a "full frame" master, they may make it full frame in the aspect ratio they're going *to*, not that the material is coming *from*. You don't want this. It means that the lab—and not you—will crop either the sides or the top and bottom. In other words, the lab will make decisions about what content to include and eliminate. Unless you are there to supervise, you are much better off getting the entire image content from them in the same *resolution*—not aspect ratio—that your project is in overall.

Dealing with Aspect Ratio in Post

Maintaining the aspect ratio when you order masters gives you more flexibility in post. Let's assume, for example, that you need to deliver your project for broadcast in 4K. The footage your team shot has a consistent aspect ratio of 16 (width) × 9 (height), which is similar to (but not exactly the same as) the current theatrical standard film format of 1:1.85. Nowadays, 16" × 9" is a fairly common aspect ratio for television and computer monitors, and also aligns with some international HD standards. If your archival materials were shot fairly recently on 35mm film, they're also in an approximately 1:1.85 format, and will therefore closely match.

However, if your archival materials are older, the aspect ratio of the original will be different. 16mm footage, or 35mm footage from decades ago may have a format of 1:1.33 or 1:1.37. Older television shows generally had an aspect ratio of 4" × 3". But you want to ensure that, when edited and used full screen in *your* aspect ratio, the material will appear without distortion and without part of the image being lost.

One solution is to frame the original within the new screen. *Letterboxing* is a technique that shrinks the entire frame of a wider original, so that no content is lost, but viewers will see black bars at the top and bottom of the screen and the image is smaller. Conversely, *pillarboxing* maintains the full size of an original, squarish image, but leaves black bars to the left and right of the screen.

If you're using a lot of older 1:1.37 material, you might choose to shoot your *original* footage in a square format to match up with your archival material. The advantage is consistency, but your distributor or broadcaster may not be willing to accept your film for theatrical release if the aspect ratio is 4 × 3 (1.37) rather than today's 16 × 9 (1.85). Most modern movie theaters can no longer properly project these older ratios, although an art house cinema that routinely shows older films probably can.

The choice is yours. You can retain content information, with some shifts in frame size because of the black boxing, or you can crop out

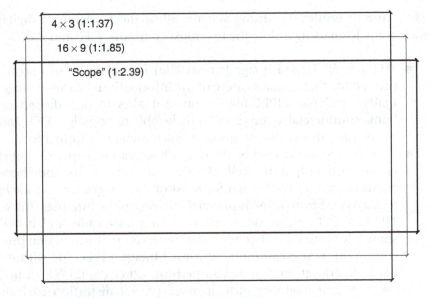

The three most popular aspect ratios. To retain visual information, pillarboxing is used when presenting 4" x 3" on a wider format medium, and letterboxing for fitting a wider format into a 4" x 3" frame.

some of the archival frame but have more consistency overall. With documentary, Kenn usually advocates for the first choice, keeping the archival visual intact. Most producers, however, opt to enlarge the archival imagery.

Frame Rate

Frame rate, as discussed in Chapter 2, is the rate at which film or video is recorded—which is also the ideal rate to play it back, if your goal is natural-seeming movement. *Overcranking,* or intentionally recording at a higher rate than normal, results in slow-motion when played back at normal rate and *undercranking,* of course, has the opposite effect. These effects can be accomplished in post-production.

Ordering Still Photographs

Many public and commercial archives have at least a large part of their collections available online for searching, purchase, and download. Some of these images are in the public domain, while others are either *royalty-free* (you pay a flat rate for unrestricted use) or *rights-managed* (you negotiate a license for specific use), as described in Chapter 11.

Most current nonlinear editing systems allow the insertion of digital picture file formats including the two most common, *TIFF* and *JPEG*.

- TIFF (or tif: Tagged Image Format File) is essentially an uncompressed file that contains more of the information the camera originally "saw" than a JPEG file. Of course, it takes up more disk space. Some commercial archives will only be able to provide a TIFF, and in any case, this is almost always a much preferable format to
- JPEG (or jpg: developed by the Joint Photographic Experts Group) is standard output for cell phones, consumer point-and-shoot cameras, and it's the format for most of the images you are likely to download from noncommercial sources on the internet. Unlike TIFFS, a JPEG image starts out as a compressed file, and it will show additional disintegration the more you perform digital processing on it. You can rotate or mirror-image a JPEG file without likely deterioration, but as you perform other digital "clean up" on it, it will begin to pick up *noise* (visual distortion such as graininess, color artifacts, and other anomalies). With that said, a high-resolution JPEG image of an 8" × 10" or larger original that is not heavily manipulated prior to use is generally fine to use as a master.

Other formats, such as PNG (Portable Network Graphics), which is smaller but often suitable for the web, may be recognized by your editing software, but we don't advise using these formats unless you have no choice.

Ordering Stills from the Library of Congress and the National Archives

Both the National Archives and the Library of Congress have extensive stills collections, which are increasingly available for online viewing and downloading, even in very high-resolution formats. What's online is still only a fraction of what's in their stills collections, however. At both agencies, images that are not already digitized (or have online copies that aren't high enough resolution) can be viewed and ordered in person, by you or a researcher hired by you. Alternatively, the Library of Congress has high-quality color copiers available on site, and with them you can make excellent hard-copy reproductions to take away with you. At both archives, it's also possible to go in person with a camera (or send a professional photographer with a high-quality digital camera) to re-photograph public domain materials.

Ordering Stills from Commercial Sites

Getty Images, AP Images, Shutterstock, and Alamy are just a few examples of commercial archives that offer extensive online collections of still images with a range of licensing options. If you downloaded comps from sites like these, obtaining masters and licensing them can be quite easy. As with motion picture footage, you simply go back to the image on the site where you downloaded the comp, click the button to order the master (sometimes you are given a choice of resolutions for different fees), and put in your credit card information. A button will activate that allows you to download the high-resolution version of the image, and usually a confirmation email (which often also serves as a confirmation of permission) will be sent to you. As with footage, remember to check the online license agreements to make sure they cover your needs, and always print them and file a copy. If the default license agreement is not adequate, contact the archive directly to ask for changes.

If you want to save money, and you're not using the images for a high-budget project—and especially if you're using multiple images from the same source—rather than order online, you're better off calling to speak with a sales representative. You may get a lower quote based on the type of project you're doing and the quantity of images involved, and the order can be placed by phone. The sales rep will then provide a license agreement and put all of your selected images into a folder that you can download. Note that the folder may also remain on the provider's site, so if you accidentally erase one of your masters, you can go back into your account and re-download the image.

Ordering Stills Offline

Smaller archives, such as historical societies and public libraries, may have provided you with photocopies or low-resolution scans to use for rough editing, or you may have made copies or shot photographs yourself. Now that you need masters, you should contact them again and obtain high-resolution scans, which they will do for you (unless they allow you to visit with your own scanner, which is rare). You will probably pay a fee for the scan as well as for permission to use the item, but these fees are usually nominal.

Ordering Masters of Visual Art

During editing, you may have obtained quick copies of artwork, such as paintings from books or posters. Now that you need good quality masters, you'll likely need to go to an art archive, such as Art Resource, Getty, or Bridgeman. These operate like photo archives; you find the image and purchase the rights you need in order to obtain a high-resolution download. If you can't find the artwork in an online commercial collection, you'll have to locate the artist's representative to find out who can grant permission to use the image and how to obtain a good scan.

For artwork that's no longer under copyright (Rembrandt, for example), you may need to contact the museum that owns the work to get a high-quality scan. They are likely to charge a fee for scanning the work and for "licensing" it, and it's likely to be quite steep. For that reason, if you know the work is in the public domain and you can get a high-quality image in some other way, do so. You don't need to pay or even credit the museum that happens to own the work.

If the work is subject to copyright, you will need to license it, as discussed elsewhere, and you can usually obtain a high-quality scan through whomever provides the license.

Technical Specs for Creating Your Own Stills Masters

If you have prints, transparencies, or books in hand with images that you want to use in your finished film, it's up to you to scan them at an appropriately high resolution. In an HD project, this means 1920 pixels along the larger dimension of the original source image (because HD's ratio is 1080 × 1920). Since nowadays most broadcast, streaming, or theatrical projects are done in 4K, filling the frame will take 4096 pixels along the original's larger dimension (because 4K for theatrical is 4096 × 2160). An important caveat: if you are scanning (or having someone scan) an image that you plan to also shoot close up or do camera moves on, the resolution should be significantly higher than these, so you can fill the frame with just a portion of the picture. Remember also that it's not just the resolution of your scan that matters. The physical dimensions of the original are even more important, because they affect how much cropping and/or moving around on the image will be acceptable. A scan of an 8" × 10" photo at 300 pixels per inch (ppi)—3000 pixels in the longer dimension—may be sufficient for an HD production if there's a little cropping. But if your program will be 4K and you plan to move on the image, you're better off with at least 720 ppi. To demonstrate how the dimensions make a difference, a 1440 ppi scan of a 4" × 5" drugstore print or snapshot will give you the same 7200 pixels, but the quality will be much less because of how much you'll be enlarging the original.

The higher the resolution, the longer the scan takes and the larger the image file that results. But disk space is cheap; if it's under your control, scan at 720 ppi or higher for your final master if at all possible, and scan to a TIFF as opposed to a JPEG file.

Improving Scans

Whether you're scanning or receiving a scan from an archive, you can use software such as Photoshop to improve the resulting image quality. Brightness, contrast, color saturation, and flaws or damage in the original image can all be corrected. Some scanners include software like *Digital ICE*, which uses complex algorithms to do sophisticated restoration during a scan (usually at the cost of some sharpness). Remember that TIFF files can tolerate these adjustments much better than JPEG files can. Be sure that your system is *calibrated*, so that what you are seeing on your computer monitor is consistent with what will end up in the final project. (If not, you may have to do some color, contrast, and brightness correction later on, on a calibrated monitor.) And remember that most photography and artwork under copyright *cannot be altered* in any significant way. There are legal as well as ethical issues involved.

Obtaining Masters of Graphics, Maps, and Newspapers

In most cases, graphics (political cartoons, published maps, 19th century news illustrations, and the like) are researched and obtained exactly as any photograph would be. If you hire a graphic designer to create or animate maps for you, they will most likely use digital animation, so the editor won't have to do it. Graphic designers or editors might also treat newspapers, such as highlighting certain headlines or text, or adding them on top of or behind other images. Often they will deliver these as QuickTime movies.

Sound and Music

It's possible to locate and order audio from a wide range of sources, such as an oral history project, the Archive of American Poetry, police recordings, the Library of Congress, a local radio station, or a sound library. As with visuals, early recordings may have been created in a variety of formats, from wax cylinders to magnetic tape. Many archives have already digitized their audio collections and posted material online (if it's not under copyright). If you're going to license from an archive, however, find out if they can make you a copy that's better quality than the one that's posted; to preserve bandwidth, they may have posted audio at a lower resolution than what's in their collection.

Most online audio consists of *mp3 files* (Moving Pictures Experts Group). These files are often highly compressed; if the archive can provide you with a WAV or AIFF file (both of which are much less compressed), the quality may be significantly better.

Music

For editing purposes, your *temp track* may contain music from a range of sources that you've likely downloaded or digitized yourself. If you end up seeking to use and license third-party music, the copyright holder should make available to you a master (in the form of an AIFF or WAV file).

Sources and Notes

156 Information about the Teranex Standards Converters can be found at www.blackmagicdesign.com/products/teranex. *Vietnam: A Television History* is a 13-part series that premiered on PBS in 1983. In 1997, underlying rights were renewed to allow for a rebroadcast of 11 of the 13 episodes. *OJ: Made in America* is a five-part series released in 2016 by ESPN Films. For information about SHOWLOG, contact Kenn's company, Fulcrum Media Services, www.fulcrummediaservices.com. *The World at War* was a 26-part documentary series that premiered on ITV in Britain in 1973. The National Archives "Item Approval Request Form" can be found at www.archives.gov/research/order/item-approval-form.html. Information about contacting the Library of Congress to request copies of film and video can be found at www.loc.gov/rr/mopic/copies.html.

CHAPTER 9

Creative and Ethical Considerations

In Chapter 4, we looked at ways in which those who draw upon third-party audio and visual material, whether created yesterday or in the early 1900s, might evaluate the value and credibility of that material. In this chapter, we look at some of the creative choices and ethical decisions involved when media makers seek to incorporate third-party materials into their own original work, dramatic or documentary.

Codes of Ethics

For those whose nonfiction work is intended for an established venue, such as the Public Broadcasting System (PBS) in the United States, or the British Broadcasting Corporation (BBC) in the United Kingdom, a code of ethics or values is generally available. There also may be a code of ethics written specifically for the host series. The PBS series *Frontline* for example, a leading long-form news and current affairs series since it was launched in 1983, offers guidelines online at www.pbs.org/wgbh/frontline/about-us/journalistic-guidelines/.

For independent media makers, especially those whose work is not strictly journalistic but is nonetheless billed as nonfiction, the guidelines are less clear. For that reason, in 2009 American University's Center for Media & Social Impact, with support from the Ford Foundation, conducted research leading to publication of *Honest Truths: Documentary Filmmakers on Ethical Challenges in Their Work*. The report's authors—Patricia Aufderheide, Peter Jaszi, and Mridu Chandra—conducted interviews with 45 filmmakers, asking them to describe ethical challenges they faced in their work. "Documentary filmmakers identified themselves as creative artists for whom ethical behavior is at the core of their projects," the authors noted in an online preamble to the report. "At a time when there is unprecedented financial pressure on makers to lower costs and increase productivity, filmmakers reported that they routinely found themselves in situations where they needed to balance ethical responsibilities against practical considerations." They grouped these responsibilities into three sets: the subjects, the viewers, and the filmmakers' "own artistic vision and production exigencies." Filmmakers "argued ... for situational, case-by-case ethical decisions"—and at the same time, they "widely share some basic ethical principles."

The overall message: when it comes to subject, "do no harm" and "protect the vulnerable;" when it comes to audiences, "honor their trust." What does this mean in terms of archival use?

158   *Protecting Subjects*

Preventing or Limiting the Resale of Images
It's expected that you'll have acquired an *appearance release* from each of the people who you've filmed for your documentary. These generally grant you permission to use their words and image, and some may be written broadly enough that you have the right to share that footage, in the future, with other filmmakers. But how do *they* want to use it, and to portray what? Chicago filmmaker Gordon Quinn described this scenario to the authors of *Honest Truths*:

> 'I made a film in the '70s about an 11-year-old girl growing up. Twenty years later some people making a film about abortion wanted to use some of our footage to set the historical context of the times. I insisted that they show me the cut and when I saw that they were implying that the girl had had an abortion, I said, "You have to change that. She's a real person and you can't imply something about her that never happened."

Sharing Cuts with Subjects
Some filmmakers retain editorial control while agreeing to share edited material with subjects prior to a film's release, although this is somewhat controversial. Protecting the subject, at times, can mean protecting the privacy or legacy of someone even after they're deceased. This is very

much a case-by-case issue, and depends in part on who the individual is, how powerful and/or public they are, and what the film is about. But there are circumstances in which you want to consider the impact your use of the footage might have.

As an example, consider filmmaker Stanley Nelson's *Jonestown: The Life and Death of Peoples Temple* (2006), a sympathetic look at the people caught up in a church and social movement led by the Reverend Jim Jones that steadily devolved into a terrifying cult. Ultimately, Jones convinced or coerced followers (many of them with young children) to settle in Guyana, South America, away from U.S. government investigators and family members. There, in November 1978, more than 900 people were shot or poisoned with Kool Aid laced with cyanide, at Jones's behest. "One of the things that happened early on was that the survivors of Jonestown, a bunch of them said to us, 'Could you please not use that shot with the big gallon of poison and the dead bodies lying there?'" Nelson said in a roundtable we convened for the first edition. "Now, I didn't really feel like I owed them anything not to show it, but it did start me thinking that that image was so iconic, it was almost a cliché. And so we didn't use that image." When the editing on *Jonestown* was complete, the filmmakers had a preview screening with former members of Peoples Temple who'd survived. "We realized that we had pictures and footage that they probably had never seen, and in those pictures and footage would be their loved ones and friends,"

The Reverend Jim Jones in *Jonestown: The Life and Death of Peoples Temple*. Photo courtesy of the California Historical Society.

Nelson said. The filmmakers hadn't ceded editorial control, but they had worked to prevent harm.

There is no obligation to reach out to family members, and to do so with an extensive archival series—to identify and locate relatives of people depicted—would be prohibitive, even after the rise of the internet. Still, decisions about the inclusion or exclusion of images can be difficult. This is not an argument for self-censorship; it *is* an argument for awareness and sensitivity.

Honoring Viewers' Trust

As the 2009 *Honest Truths* report summarized, documentary filmmakers feel "an ethical obligation to deliver accurate and honestly-told stories." If a film is billed as nonfiction, it needs to be nonfiction. "You know what your film is saying … and you know what your footage is implying," Stanley Nelson told us. "If it's not true, then I think there's a problem." Accurate and creative use of archival materials was one of the ways in which those interviewed for *Honest Truths* said they felt ethical challenges.

Using Archival Materials Specifically vs. Generically

Historical materials, as the report notes, "document specific people, places, and times." Yet it's fair to say that across the filmmaking spectrum, the use of *generic* audio and imagery—historical or not—is common. A shot of a carnival in London in 1893, provided there are no clearly identifiable characteristics that viewers would recognize immediately as London, might be used for a discussion of a carnival in Berlin in 1910. Footage of steelworkers protesting in Kentucky in 1930 might substitute for footage that couldn't be found of meat packers protesting in Kansas around that general time. And so on. Does it matter? The answer is sometimes yes, sometimes no.

Using Archival Material as Evidence: *Vietnam: A Television History (1983)*

The most important reason not to use footage generically is when it's being used directly as evidence of the past. One of the strictest examples of this can be seen with the production of *Vietnam: A Television History*, a 13-hour series that premiered nationally in October 1983; it was the first long-form historical documentary series mounted by PBS. The visuals consisted entirely of new interviews (filmed by the series' production teams from WGBH-TV and the U.K.'s Channel 4), a few maps and graphics, and archival materials.

PBS itself had only existed since 1970, and the war ended in 1975. Production on the series began in 1979, and conservative watchdog groups were paying close attention to how the war was presented in the media. Because of this, the series' production team at WGBH-TV in Boston, led by executive producer L. Richard Ellison, established rigorous rules for fact checking *everything*, including not only words spoken but also all archival materials. Considering that any single archive might be the source of biased coverage, they sought footage of the same event from multiple sources, eventually reaching out to more than 90 archives worldwide. The footage was carefully tagged and checked to reflect accurately the date, time, and location of the events seen on screen; there was no using footage simply because it was "more dramatic," for example. As a result, viewers watching the film and being told by the narrator that they were seeing a certain battle or a certain meeting could trust that what they were seeing was exactly that. And if they saw archival footage of planes taking off, accompanied by narration that said, "B-52s took off from Andersen Air Force Base on December 26, 1972," viewers could trust that they were seeing *those* planes taking off from *that* airstrip on *that* day.

Additional rules were put in place to govern the use of music and sound. Because music can significantly alter the emotional impact of footage and could thereby be viewed as editorializing, absolutely no non-diegetic music was added to the films. Short instrumental cues, composed by The Grateful Dead percussionist Mickey Hart, were used during the opening and closing credits. In a few cases, music was *part* of the archival material. For example, in one episode, there was footage showing a group of soldiers singing in a chorus. This *incidental capture* of diegetic music was true to the footage, not an editorial add-on.

As with music, no additional sound effects were added to enhance the footage because to do so might alter a shot or scene's emotional impact. Screams, babies crying, weapons firing, airplanes buzzing overhead, and other sound effects were strictly prohibited unless they correlated to what was seen in the original footage. This also meant that when sound was added to silent footage—much of the military footage of the Vietnam era was shot without sound—the audio was carefully researched. Only sounds that correlated to the exact weapons, tanks and helicopters seen on screen could be added. In some cases, these sounds had to be created for the *Vietnam* series by the Imperial War Museum in London, using the accurate hardware. This was a rigorous and time-consuming process, but it meant that the images and sounds could be viewed as authoritative.

March on Washington for Jobs and Freedom (August 28, 1963).
Photo by Warren K. Leffler. From the U.S. Library of Congress.

162 Using Archival Material as Evidence: *Eyes on the Prize* (1987; 1990)

These same archival guidelines were brought into the production of the 14-hour archival history of the modern American civil rights movement, *Eyes on the Prize*, created and executive produced by Henry Hampton and the production staff at Blackside, Inc., in Boston. Roughly 60 percent of *Eyes on the Prize* consists of period images, including footage, photographs, and headlines. This material was assembled according to time and place, and edited into visual sequences that advanced the storytelling even before interviews and narration were added. *Eyes* covers history between 1954 and 1984, and the first two decades, especially, offered a wealth of footage from the in-depth, 16mm film coverage of the networks.

As on the *Vietnam* series, researchers scoured multiple sources for footage of the same event, to not only help ensure that the visuals could often be edited into compelling scenes, but also to ensure their accuracy. The major difference between the two series' productions, however, was their use of music. *Eyes on the Prize* includes about 130 pieces of copyrighted music, including diegetic music, such as protestors seen in archival footage singing "We Shall Overcome." A lot of additional music is drawn from the hits of the era, the music that participants insisted was essential because it had informed and energized the movement. "I don't know that you could have had a movement in the way that we had the movement without the music," former SNCC activist and *Eyes* series associate producer Judy Richardson said in an article for *Documentary* magazine. "Music took you outside of yourself. It made you feel that you were absolutely invincible. It made you feel that you were with this crowd of people—and it could only be maybe five people—but you were so united in singing." With *Eyes*, as with *Vietnam*, there were no sound effects added unless there were visual cues to justify them.

With some projects, the extent to which archival details matter may vary. Stanley Nelson described using archival in *We Shall Remain* (2009), about the siege of Wounded Knee (the 1973 conflict between the American Indian Movement and the federal government):

> It went on for 71 days. And there's tons of shooting, people just shooting at each other. And you don't know what day it is, and it doesn't matter for us a lot of times what day it is. It does matter the day the federal marshal gets shot and gets paralyzed. That happened on a certain day, and certain things happened before, and certain things happened afterward. But [the rest], we have no idea, and the footage isn't even cataloged in that way. We do our best to figure out when it is, and if we do know—"well, wait a minute, they didn't have the tanks this early on"—then we can't use that footage. It's just that simple. We know, and so we just can't do it. And part of it is because we all work too hard on making films to have something like "when the tanks showed up" come back and bite you. Because it *will* come back and bite you.

163

Are You Obligated To Use Archival Materials, If They Exist?

Just because archival coverage of a person or event can be found doesn't mean a filmmaker is obligated to use it. As filmmaker Ric Burns told Sheila while she researched the first edition of *Documentary Storytelling*,

> [T]here are historical documentary filmmakers who apparently believe that having the original photograph is all you need to bring somebody into the truth and to make the film powerful. That's nonsense. It may well be that the shadow of a hand of a live actor, at a certain moment, will bring you closer to the truth of Abraham Lincoln than all the Brady photographs in the world. Conversely, maybe it won't … Sometimes, you might actually choose to use an element that's less historically authentic, because it works better and is therefore a better thing to do.

CREATIVE AND ETHICAL CONSIDERATIONS

Burns noted, however, that decisions were made while working closely with academic advisors. "Tampering with the facts is absolutely inconceivable," he said. "When filmmakers begin to play fast and loose with a fact, they begin to rupture the essential contract that they make with the audience. Even though the audience can't quite tell where or how or why, they may not have that knowledge, they swiftly and intuitively understand that somebody's bullshitting them. You need to feel the integrity of a film."

What Are Your Options When Archival Stills or Footage Are Very Limited or Don't Exist?

The interesting thing is that there are *two* ethical issues involved with this question. The first is less obvious: if we only tell stories for which visuals—and good visuals at that—are available, whose stories are not being told? And the answer is clear: it's the people who have been marginalized, imprisoned, enslaved, or in some other way stripped of an opportunity to leave a historical record of themselves—told *by* themselves. Having visuals *about* marginalized communities is not the same. One of the interesting challenges filmmakers face is telling or helping to tell stories for which the record is limited, whether it's family histories or stories where the archival record either never existed or was destroyed, either deliberately or not.

On a practical note, one solution may be to use non-photographic visuals, such as newspaper headlines, artifacts an individual used or lived around, or lithographs or other artwork. Some media makers use animation; an interesting example of this is Israeli filmmaker Ari Folman's *Waltz with Bashir* (2008). Others use re-enactments.

Working With a Limited Archival Record: *Alexander Hamilton* (Middlemarch Films)

Founded in New York 30 years ago by filmmakers Muffie Meyer and Ellen Hovde, Middlemarch's credits include more than 100 documentary films and videos, for which they've earned an Academy Award nomination, two Emmys, the Columbia-duPont Award, the George Foster Peabody Award, and recognition from film festivals in Europe, Asia, and North America. While their work is not solely historical, Middlemarch has gained a reputation for its historical film storytelling using a variety of approaches, including the use of archival materials and anachronism

164

(such as imagining televised news coverage of the 1891 ratification of the U.S. Constitution).

Middlemarch is perhaps best known for its innovative casting of modern-day actors to portray historical figures on screen, as they did for *Alexander Hamilton* (2007), a two-hour special; *Benjamin Franklin* (2002), a three-part series; and *Liberty! The American Revolution* (1997), a six-part series, all for PBS. Dressed in period costumes, the actors appear to be "interviewed" in period settings, when in fact they're filmed at a studio. High-resolution slides of historic locations (such as interiors of 18th century homes) are projected behind each actor, and careful set dressing and lighting creates an illusion of space and unity. In addition, the filmmakers use digital technology to create limited but vibrant exterior motion picture footage.

The idea behind this style, which they inaugurated with the 1997 *Liberty!* series, was to "bring alive the words and the ideas and the experience of the historical event," said Ronald Blumer, who wrote all three films and co-produced *Alexander Hamilton*. "The participants in this movement of history, or in any movement of history, didn't know what was going to happen next: There is nothing inevitable about it. In the case of the American Revolution, the only thing inevitable was that the Americans were going to lose and the British were going to win."

165

The principals at Middlemarch experimented with limited use of dialogue, with actors interacting based on period transcripts, "but it just didn't work," Blumer said, "so we decided to go for this very stark direct dialogue method." The actors are filmed alone, speaking directly to camera. "They're talking to *us*, and they're telling us what they're thinking, what they're feeling at the time," he says. "It's like a Shakespearean monologue."

Creating a script that's heavily based on period documents, according to Blumer, involved not only extensive reading of primary and secondary sources, but also detailed exploration of footnotes. "So if [a reference says] 'he's feeling this' or 'he's doing this' I want to know how exactly they know that, what is their source, and then I trace back their sources. Frequently, it's a gold mine; I find—and I don't know why it is—that the most interesting things are not used." Blumer has found this to be the case even with books that purport to be transcripts of actual events, such as meetings or trials. While researching *Benjamin Franklin*, Blumer explains, "I went to a book that purported to be the complete transcript of all the letters and dialogues and everything concerning the peace treaty in France, with the final negotiations to end the American Revolution. I noticed that there were a few [ellipses]. And so I went to an even more primary source and found that the person who was putting

166

Bryan F. O'Byrne on set as Alexander Hamilton. The background is projected from a large-format transparency. Photo courtesy Middlemarch Films.

together this book didn't think that something was important because it was basically emotional. Of course that's what one wants in the film."

What liberties does Blumer take when breathing life into original documents that were written to be read but now must be spoken aloud? "The important thing is that the audience has to believe that the people are experiencing and feeling what you're hearing. If it sounds as if they're reading something, it just doesn't work." To compensate, Blumer will rework period documents, adding contractions, replacing references nobody will understand, and even giving modern meaning to outmoded words. "Our language has changed, what did they actually mean by saying that? So I'll look it up in Samuel Johnson's 18th century dictionary, and give a modern meaning to the words. Translate it. But I can always justify every word with a source."

Working With a Limited Archival Record: *The Civil War* (Florentine Films)

At times, an archival record exists but is either very limited or doesn't support the carefully-researched story being told—or both. This was the case with the very successful nine-part PBS series *The Civil War* (1990), directed by Ken Burns. The series, which covers events from 1861 to 1865, tells its story through the use of present-day evocative imagery (landscapes, wagon wheels, images of historic artifacts, etc.), archival still photographs, voice-overs from period documents, and on-camera interviews with historians. With only a few exceptions, none of the historic photos depict what the voices and narrator are discussing, a decision driven not only by the scarcity of *any* visuals, but also by Burns's decision to allow the words to take precedence. As he wrote in a preface to *Ken Burns's* The Civil War: *Historians Respond*, "We [Ken Burns, Ric Burns, and Geoffrey C. Ward] wrote our script unconcerned with whether there were images to fill what we wanted to write about. We shot the old photographs unconcerned about whether there might be a scene in the script which these images could illustrate."

As he explained at a 1993 conference on media and history that focused largely on *The Civil War*, Burns and his team chose images for their evocative, rather than illustrative, value. Burns presented a clip from episode six, "Valley of the Shadow of Death," focusing on a segment that begins, he said, "after Lee and Grant have really fought to this horrible stalemate at Petersburg." He then dissected its use of archival images:

> With the exception of the illustrative pictures of Dorothea Dix and Walt Whitman, there's absolutely not one image that is "truthful" in this scene. There is a street scene taken in the 1850s of a small Connecticut town, which is used to illustrate Horace Greeley's 1864 lament about the bloodshed of the Civil War. There are Southern quotes over pictures of Northern soldiers. None of the hospitals specifically mentioned are actually shown, particularly Chimborazo in Richmond. We had only one photograph of it that did not work. There's a Southern hymn, "When Johnny Comes Marching Home," to introduce Walt Whitman's story, and is used throughout the scene. The picture of Walt Whitman is, in fact, several years too old, as is the illustration for Dix. ... There's not one

photograph of action or battle during *The Civil War*, and yet nearly 40 percent of the series takes place while guns are actually going off. What do you do? What are the kinds of licenses you take?

Filmmakers substitute images for the real thing for a range of reasons, from an absence of material to creative choices. A filmmaker quoted in *Honest Truths* argued, as Burns had, that his own creative, non-specific use of archival imagery supported an otherwise researched, authentic story. One of the characters in his documentary did not have footage or photos from his childhood. "I at this point had a hobby of buying Super 8 films at a flea market, found some home movies from the '50s of a family, it worked perfectly, a kid his age, house, it was perfect," he told the report's authors. "I'm sure 99 percent of the people who watched the film thought it was him and his family," he acknowledged. "There are purists who would feel that's not right. Ultimately I'm not of that position ... One struggles enough in making a good film."

168 Other Uses of Archival Materials

There are, of course, myriad ways in which third-party footage is used in documentary and non-documentary works, including art and experimental works, dramatic features, and even fictional television. (An example of this is the American television comedy *Dream On* (1990–1996), created by Marta Kauffman and David Crane, which used clips from old black-and-white films and television shows to reveal the main character's inner life.) Archival footage and stills appear in television commercials, mashups, collages, museum installations, and other new works. As archivist Rick Prelinger notes, "Many younger makers don't work with stories as older makers do. They remix and recombine fragments from many sources in real time. The notion is that there's a dynamic, living collage that's going on, that's shared; it's communal." He cites the three-part BBC documentary series, *The Power of Nightmares: The Rise of the Politics of Fear* (2004, directed by Adam Curtis), as an example of this idea. Against fairly traditional storytelling on the soundtrack, archival visuals are collaged—sometimes speeding by so fast as to make only a subconscious impression.

A major source for this type of work is *found footage*. Found footage is moving image material acquired through various nontraditional means, and it's a staple of works by filmmakers including Alan Berliner, Jay Rosenblatt, and Craig Baldwin. Perhaps it's found in the trash or acquired from or traded with private collectors who specialize in obscure material, such as old educational films or unusual film memorabilia. The copyright may have expired or the rights holder may be difficult or impossible to locate. Although it can be risky, filmmakers using found footage sometimes pursue a philosophy (borrowed from the technology arena) of "asking forgiveness" for unauthorized use rather than "asking permission" for use beforehand. In some cases, even if the rights holder does come forward, the new use of the material may be sufficiently transformative as to be protected as fair use.

What About Manufacturing "Fake" Audiovisual Evidence?

Although it may seem tempting to simply *create* what seem to be archival materials, most filmmakers—working in both fiction and nonfiction—agree that this isn't ethical, unless it's clear to the audience that what they're seeing is an invention. In *Honest Truths*, a documentary filmmaker described taking a campaign ad created for radio and making new visuals to go with it, as if it had been a television ad. To their credit, executives presenting the film on television "asked if it was real," the filmmaker reported. "And it wasn't, so we had to take it out. It's too misleading to the audience." Examples abound, particularly in films that are considerably didactic in forcing a point of view, of fake "redacted" documents offered as "evidence" of what "they" don't want you to know, and of footage misused to represent something it simply doesn't represent.

Honesty is important for two reasons: first, it respects the intelligence of the audience and allows them to come to their own conclusions, based on a truthful presentation of evidence—not cherrypicked, but warts and all. Second, it's important because of how the project may be used over the long term. As MacArthur fellow and filmmaker Louis Massiah (founder of the Scribe Video Center in Philadelphia) told the authors of *Honest Truths*, "A good film often has many lives, and one of the lives is in educational institutions, within schools and libraries. The film becomes a historical document."

Additionally, films—especially documentaries—have long been an important source of information for policymakers, voters, educators, and the public. "It's profoundly true that a lot of our films do in fact drive policy and they do inform public debate; they do inform the national conversation," said documentary filmmaker Jon Else. "And with that voice that we give to ourselves and others comes a responsibility to deliver the genuine article." In a roundtable for this book's first edition, he explained: "What appears to be true should be true, and what appears to be real should be real." In part, this issue comes down to transparency as well as accuracy. "When the lights come on in the theater, what does the audience believe to be true? What do they believe happened? What do they believe is real?" As we've seen throughout this book the public's understanding of what constitutes a documentary has changed over the years. But as Else noted, "That said, there are untruths, and untruths have no place in documentary."

Check Your Facts

When working with third-party audiovisuals, it's important to do your own, independent fact checking, especially if the content seems too good *not* to use. "When we were doing *The Great Depression* (1993), we found a lot of newsreels of hoboes in California, talking about what a terrible jerk Upton Sinclair was when he was running for governor," Jon Else told us. "It turned out they were all actors that had been hired by [MGM studio head] Louis B. Mayer, who was opposing the campaign of Sinclair, and then this stuff had slipped into the archives as real interviews." Unfortunately, media makers often face pressures that can lead to short cuts that compromise a film's integrity. Executives at some outlets have been known to discourage consultation with historians or other experts. Resist this pressure, and get it right.

Using Footage Originally Created as Propaganda

How do you handle footage that exists and might be useful, but has a terrible provenance? Consider, for example, director Leni Riefenstahl's *Triumph of the Will*. Filmed in 1934 at the second Nazi Party Congress in Nuremberg, Germany, "produced by order of the Führer" and "created by Leni Riefenstahl," the entire film is framed as an homage to the healing powers of Germany's leader. Opening title cards read: "Twenty years after the outbreak of the World War, sixteen years after the start of the German suffering, nineteen months after the start of Germany's rebirth, Adolf Hitler flew once again to Nuremberg to hold a military rally." In fact, as author Morris Dickstein wrote in his book, *Dancing in the Dark*, while the film "presents itself duplicitously as a mere record of the 1934 Nuremberg congress of the Nazi Party ... in fact the whole event was staged as a spectacle for the camera, using the largest cast ever assembled for any film." Under Riefenstahl's direction, he wrote,

> Every image in the film is cunningly designed for indoctrination into the new order ... The rally itself is the culmination of this genuinely Fascist piece of filmmaking. Not only do we see Hitler from below, standing behind his massively monumental platform—the very image of the god-like, distant figure—but his vast army of worshippers is organized into strict geometrical formations that subsume individual humanity into one collective, and frighteningly impersonal, mass.

"It's fiction," scholar Bill Nichols told us, "in the sense that it was choreographed and planned in minutiae but given the guise of a reality. And that removed from the equation a sense of trust in the audience to assess and judge." How should filmmakers approach this footage for archival use?

In Chapter 10, filmmaker Roberta Grossman discusses her own considerations when using propaganda footage created by the Nazis in her film *Who Will Write Our History*. Based on the book by historian Samuel Kassow, the film tells the story of people trapped and starving in the Warsaw Ghetto, who fought back by creating a record of Jewish history, the *Oyneg Shabes* Archive.

Colorizing Archival Visuals

With improvements in technology, filmmakers may choose to return to the archival record and add color to images initially photographed or filmed in black-and-white. With historic footage, the transformation can be startling, as evident in Peter Jackson's *They Shall Not Grow Old*, discussed later in this chapter. To some viewers, color imagery makes an event feel more real and immediate, taking on new and vibrant life.

Old black-and-white fictional films, too, have been colorized, in part as a means of transforming them enough to warrant a new copyright, when the original work is about to enter the public domain. In 1988, for example, Ted Turner's Superstation presented a colorized version of *Casablanca*, the 1942 classic drama starring Humphrey Bogart and Ingrid Bergman. Some critics approved, but renowned critic Roger Ebert wasn't having it. "There are few issues in the area of film preservation that arouse more anger than the issue of colorization," he wrote.

171

That is because it is an issue involving taste, and, to put it bluntly, anyone who can accept the idea of the colorization of black-and-white films has bad taste. The issue involved is so clear, and the artistic sin of colorization is so fundamentally wrong, that colorization provides a pass-fail examination. If you "like" colorized movies, it is doubtful that you know why movies are made, or why you watch them.

For scholars and media makers, however, there are ethical as well as aesthetic issues involved in colorizing material that was created in black-and-white. In his 2014 article in *Gizmodo*, "Are Colorized Photos Rewriting History?," Matt Novak argued that "there's a danger that the colorized photos could become more popular in search engine results than the black-and-white ones"—a concern in part because there is no guarantee that the color choices made are accurate. As an example, Novak posted a photo of Steve Jobs, taken in black-and-white around 1985 by Norman Seeff. He compared it to a colorized version by Jordan J. Lloyd (r/ColorizedHistory, a Reddit site). Novak noted that in posting the color image, Lloyd said that he had done his best with the color of the striped sweater Jobs is wearing. "But who's to say what the color of that sweater really was?" asked Novak. "And what about the books on the shelf or the art on the wall?"

Yet colorization is popular, in part, because it can help to bring the past to life, especially for younger audiences. The issue, then, becomes one of rigorous research. In 2017, for example, the Smithsonian Channel premiered *America in Color*, "which explores the nation's history through colorized, largely unaired footage from the 1920s through '60s," according to Meilan Solly, writing in *Smithsonian* magazine.

Researchers spent more than 5,800 hours digging through obscure archives and home movies, and more than 27 miles of film were transferred. The team also created a methodology for ensuring historically accurate colorization. For the 1920s and 1930s episodes, researchers relied on sources including postcards, modern-day color images ... and the few chromatic photographs taken during the era.

(A benefit of the Smithsonian Channel's work, and that of others who undertake colorization responsibly, is that they use digital technology to restore footage that is scratched or otherwise damaged, a boon for those seeking to use the original black-and-white material as well).

Using Technology to Bring the Past to Life:
They Shall Not Grow Old

In 2015, New Zealand filmmaker Sir Peter Jackson, a leading expert in digital special effects features (*The Lord of the Rings* trilogy), was commissioned by the World War I Centennial Commission (14–18 NOW) and the Imperial War Museum (IWM) of London, in association with the BBC, to create a film that would commemorate the centennial of World War I (1914–1918). The commission was simple: Apply all the technological wizardry at your fingertips to the IWM's collection of 100-year-old archival film from the war, and in some new and dynamic way create a testament to that important and horrific event and the brave men and women who participated in it. Make them live again.

The result, *They Shall Not Grow Old* (2018, 99 minutes) was not only a critical success, but it also provides a valuable case study in the ethical and effective exploration of archival use in the digital age. Footage was not only colorized but painstakingly remastered to project at lifelike speed, and to allow for the kind of closeup photography not technically possible in the early decades of the 20th century.

173

Elements

In press materials, Jackson outlined the elements that went into the film. These included:

- 100 hours of original footage from the Imperial War Museum. Of this, about 90 minutes was used in the film, and yet at no cost to the IWM, Jackson's crew restored everything—a tremendous gift to the archive. "Much of this material, of soldiers in training and then in the trenches, was shot for propaganda newsreels that would play in theaters between other movies," *The New York Times* reported.
- Artists' sketches from *The War Illustrated*, a weekly magazine released throughout the war. These were used to illustrate the actual battle scenes, which were too dangerous for the news cameras to film.
- Recruitment posters from the time, encouraging British men and women to join the war effort.
- About 600 hours of audio: oral histories from more than 200 British veterans, recorded in the 1960s and 1970s by the BBC. Of these, the testimonies of about 120 were used in the film. The filmmakers decided not to identify the speakers until the end credits, as "names would be popping up on screen every time a voice

appeared," Jackson told Australian e-zine *Flicks*. "We also edited out any references to dates and places ... There's hundreds of books about all that stuff. I wanted the film to be a human experience and be agnostic in that way." Jackson also decided to "focus on one topic and do it properly," he told *The New York Times*. His choice was "the experience of an average [British] soldier infantryman on the Western front."

Applying Technology to the Footage

The original 100-year-old footage was subjected to sophisticated technology, including computer-based restoration, speed adjustments, colorization, reframing for closeups and 3-D treatment for theatrical release. "This footage has been around for 100 years and these men had been buried behind a fog of damage, a mask of grain and jerkiness and sped-up film," Jackson said. "Once restored, it's the human aspect that you gain the most." Viewers are struck by the sense that they can get to know and recognize specific faces that were previously just blurs of black and white.

At the same time, the project retained its journalistic integrity, thanks to the efforts of Jackson, his editor, Jabez Olssen, and the technical crews of WingNut Films (Jackson's company), Park Road Post Production in New Zealand, and Stereo D in Los Angeles. There is no effort to disguise the alteration to the original footage; the restoration process was discussed extensively in the film's promotion. Furthermore, for roughly the first half hour of the film, we see the original black-and-white footage unrestored, in its original aspect ratio, with all the dust and dirt and smearing and deterioration. This footage is not pillarboxed; the picture appears onscreen surrounded by black, which signals that we're seeing the entire original frame. This framing also has the effect of holding the footage at a psychological distance, and establishes the "before" of the manipulation.

The shift to full restoration occurs around 25:21, by degrees, so that audiences can follow it. Color and sound both fade in, while a technique that mimics a modern zoom lens brings us in even closer, all in the course of a single 37-second shot—a transformation that occurs in the storyline as the soldiers, after leaving home and going through training, finally arrive at the front. "It was deadly warfare," a veteran remembers in voice-over. "We were facing the Germans." From there, nothing Jackson and his team did altered the factuality of the footage; they merely used technology to simulate what it would have looked and sounded like had it been shot with advanced film and audio technology, and had a century of deterioration not taken its toll.

Remastering Footage Shot at a Range of Frame Rates

They Shall Not Grow Old is done so effectively that the painstaking care that went into it may get lost. Plenty of filmmakers have tried to work with the mismatched technology of old footage. As explained in Chapter 2, modern film footage is shot and projected at 24 frames per second (or 25 in some countries). In the 1920s, once motors were incorporated into cameras, silent film was usually shot at 18 frames per second. But before *that*, between the 1890s and about 1920, cameras were hand-cranked, which meant that speed varied—even within a single shot—from about 11 to about 18 fps. Past restorations of silent films often addressed this by double-printing a certain number of frames each second, approximating a somewhat slower speed. However, this *step-printing* process resulted in a slightly jerky feeling, and the same correction applied uniformly over the entire film meant that motion on screen would appear to be inconsistent.

Jackson and his effects crew, in contrast, did not apply a single correction to an entire reel. Instead, they analyzed and digitally corrected each shot separately, determining its exact original speed. "We became quite good at being able to guesstimate what the original speed was," Jackson explained in a "making of" documentary aimed at American preview audiences. "We could immediately tell, even if it was one frame out ... And so we would just do it again, and adjust it, and get it bang-on. Because certainly when you get that speed spot-on, it just suddenly comes to life."

Colorization, too, was done with exceptional care. Historic uniforms and patches were provided as reference to the artists doing the colorization, and in several cases, Jackson traveled to the actual locations and took reference photographs to make sure the artists would get the color of the grass and dirt exactly correct.

In addition to extraordinary care with sound effects, such as that of weaponry and animals, the team hired forensic lip-readers to tell them what soldiers were saying in the footage (which of course was originally silent). They then hired actors for voice-over work, taking care that the actor was from whatever region the soldier's regiment, seen in the film, called home. In one well-known clip, a commander is seen referring to a scrap of paper he holds, as he rallies his men before the battle of the Somme. At an archive, Jackson and his team had come across a scrap of paper among documents left by that regiment during this time period, and wondered if it might be the paper seen on screen. On his iPhone, Jackson recorded his own voice reading the text on the paper at various speeds—and Olssen confirmed its authenticity by matching Jackson's voice to the commander's lips. They then got an

For the first half-hour of the film, the archival footage from the Imperial War Museum is framed in black, maintaining its original aspect ratio within the modern widescreen frame.

The footage is black-and-white, and the speed rate has not been corrected. Note the soldier circled as a reference point.

Now the frame begins to expand, until the image fills the standard 1:1.85 (16 x 9) frame.

While the top and bottom of the scene are cropped out, the viewer is closer to the action.

The speed begins to slow, becoming more realistic.

As the aspect ratio transition completes, Jackson introduces the digital restoration, which eliminates the graininess and scratches.

Faces can be seen more clearly, and color and sound effects fade in.

Transition from archival to digitally restored footage, *They Shall Not Grow Old*.

Colorization is complete, checked for accuracy against real uniforms and weaponry, and in some cases from location photography.

In press materials, Jackson said the dirt was the hardest thing to colorize correctly.

Computer technology allows the camera to zoom in, as if the cinematographer had access to a lens not invented for another 50 years.

The speed is now lifelike, the grain and artifacts gone, and the past is no longer floating on a much larger black frame. Viewers can easily see the soldiers' faces.

According to Jackson, the use of color and sound, as well as the effect of zoom lenses, represent technologies that cinematographers of the WWI era would have embraced had they been available.

Compare this frame with the first frame in this sequence; it's all one shot.

Transition from archival to digitally restored footage, *They Shall Not Grow Old*.

actor from that regiment's region to dub the pep talk and laid it onto the soundtrack. That clip, without words, had been used in numerous documentaries over past decades. Now, viewers and historians could see and hear it come to life.

Sources and Notes

Honest Truths: Documentary Filmmakers on Ethical Challenges in Their Work is available for download at the website of American University's Center for Media & Social Impact, https://cmsimpact.org/resource/honest-truths-documentary-filmmakers-on-ethical-challenges-in-their-work/. Sheila Curran Bernard, Jon Else, and Bill Nichols served on the project's advisory board. Stanley Nelson's discussion of *Jonestown* and *We Shall Remain* are taken from a roundtable conducted by us for the first edition of this book. Discussion of *Vietnam* and *Eyes on the Prize* comes in part from the authors' experiences, Kenn Rabin on both series and Bernard on the second season of *Eyes*. Additional information about *Eyes on the Prize* is drawn from Bernard's "Eyes on the Rights: The Rising Cost of Putting History on Screen" (*Documentary Magazine*, June 2005) and "Watching Eyes on the Prize" (*Doubletake/Points of Entry*, Fall/Winter 2006). Information about Middlemarch Films' *Alexander Hamilton* and the discussion with Ronald Blumer come from research for the first edition of this book. For more on *The Civil War*, see Robert Brent Toplin (ed.), *Ken Burns's* The Civil War: *Historians Respond* (Oxford University Press, 1996). The conference proceedings were published; see Sean B. Dolan (ed.), *Telling the Story: The Media, The Public, and American History* (New England Foundation for the Humanities, 1994). The quote from Rick Prelinger is from the first edition of this book. The official BBC page for *The Power of Nightmares* is here: http://news.bbc.co.uk/2/hi/programmes/3755686.stm. There are links on that page to the three episodes of the series as well as various comments and interviews. Leni Riefenstahl's *Triumph of the Will* can be viewed at Internet Archive. Morris Dickstein's book is *Dancing in the Dark: A Cultural History of the Great Depression* (W.W. Norton & Co., 2009). From Roger Ebert, "'Casablanca' Gets Colorized, But Don't Play It Again, Ted," October 30, 1988, available online, www.rogerebert.com/interviews/casablanca-gets-colorized-but-dont-play-it-again-ted. Matt Novak's "Are Colorized Photos Rewriting History?," *Gizmodo*, May 21, 2014, can be found online at https://paleofuture.gizmodo.com/are-colorized-photos-rewriting-history-1579276696. A video of Jordan Lloyd's colorization process is available online, www.youtube.com/watch?time_continue=352&v=vubuBrcAwtY. Meilan Solly's article, "Colorized Footage Is a Vivid Reminder that History Didn't Happen in Black and White," appeared on Smithsonian.com on June 29, 2017. The Smithsonian's colorization process can be viewed online, www.smithsonianchannel.com/videos/how-colorized-historical-foot age-is-painstakingly-made/56957. Press materials for Peter Jackson include "Peter Jackson Interview: How I Made the Visually Stunning They Shall Not Grow Old," *Flicks.com.au* (November 10, 2018), and Mekado Murphy, "How Peter Jackson Made WWI Footage Seem Astonishingly New With 'They Shall Not Grow Old,'" in *The New York Times* (December 16, 2018). Information and quotes from Peter Jackson in the chapter are from a special video created by Jackson and presented in theaters at selected screenings; Kenn Rabin recorded the material for reference and is grateful for permission from Jackson and editor Jabez Olssen to quote from it, as well as to use the frame grabs that appear in Fig. 9.4.

179

CHAPTER 10

The Power of Eyewitness Accounts: A Conversation with Roberta Grossman

On January 27, 2019, the International Day of Commemoration in Memory of the Victims of the Holocaust, producer/director/writer Roberta Grossman's *Who Will Write Our History* was screened in 55 countries. Screening sites including UNESCO's headquarters in Paris; the United States Holocaust Memorial Museum in Washington, D.C.; the Emanuel Ringelblum Jewish Historical Institute in Warsaw, and hundreds of theaters, museums, and community centers.

This 94-minute documentary, based on historian Samuel Kassow's *Who Will Write Our History?* (Indiana University Press, 2007), uses primary source print and audiovisual documentation to tell the story of a clandestine group known by the code name *Oyneg Shabes* ("Joy of the Sabbath"). "Created and led by Polish historian Emanuel Ringelblum, the *Oyneg Shabes* was an organization of 60+ members engaged in spiritual resistance against the Nazis, fighting hatred, lies and propaganda with pen and paper," Grossman notes in press materials. "On the eve of the Warsaw Ghetto Uprising [which began on April 19, 1943], *Oyneg*

Shabes members buried 60,000 pages of documentation in the ground in the hopes that the archive would survive, even if they did not, to 'scream the truth to the world.'"

The film features two primary characters, speaking words drawn from period documents. The main narrator is Rachel Auerbach (1903–1976), heard in voiceovers read by American actress Joan Allen and portrayed in re-enactments by Polish actress Jowita Budnik. The other is Emanuel Ringelblum (1900–1944), heard in voiceover read by the American actor Adrien Brody and portrayed in re-enactments by Polish actor Piotr Głowacki.

Roberta Grossman's extensive lists of credits includes, most recently, *Seeing Allred* (2018) a portrait of attorney Gloria Allred created for Netflix. This interview was conducted by phone in August 2019 and edited for length and clarity.

First, congratulations on the success of this film. It's incredibly moving.

Thank you. We had an amazing screening all over the world on International Holocaust Remembrance Day last January 27th. I think there were 350 screenings or something on that one day. It was huge; it was unbelievable. And so that feels really good, and I feel like in some places, we were getting outside of the usual [audience]. This is a story that people don't know, and even people who have seen every film—or it feels like it—say they have never experienced it like this, and I think it's because of the first-person testimony. We're used to hearing the story of the Holocaust from survivors, which is obviously powerful, moving, and important, but that's different than hearing in the moment: "Right now, I see a girl outside the window, an eight-year-old girl calling for her mommy, and the Nazis are dragging her away." It's somehow more real.

At what point did you become interested in the story of the Oyneg Shabes *archive, and why did it need to be a film?*

I was in the early stages of developing another film on the subject of the Holocaust in Poland, a Warsaw story, and I read a review of Sam Kassow's book, *Who Will Write Our History?* I was a little bit dumbfounded that I had never heard of the secret archive of the Warsaw Ghetto, and I got the book and ten pages in, I realized, "I have to do this." It took about seven years until the film came out; it took a long time to try to do the story justice.

The press materials list a range of high-profile partners—major institutions and organizations around the world. Being the first person to tell this story, what is your sense of a responsibility to get it right?

The feeling of having to do it right has come in part from high-profile partners, and it comes in part from the donors, because the whole film was very expensive. It was all raised through grants and through donations through our 501(c)(3), so there's this feeling of incredible responsibility to those people. But most importantly, it's a feeling of responsibility to Emanuel Ringelblum and Rachel Auerbach and the people who created the archive. It's upsetting because in a way, the archive remained buried, right? Sam Kassow's book—one review called it a work of historical rescue, which I believe it was—was very well respected among scholars, but it didn't break through to the consciousness of the world at large. And not that the movie has, but it certainly has gone further.

I mean, that's why we make films, I think—to tell stories in the hopes that millions of people around the world will hear about the experience of the characters in our films, and that in some way, that will make a difference. And so in terms of responsibility, I just felt that there probably was not going to be another documentary about the *Oyneg Shabes* archive in the near-term, because of the amount of resources that were going into my film. If it fell flat, if it didn't do them justice—that was going to be something I would regret for the rest of my life.

When you and I first talked about this project, a few years ago, there had been some pushback from scholars about your use and potential treatment of archival visuals. You were considering "colorizing" black-and-white footage to make it feel more immediate, especially to younger viewers, and using green screen technology to insert actors into archival imagery. Also—as historian Barbara Kirshenblatt-Gimblett points out on screen, early in your film—most of the footage of the Warsaw Ghetto is propaganda shot by the Nazis. Could you talk about this a bit?

Well, I did not end up colorizing any footage. There was extant color footage that was shot in the Jewish community in Warsaw shortly before the war, and there were some snippets of color footage that were shot by the German propaganda units in the Ghetto. But I did not colorize any archival footage; I just decided that with using green screen and using recreations, I didn't need to do a third potentially questionable thing.

That's interesting; I assumed the 1930s footage was colorized, both because it's rare and because it aligns so well with Auerbach, post-war, remembering the strength and vibrancy of the Jewish community in that earlier time. What was the historical argument against colorization, had you gone down that route?

Well, I don't necessarily agree with it because, as we just discussed, there was color footage at the time. So, if a cameraman put a roll of color footage or a roll of black-and-white in the camera, it's an arbitrary decision. But the pushback was, "You're making a film about an archive whose singular goal was the truth, and then to 'falsify' footage or photographs undermines the veracity of the story, of the truth, of the footage itself." Somebody said to me, "Footage and photographs from the Holocaust are sacred and you can't touch them." On the other hand, they're all shot by Nazi propagandists, right? So it's complex. I mean, when I talk to audiences about this, my standard pushback is [against] the common idea that archival footage is true, honest, real, authentic, and that recreation is on the opposite end: fabricated, false, suspect.

In this film, the common assumptions are flipped: The archival footage and photographs, 98 percent of them, were shot by Nazi propaganda units—and we can talk about using that in a minute. All the recreations were shot with extreme, extreme care for authenticity, and all are illustrations, if you will, of the writing that's directly from the archive. I'm trying to give more expressive voice to the writing in the archive, and there's nothing to show of the inner lives of these people, their homes, their families, the meetings of the archive, the act of creating the archive itself—but I didn't make anything up, even when there's dialogue. In the early scene where Auerbach meets Ringelblum at his office, and they speak to each other—it's one of the few places where there's actual dialogue in the film—it comes directly from Auerbach's writing, in which she said, "A Yiddish poet came to see me. She said, 'Ringelblum is looking for you.' I went to see him. I told him I'm leaving. I'm going to my family. He said, 'No, you can't leave, we can't all run away.' And this changed my fate." It all comes from her writing, with the writing from the archive. So I feel comfortable that it's authentic.

Can you talk a bit more about your decision to use green screen?

I'm always thinking about how you bring archival photographs and footage to life; one of the challenges of working with archival material is, *how do we really see what we're looking at?* We're so inundated with archival images that I feel like we don't see it. Visually, there are really simple techniques, like seeing the whole photograph, and then looking at different parts of it, taking more time. People have used the strategy of making 3D images, which is already cliché.

In this film I used the strategy of green screen, literally inserting actors into archival footage.

You used green screen only occasionally, to place actors into the archival footage. For example, there's a scene in which the actress playing Rachel Auerbach joins a black-and-white archival shot of people entering a building, and the film cuts, as if it's continuous motion, to a re-enactment shot inside the building. Now in full color re-enactment, we see a group of people, including Auerbach, entering.

So she starts in black-and-white, like everybody else in the footage, and then she comes to full color [and the footage remains black-and-white] as she crosses the threshold. There's never an attempt to hide the fact that it's a composite of actor and archival. Sometimes it was a still and sometimes it was footage. You'd think it would be less expensive, but it takes so much time. My editor, Chris Callister, directed the green screen on a separate stage when we were shooting in Poland. We only did four shots, and he was in the studio for a week or so; we had special effects people from England that were there helping us. It's not cheap and it's not fast. But it's very cool, in my opinion.

How did you make decisions about balancing the archival and re-enacted scenes, and why not do a 100 percent dramatic film?

Very simply, I wanted the film to have the gravitas of a documentary and the emotional impact of a dramatic feature. I wanted us to be able to get to know the characters and care about them in a way that we might not just from still photographs of them, and yet I wanted people to know, on a really visceral level, that this was a true story. My intention was to make something of a hybrid, but if I had to choose, I'd say it's a documentary. I have no doubt that it is.

What did it take to ensure that the re-enactments were authentic?

I had two production designers. One was Polish, from Warsaw, and one was from Israel. The production designer from Israel went to Warsaw [about] six months before we started shooting, and they started searching for locations and costumes—wardrobe, with the wardrobe department, and props, working with a very prominent, well-respected scholar in Warsaw who looked at every prop, every piece of clothing, every pen,

Director Roberta Grossman and Director of Photography Dyanna Taylor on set in Poland. Photo by Anna Wloch, used courtesy of Roberta Grossman.

so that it would be as accurate as possible. And of course, looking at photographs from the time for interiors and street scenes. We went to great lengths for accuracy.

Can you talk about your use of archival music? You worked with a composer, Todd Boekelheide, but there are also seven pieces of third-party music listed in the credits.

I worked with a great musical scholar, Henry Sapoznik. His parents were both survivors, and he's a scholar of Yiddish music and music from Poland. He's also a Klezmer musician, and he tried to find things that were authentic to the period but not stereotypical—like there was a huge craze at that period for tangos, recorded by Polish musicians, and so there's some tangos that were recorded by Jewish-Polish orchestras at the time. There also is the Partisan Song, which doesn't come from the ghetto, but during the war and afterwards was used to evoke the overarching spirit of resistance amongst the Jews. Some of the pieces that are classical music are from the period. One of them was written by composer Mieczysław Weinberg. He was a Polish Jew who survived the war by going to the Soviet Union and then lived there for the rest of his life. And then there's a scene in the film where Hersh Wasser [another

Oyneg Shabes member] stops to listen to a violinist in the street. That comes from his writing, where he says that Warsaw was filled with music; the belly's empty but the ears are full.

Returning to the subject of Nazi propaganda footage, can you talk more about the arguments against using it, the controversy?

I'm sure you know *A Film Unfinished*. That film peels back the conceit that this is somehow documentary footage, *vérité* footage—there's an agenda behind it. And the agenda is to make the Jewish people look as bad as possible. On the other hand, it is footage shot in the ghetto of the Jewish people who were incarcerated there at the time, in the place with the actual people, and it's all we've got. The bias—the way it was shot and what it was trying to do—doesn't mean that there isn't a lot of incredibly valuable archival material in there. There is; you just have to be careful, and you have to be aware of what you're showing and why.

We didn't use any of the really overtly propagandistic stuff without talking about it in that context. The members of *Oyneg Shabbos* were aware of the filming and were talking about it all the time, and they were aware that what they were doing was an act of resistance against that portrayal of the Jews. So when you see, for example, a wealthy woman who's being forced to stand next to an impoverished older woman in threadbare clothes, and the wealthy woman looks so pained and uncomfortable, we don't use that just as is. I mean, we know what the intent was. It's to show that the Jews didn't care for each other; that wealthy Jews didn't care for the poor, which is not true. So whenever we use anything that was clearly meant to have an impact like that, we call it out. It says "Nazi propaganda footage" right on the screen, and that's what's being discussed through voiceover or by the scholars.

Was there any resistance in Poland to bringing up this history, recreating these events?

Well, film crews tend to be progressive and interested in digging up the truth, so the crew was extremely supportive, very invested in helping to tell the story. The Polish government changed hands right before we started shooting, but we did get grants from the Polish Film Institute and from the City of Łódź and other Polish organizations and foundations. So I would say, on the whole, no. But the government became this right-wing government, and I don't think we would've gotten that support had that government been in place when we applied for those grants.

Bartek Kotschedoff as Leyb Goldin in *Who Will Write Our History*. Photo by Anna Wloch, used courtesy of Roberta Grossman.

It's interesting, because the U.S. government also changed significantly while you were making this film.

Right. I always think that it is important to keep telling the stories of the Holocaust, but I could not have imagined, when I started making the film, that it would come out at a time when it would be so relevant and so urgent, sadly, in terms of just the idea of propaganda. I keep this quote on my desk, it sort of starts mid-thought:

> The attraction of the Nazi conspiracy thinking is that we can feel like victims when we attack. Its vulnerability is that the world is full of facts. Hence Hitler's hostility to journalism. In the Germany of the early 1930s, the newspaper industry was suffering after a financial crisis. Hitler and other Nazis used the idea of the "Lügenpresse" ("fake news") to attack remaining journalists who were trying to report the facts. In Germany and Austria today, the far right once more speaks of the Lügenpresse, in part because the American president has made the idea respectable. The extreme right in Germany and Austria knows perfectly well that "fake news" is American English for "Lügenpresse." [Timothy Snyder, *The Guardian* (October 30, 2018).]

Early on in the film, we see footage of people going about their daily lives, and in voiceover Rachel Auerbach says, "We protected ourselves from the truth. We didn't want to see it."

Right.

You worked with eight archival researchers and used material from numerous archives and other sources. Were there any rules that you had governing your use of archival images? Did images have to be specific to the date and place they're used to represent?

No, and I got pushback from scholars about that. They wanted that kind of direct correlation. So, for example, just to call myself out—we tried very hard not to do this, but we did in this instance, and in a (very) few others—the ghetto was closed on November, 15, 1940. You see a shot of a ghetto gate being closed, and one of the scholars jumped at me and said, "That's not Warsaw, that's Łódź," and I said, "I'm sorry, but I'm going to use it." It was a fairly specific, fairly tight shot of a gate being closed in a ghetto, and they knew it wasn't Warsaw, and I used it anyway because there was a shot of a gate closing and I needed that to help make that point: the ghetto is closed.

So in some ways you're using the image as much for the emotional and essential truth of what's being, rather than as specific visual evidence. I imagine that you also are working around a very limited choice of visuals.

Very limited. I think there may be one or two shots when we're talking about Jews who are internal refugees, Jewish Polish refugees, being pushed from the provinces into Warsaw, and we used a shot or two from—I think it's Łódź. In that city, when the Jews were kicked out of their homes and pushed into the ghetto, there was a German cinematographer present. Not in Warsaw.

We really tried to avoid anything like that, but it's the same action, essentially the same population, in the same couple of months, and we felt like it was important.

What about making decisions about when images are very graphic, such as dead bodies and just terrible imagery? Were there ever times when you thought, "We don't want this on the screen for any longer because it's just too much," or, "We don't need to use this shot because it's undignified for this person who's deceased," any conversations like that?

Yes, of course. Statistics show that an ever-growing number of people don't really know anything about Holocaust, so, there's a very serious discussion that happens. "Is this an important image for us to see and confront and understand, that this is what happened and this is how far human beings will go to harm one another, degrade one another?" Or, "Is this 'Holocaust porn'"? We didn't use anything for shock value. Well—that's not true. It's shocking to see cart after cart after cart of naked dead bodies. We do use it. My partner, Sophie Sartain, who ended up being a consultant in the editing phase, would say, "You have to calibrate. You don't want to completely desensitize people because it's so overwhelming right at the beginning." We calibrated it so that it built, which is, in a way, historically inaccurate—this was terrible violence on Jewish communities and Jewish bodies that went on right from the very beginning—but of course, it did build in scale. And there are things we didn't use. There's horrible footage the Nazi shot; they forced rabbis to stand where bodies were being dumped down chutes into mass graves. As Barbara Kirshenblatt-Gimblett talks about, the intensity and specificity of the Jewish burial rituals are all about dignity of the deceased, and this is the exact opposite.

190

One of the strengths of this film, in my view, is that you let the truth reveal itself over time. You remain in the moment with the people in the Warsaw Ghetto, the people compiling the archive. Even though the outcome is known, the viewer is still able to suspend disbelief and somehow believe an alternative outcome remains possible.

That's the power of the eyewitness accounts. They're being written in the moment by people who are experiencing these events, and they don't know the end. They don't know how it's going to end.

Can you talk about your decision to frame the story around Rachel Auerbach, which is not the structure of Samuel Kassow's book?

It was pretty simple to me, because she knew Ringelblum; she was part of the same intellectual, Yiddishist, leftist, literary milieu before the war. She was part of the *Oyneg Shabes* archive during the war, and she lived to tell the tale. She was one of the few who did, and then spent the rest of her life writing about Ringelblum and the archive, the Jews of Warsaw, and wanted so much to bring the story to the world, have people be aware of it. Her arc had a beginning, middle, and end, and she's a great writer. All of her writing is great, and her post-war writing is just fantastic. So it was a natural choice.

There's a misconception, sometimes, that adaptation is somehow "putting the book on screen," which is rarely the case.

One of the reasons it took seven years was not just raising the money, it was figuring out how to tell the story. Despite the invaluable resource of Sam's book, as a filmmaker, you basically have to start over. Going into the archive, going to the original writing—and Rachel Auerbach's writing, except for a couple of pieces, had never been translated out of Yiddish and Polish; I had a great deal of her writing translated. And unlike a historical book, which can just go chronologically, a film has to have a dramatic arc. A documentary is no different from a drama: it's a story with a beginning, middle, and end. It has to have an arc for each of the characters and an arc for the overall story, and then there's the background and the foreground. It follows the rules of drama. So, it's a very different craft from writing history. The hardest part of the script writing process was what to leave out. That's really what took such a long time. The structure was hard, too—but it's what to leave out that kept me up at night.

Sam's book is about 700 pages. A film, when it's very condensed, just the information, just the script, it's about 30 or 40 pages. So we need both, in-depth historical writing and historical films. But, especially for trying to reach students and young people around the world, there's no better medium than film. It's the most powerful communication medium—that's why it's the most popular art form—because you have images and music and words and the inexplicable magic of the combination of all of the above. And then you have, hopefully, something that really teaches history in a very emotional way.

You've done films on a range of topics, but your undergraduate degree is in history (your graduate degree is in film). What do you see as the connection between the professions of filmmaking and history?

They're the same thing using different tools of communication. You could write a book on the subject as Sam Kassow did, and heavily illustrate the story with photographs, maps, documents, and other things. Or you could make a film, and you are telling the story using the tools of that craft. For me, I'm obviously very biased, but there is no better way to tell a historical story than in a film, although you perhaps can't go into as many details … I think we need both, right?

Sources and Notes

The website for *Who Will Write Our History* is https://whowillwrite ourhistory.com/. The entire Ringelblum Archive is available to researchers in digital format through the United States Holocaust Memorial Museum, www.ushmm.org/, and through the Jewish Historical Institute of Poland, www.jhi.pl/en. *A Film Unfinished* (2010, 90 minutes), by Israeli director Yael Hersonski, aired on PBS's *Independent Lens*, www.pbs.org/independentlens/films/film-unfinished/.

RIGHTS AND LICENSES

CHAPTER 11

Introduction to Rights and Licenses

Filmmakers, writers, scholars, and others who want to incorporate the intellectual property of others—such as images, footage, or music—into new works need to consider issues of *copyright*. Most likely, they need to get permission, in the form of a *license*, to use that property, and failure to do so may result in costly legal problems. Also, once they've created their own new works, they'll want to protect that work from unlicensed use by others. What are the processes involved in making this happen, and in what situations might third-party materials *not* need to be licensed? This chapter and those that follow seek to answer these questions. Understanding how material is cleared for use and the challenges that may arise can inform media production and scholarship. At the same time, it can advance discussion about the need to make archival materials affordable and accessible, as well as the need to support the important and expensive work that archives do.

The basic information presented here applies to any type of production, from Hollywood blockbusters to independent archival histories or roll-in video for a museum or website. There are, of course, myriad special circumstances, and each license agreement is unique. When faced with legal documents, always consult a qualified legal professional.

Rights: The Basics

According to the World Intellectual Property Organization (WIPO; an agency of the United Nations), intellectual property (IP) "refers to creations of the mind, such as inventions; literary and artistic works; designs; and symbols, names and images used in commerce." WIPO divides IP into three categories:

- *Copyright*, which describes "the rights that creators have over their literary and artistic works. Works covered by copyright range from books, music, paintings, sculpture, and films to computer programs, databases, advertisements, maps, and technical drawings";
- *Patents*, "an exclusive right granted for an invention, which is a product or a process that provides, in general, a new way of doing something, or offers a new technical solution to a problem"; and
- *Trademarks*, "a sign capable of distinguishing the goods or services of one enterprise from those of other enterprises."

Each nation has its own laws regarding intellectual property. In the United States, IP is covered by Title 17 of the U.S. Code and is generally governed by two agencies: the U.S. Copyright Office (www. copyright.gov) and the U.S. Patent and Trademark Office (uspto.gov). Title 17 defines *copyright protection* as subsisting in "original works of authorship fixed in any tangible medium of expression, now known or later developed, from which they can be perceived, reproduced, or otherwise communicated, either directly or with the aid of a machine or device."

The U.S. Patent and Trademark Office definitions essentially echo those of WIPO. That is, a trademark is a word, phrase, symbol (like a logo), or design (or combination of these) that uniquely identifies one product or service from another. A patent, meanwhile, confers property rights to someone who has *invented* something, including a *utility patent*, "granted to anyone who invents or discovers any new and useful process, machine, article of manufacture, or composition of matter, or any new and useful improvement thereof"; *design patent*, "granted to anyone who invents a new, original, and ornamental design for an article of manufacture"; and *plant patent*, "granted to anyone who invents or discovers and asexually reproduces any distinct and new variety of plant." Media makers do sometimes venture into non-copyright areas of intellectual property law; they may seek to patent an innovation in camera technology, for example, or they may want to trademark characters, titles, production company logos, and other appropriate elements of a project. Additionally, they may need permission to incorporate materials to which others hold the patent or trademark.

A Brief History of Copyright

In the United States, copyright law is written into the U.S. Constitution, ratified in 1788. In Article 1, Section 8, the nation's founders asserted: "The Congress shall have the Power ... To promote the Progress of Science and useful Arts, by securing for limited Times to Authors and Inventors the exclusive Right to their respective Writings and Discoveries." The initial copyright term was 14 years, renewable once for an additional 14 years from the date of first publication. The law was originally designed to encourage and motivate creation and invention by allowing those who *performed* (created and made tangible) this work to profit from it for a limited period of time. After this point, the work would be copyright free, entering into a "public domain," where it could be used and drawn upon by others without restriction, thus fueling further creation and invention.

It's important to understand how copyright law has evolved, and in particular, how the *term* or length of copyright protection has expanded. This information is useful not only when considering U.S. law, but also differences in copyright around the globe. As stated, the initial copyright term was 14 years, renewable for another 14 years. In 1909, Congress extended the copyright term to 28 years, renewable for another 28, for a total of 56 years. Author Samuel Clemens—known by his pen name, Mark Twain—was among those arguing in support of this extension. According to *The New York Times*, he told Congress that 50 years seemed about right: "I think that ought to satisfy any reasonable author, because it will take care of his children. Let the grandchildren take care of themselves."

Until 1976, when the law was changed, copyright protection—either the initial copyright, or the renewal—had to be claimed by putting a copyright notice on the work and by *registering* the copyright—in other words, by filing the proper paperwork with the U.S. Copyright Office, part of the Library of Congress. If creators failed to do this, their work was not copyrighted. Similarly, if the copyright was not renewed before the initial period was up, it fell out of copyright protection. (According to the Copyright Office, between 1909 and 1961, only about 15 percent of all 28-year copyrights were renewed.) What this means is that a significant amount of early material was considered to be in the *public domain*, meaning that it was no longer copyrighted and could be used by anyone for any purpose.

In the meantime, however, owners of valuable copyrights—such as The Walt Disney Company, whose 1928 animated short, *Steamboat Willie*, marked the debut of Mickey Mouse—were pressuring Congress to expand and extend copyright terms. Congress complied, modifying copyright law several times between 1962 and 1974, and then making major changes in 1976 and 1998.

The 1976 Copyright Act

In 1976, U.S. copyright law was overhauled entirely, with changes that took effect on January 1, 1978), including the following:

- Copyrights that *had* been renewed for a second 28-year term and were in a legal "holding position" pending the 1976 law were automatically extended for a total of 75 years from date of first publication (rather than the previous 56), keeping more works out of the public domain for longer.
- For works created in or after 1978 (when the law went into effect), protection lasted for a total of 75 years from publication if they were corporate works or works for hire (created for a company or employer). Personal creative works would no longer be based on publication, but rather they were protected for the life of the artist plus 50 years.
- For works created in or after 1978, copyright became automatic. In other words, while registration brings certain benefits (and is still encouraged), from 1978 forward, the mere act of creating the work is enough to initiate its copyright protection. One key drawback is that because fewer creators now register, it has become much more difficult to locate a copyright holder when permission to use protected works is needed.
- Certain foreign works that had been in the public domain in the United States, if not in the public domain in their countries of origin, were restored to copyright protection.

The Copyright Clock

One of the most far-reaching revisions of the U.S. Copyright Act of 1976 was its change to the start of the "copyright clock;" the countdown of years during which something is protected. Prior to 1978, when the act took effect, copyright protection began as of *first publication*. Now, it would begin when a work was *created*. This poses challenges for those trying to determine whether or when a work has or will enter the public domain.

Another aspect of the complexity is the definition of what it meant, prior to 1978, for a work to be published; publication was determined by *mass production*. In other words, whatever the type of work, it wasn't considered "published" until multiple copies had been disseminated by some means. The law stated that "a public performance or display of a work does not of itself constitute publication." This can make a difference if you're trying to clear works created prior to 1978. A television show that was broadcast live or aired a single time would not be considered "published," and instead was only publicly performed or displayed. To explain: the single broadcast may have been seen by millions of people, but the program had not yet been *mass produced* in a tangible form. Only when a show was *syndicated*—requiring that multiple film prints or, later, videotape copies, were physically distributed to television stations—did the copyright clock begin ticking.

With theatrical films, the countdown even for pre-1978 works is more straightforward. It has always begun when the film is released because film prints (or today, digital copies) have always needed to be mass produced for physical distribution to theaters.

The 1998 Copyright Term Extension Act

In 1998, the U.S. Congress passed another change to American copyright law, the Copyright Term Extension Act (CTEA), known informally as the "Sonny Bono Act." Named for California entertainer and Congressman Sonny Bono, who died in 1998, the CTEA was championed by his widow, Mary (elected to complete his term), and by the estate of American composer George Gershwin, who died in 1937. Once again, the bill's supporters included Disney, as Mickey Mouse's debut was now due under existing copyright laws to enter the public domain in 2003. Ironically, critics noted, many of Disney's most popular works were themselves drawn from public domain material. Attorney Chris Sprigman, writing in *FindLaw Legal News and Commentary*, noted that these works include "*Snow White and the Seven Dwarfs, Cinderella, Pinocchio, The Hunchback of Notre Dame, Alice in Wonderland,* and *The Jungle Book* (released exactly one year after [author Rudyard] Kipling's copyrights expired)."

The CTEA added two decades to the copyright period, meaning that works were protected for 70 years after the death of the author or, in the case of corporate authorship, 120 years after a work was created, or 95 years from first publication, whichever came first. Thousands of works created after 1923 (if still under copyright in 1998) would not enter the public domain for an additional period of at least 20 years.

In January 1999, just 10 days after the Act took effect, lawyers filed a complaint arguing that the retroactive extension of copyright was a violation of the U.S. Constitution, citing two key reasons. First, that the Act contradicted the intent of the founders in securing copyright for "limited Times" as specified in Article 1, Section 8. Second, it violated the First Amendment by weighing the interests of copyright over freedom of

199

speech. By 2002, the case had reached the U.S. Supreme Court (*Eldred et.al. v. Ashcroft, Attorney General*), where attorney Lawrence Lessig argued for the petitioner. "When we brought *Eldred*, we were really focused on a very basic and obvious point about the structure of copyright," Lessig told us, adding:

> If copyright is to be an incentive to create works, the one thing we know about incentives is they're prospective [forward looking]. And when you extend the term of existing copyrights, you're not creating any new incentive to do anything, you're just giving more power or more reward to somebody who has already produced something. No matter what *I* do, ... George Gershwin will not produce anything else ... If you think about the purpose the framers had in being very restrictive around what they thought of as monopolies, it was to avoid exactly the dynamic we see right now: rich people, or powerful companies, or powerful interest groups basically buying off Congress to extend the term or extend the reach of copyrights.

Lessig lost the case and a subsequent appeal, but so far, since 1998, no other major changes have been made to the U.S. copyright law. The effect of the 1998 CTEA was to put a 20-year freeze on works entering the public domain. Finally, on January 1, 2019, works copyrighted or renewed in 1923 were no longer protected. A year later, on January 1, 2020, works from 1924 entered the public domain, including George Gershwin's *Rhapsody in Blue*.

Provided there are no further changes to U.S. copyright law, Disney's short, *Steamboat Willie*, will enter the public domain in 2024, 95 years after the corporation published it. However, Mickey Mouse, as both a company logo and a trademarked character belonging to The Walt Disney Company will be protected for as long as the company keeps renewing their trademarks.

Copyrighting Your Own Work

How do you protect your own work from theft? If you have created materials that are "original works of authorship" and "fixed in a tangible form of expression," they are eligible for copyright protection. The U.S. Copyright Office lists the following categories of eligible works:

- Literary works;
- Musical works, including any accompanying words;

- Dramatic works, including any accompanying music;
- Pantomimes and choreographic works;
- Pictorial, graphic, and sculptural works;
- Motion pictures and other audiovisual works;
- Sound recordings;
- Architectural works.

The site also notes that "categories should be viewed broadly. For example, computer programs and most 'compilations' may be registered as 'literary works'; maps and architectural plans may be registered as 'pictorial, graphic, and sculptural works.' As the *author* of these works, whether the work is published or unpublished, registered or unregistered, the 1976 Copyright Act generally gives you the "exclusive right to do and to authorize others to do the following:

- To reproduce the work in copies or phonorecords;
- To prepare derivative works based upon the work;
- To distribute copies or phonorecords of the work to the public by sale or other transfer of ownership, or by rental, lease, or lending;
- To perform the work publicly, in the case of literary, musical, dramatic, and choreographic works, pantomimes, and motion pictures and other audiovisual works;
- To display the work publicly, in the case of literary, musical, dramatic, and choreographic works, pantomimes, and pictorial, graphic, or sculptural works, including the individual images of a motion picture or other audiovisual work; and
- In the case of sound recordings, to perform the work publicly by means of a digital audio transmission."

Works for Hire
Note that in cases where a work falls under the legal definition of "work for hire," the copyright is held by the employer and not the employee. Thus, if the employer is a company and not an individual, the work is subject to the term limitations for corporate ownership as opposed to personal ownership. If you hire a production staff and/ or crew to work on your own film, it's likely that you'll want them to sign a work-for-hire agreement, so that it's clear that you own the rights to whatever you hired them to do. Otherwise, they could have a copyright claim on it, since they, not you, actually "created" it. Sometimes media projects fail to do this, and it has caused problems for them.

Registering Copyright

While copyright is now automatic, there are multiple benefits to registering a work with the Copyright Office, and we encourage you to do so. Most distribution outlets require you to register the copyright to your film. Most importantly, someone who may want to license your work will have a better chance of finding you and vice versa. For details, visit www.copyright.gov and/or consult with a copyright lawyer.

Exceptions to Copyright

In the United States, there are two notable exceptions to copyright law, *public domain* and *fair use*, discussed in the following chapters. Other countries may have related exceptions, such as *fair dealing*, as discussed by attorney Hubert Best in Chapter 14.

Creative Commons

One way for creators and users of material to avoid the copyright tangle is to utilize what are known as "Creative Commons" or similar licenses. Established in 2001 by Lawrence Lessig and others, the CC website (https://creativecommons.org/) now claims a global network involving "1.6 billion works and counting." There are six main licenses that creators can choose from in making their works available. These are derived from different combinations of the following basic conditions that may apply to re-use: Attribution, ShareAlike, NonCommercial, and NoDerivatives, described on the Creative Commons website.

More about Trademarks

Trademarks, often considered a part of *branding*, affect media makers and the use of third-party materials in a number of ways, in part because trademark law covers a wide range of issues and materials, both historic and present day.

Trademarked Characters

The Nike *swoosh*, the Pillsbury Doughboy, and McDonald's golden arches are obviously trademarked. Certain fictional characters and real personalities, including actors and athletes, may also be protected (not only by trademark, but also because of their *right of publicity*, discussed later). Some of the most iconic (and long-deceased) characters of the 20th century, including Charlie Chaplin's Little Tramp and The Three Stooges, are protected. Notable *animals*, both real (such as the Depression-era racehorse, Seabiscuit) and fictional (such as Lassie, a dog whose television show ran for nearly 20 years on CBS), are protected and their rights of publicity administered by companies that act as agents.

What this means is that in addition to obtaining a license to use a copyrighted photo or clip, you may need to license your use of the trademark. If you license a clip from a Three Stooges film from Sony Pictures (formerly Columbia, which produced The Three Stooges films), you must also contact C3 Entertainment, Inc. and work out a licensing deal. If you want to use a clip of Chaplin from an old comedy short that has fallen into the public domain, you may still need to clear your use of his trademarked character through Association Chaplin in Paris. (Likewise, as noted, even if the 1928 short *Steamboat Willie* enters the public domain in 2024, you will still need to clear your use of the trademarked Mickey Mouse character.)

It can cost as much to license the use of a trademarked character as to license the clip in which they appear, so beware. Note that you only need to clear trademark if you are presenting the characters *in* character. If you are showing not the characters but the actors who portrayed them, in a real-life setting—for example, Chaplin as himself, seen arriving at a movie premiere in newsreel footage—you don't have to clear trademark. Also note that if a trademarked character is embedded in a clip that qualifies as fair use, you do *not* need to clear the trademark.

203

Licensing: The Basics

Whether the rights are protected under copyright, trademark, or another IP law, the term *licensing* refers to the process of clearing those rights. This means securing and usually paying for permission to use third-party owned materials in a new work, such as your film, video, or YouTube post. Licenses are not optional. You must have signed releases in hand for the appropriate markets before your work can be insured, and before it will be shown or picked up by distributors. If you don't clear the necessary rights, you will not be able to reach audiences at film festivals, on broadcast or cable television, on streaming services, in theaters, in classrooms, or on the web. If you try to distribute in any venue without the appropriate clearances, you may be subject to financial and even criminal penalties, and your film may be taken down from a site and/or enjoined from being shown anywhere.

The Materials Release

Releases are a fact of life for filmmakers, authors, and those in similar professions. (News gathering has somewhat different legal issues; consult an organization such as the Reporters Committee for Freedom of the Press, www.rcfp.org, for details.) Filmmakers will likely need to secure *appearance* releases for people who appear as themselves on camera, or guild clearances if they're hired actors. Often, depending on circumstances, filmmakers may need to obtain *location* releases or filming permits. If you are licensing work from someone else, you should make sure that they secured whatever clearances they needed for their work, *and* that the wording of those clearances gives the licensor the right to extend those permissions to you.

Lastly, you will need to secure *materials* releases, which relate to the third-party *content* you are acquiring. It can be a fairly straightforward transaction, such as when you're requesting permission to use material owned by a friend, an interview subject, or a noncommercial archive. Provided they own the rights, they can grant you permission simply by signing a standard materials release that you provide. (See the following page for an annotated sample.) If the copyright holder provides the release or license for *you* to sign, be sure to consider it carefully to make sure it matches what your employer or distributor requires. In either case, these are legal documents; be sure to seek advice from a qualified professional.

Also, a word of caution: just because a photo or film clip or audio recording is in someone's *possession* doesn't mean they hold the rights to it. A famous person might have a collection of press photos that were taken of them over the course of their career that they're happy to let you film or scan for use in your project, but they may not own the copyright.

"Seating now in all parts of the house. Chicago, Illinois." July 1941, photographer John Vachon. U.S. Library of Congress.

SAMPLE MATERIALS RELEASE

I, [copyright holder] ("Licensor") hereby grant to [your production company or distributing LLC] ("Licensee") non-exclusive **(1)** , one-time **(2)** permission to include the materials listed below ("Licensed Material") for use in the [type of project such as feature, documentary or other] entitled [name or working title of your production] (hereafter "Production").**(3)** I hereby authorize the producers to reproduce on film, tape, digital media or otherwise the materials I provide for purposes of creating the Production. I further grant Licensee, on a non-exclusive basis, all rights in all media now known or hereafter devised, in perpetuity, worldwide and throughout the universe **(4)**, for use in the Production and in the promotion of same ("in-context promotion").**(5)**

I agree that the producers shall have sole editing discretion **(6)** in determining the extent and manner of use of the Licensed Material. It is also understood that the producers are not obligated **(7)** to use the Licensed Material in the Production. Producers and their assigns shall have sole discretion in creating, advertising, promoting and marketing the Production.

I warrant that I have the right and power to enter into and fully perform this Agreement and to grant the producers and Licensee the rights herein discussed. I further agree that if there is any claim or litigation involving any materials submitted for use in the Production, I will hold the Licensee, the producers, and their licensees, successors and assigns **(8)** harmless from liability, and indemnify **(9)** producers for any and all losses or expense arising from the defense of such claims or litigation. I hereby waive the right to seek to enjoin, restrain or interfere with the reproduction, distribution, exhibition, marketing or promotion of the Production **(10)**.

205

I acknowledge that the Licensee and their assigns own all rights to the Production, including all allied, ancillary and subsidiary rights **(11)**. Licensee may freely assign the rights contained herein to any third person, firm, or corporation, specifically for the purpose of facilitating distribution and/or publicity of Production. Such person, firm or corporation will assume all of the executory obligations herein **(12)**.

I have read, understand and agree to the above terms and conditions. I understand that this contains the entire understanding of the parties relating to the subject matter and cannot be changed or terminated orally. The provisions shall be binding upon me and my heirs, executors, administrators and successors. All rights, licenses and privileges herein granted are irrevocable and not subject to restraint or injunction under any circumstances. This Agreement is subject to the laws of the State of [primarily business address of contract creator], and I acknowledge that a facsimile or digital image of my signature **(13)** will be considered an original signature for purposes of this Agreement.

Licensed Material: **(14)** _____
Signature: _____   Date: _____
Print Name/Organization: _____
Contact Information: **(15)** _____
Requested on-screen credit **(16)**: _____

SAMPLE MATERIALS RELEASE: Annotations (see bolded numbers in document)

1) "Non-exclusive" means that the licensor can license the same material to anyone else at any time. A licensor will almost never grant exclusive access.
2) "One-time use" means in the one production specified. If the agreement is on a royalty-free basis, it should not specify one-time use.
3) The agreement starts with definitions, so that names and descriptions aren't needed throughout.
4) "All rights, all media, in perpetuity, worldwide…" It's almost always necessary to obtain a comprehensive rights package for a project destined for streaming on services such as Netflix, for downloading, and often even for broadcast.
5) "In-context promotion" means that the licensed material may be included in a trailer or other advertising for your film. If you can't get these rights, be sure that everyone involved in your project's promotion knows not to use that material.
6) "Sole editing discretion" – it's up to you how you include the licensor's material in your project. However, some commercial archives may insist on seeing the context in which you plan to use their material before granting you permission.
7) You are under no obligation to use any of what you've licensed.
8) "Assigns" (and "successors,"etc.) provides that any distributor, partner in your business, company you're making the film for, or those who assume these roles later on are also protected by, and responsible for honoring, the terms of the agreement.
9) This is a warranty that the licensor has the right to sell you the clip; it protects you against any legal action that might be taken by any third party who may claim otherwise.
10) Waiver of injunctive relief means that if the licensor thinks you violated the agreement, they still can't stop you from finishing and distributing your film.
11) The licensor is acknowledging that you own the project and can assign it to others, including material you have licensed for inclusion in the project.
12) If you do assign the project to others, they must honor the terms of this agreement.
13) A signature gathered electronically is to be considered the same as an "original signature" for legal purposes.
14) Here, you list very specifically the material that's covered by the license agreement. If the list is extensive or requires more detail, add another page as an attachment. (This can be the same as, or similar to, the report you make to the archive after you've locked your film.)
15) Current contact information is important, especially if you need to make changes.
16) *Very* useful to get this right away, and be sure of spellings, etc. *All* third-party providers (licensed, public domain, fair use) should be credited in the end credit roll, whether you licensed material from them or you are using their material under fair use or public domain. Some rights holders, such as museums, record companies (in the case of music), and many photo agencies have very specific credit wording that they'll want you to use. If you use a clip from a Hollywood film or TV show, the copyright holder will also provide you with credit wording you must follow.

NOTE: This information is provided for informational purposes only, and is not intended to replace legal consultation or to be used as a contract without legal review.

Additional Notes on the Sample Materials Release

Note (4): If you are unable to obtain the "all-inclusive" rights but negotiated a window during which you can upgrade your rights for a negotiated price, you can add an optional sentence to the end of this paragraph, such as: "Licensor agrees to expand this rights package to include [*additional rights*] for the negotiated upgrade fee of [*dollar amount*], if such purchase is completed within [*length of window*]." See Chapter 15 for more information on rights windows.

Note (6): Some commercial archives, especially news entities, may need to see the context in which you plan to use their material before granting you permission. This is to guard against what they may view as misrepresentation of the content, slander against them or their personnel, or using their materials for pornographic purposes, to incite violence, etc. You should supply them with a *minimum* amount of context beyond their clip (usually 30–60 seconds on either side of the clip used). All they can do is allow you or not allow you to use the clip. If they disallow you, but you haven't violated any basic conditions—they simply don't like you criticizing or analyzing them—and you have told the truth, you may have a claim to fair use.

Note (9): This is a *warranty* (i.e., written guarantee) that the licensor has the right to sell you the clip, and, related to that, an *indemnity clause*. Indemnity clauses and warranties are important, and they're a big part of boilerplate agreements that come from larger organizations, which often want *you* to indemnify *them* against any legal action.

Note (10): Something like this waiver should be in every license agreement you have, although most initial agreements offered to you by the licensor will not include it. Simply stated, a *waiver of injunctive relief* means that if the licensor for any reason thinks you violated the agreement, they can't shut your film down or stop its release. The rights holder may resist, but this waiver should be fought for, even if it means paying a higher license fee to have it included.

In addition to adding language that *waives* injunctive relief, watch out for—and insist on the removal of—language that even implies a right to injunctive relief. This is usually a sentence to the effect that the licensor can withdraw permission at any time, for any reason or even for no reason. If you license a ten-second clip from someone and they exercise that clause, distribution of your entire film must stop immediately until you remove the offending clip (or convince the licensor to change their mind). Bottom line: your licensors must waive injunctive relief. You can't agree to language that grants the licensor the rights to *enjoin* (stop) your film, not least because if you don't have it and your film is picked

207

up by a distributor, you will need to go back and get it, or face re-editing the film or losing the distributor.

On the other hand, most license boilerplates offered by copyright holders include a statement to the effect that they reserve the right to sue you in a court of law for monetary damages. If they waive injunctive relief, this becomes the owner's only recourse, should you breach the agreement. Such language is to be expected and is acceptable to distributors. As far as the risk this presents to you, that's why you'll have errors and omissions (E&O) insurance. And a lawyer.

Note (11): Some licensors will offer boilerplate language stipulating that the rights they are granting you *cannot* be shared or re-assigned, and can only be exploited by the licensee (you or your production company). Alternatively, some rights holders will only let you re-assign if you notify them first, and they reserve the right to refuse to allow it. No distributor can live with those kinds of restrictions, so you can't agree to them. What you can generally agree to are limitations, such as assignment "only for the purposes of distribution, publicity and promotion of the production." Another variation is that you can only assign the rights to *their* materials "as they are embedded in your film for its distribution and promotion." They don't want you to sell or give their specific materials, in isolation, to any third party.

Note (13): The final contract paragraph is mostly self-explanatory and is fine. There's usually a clause saying that this agreement is the entire agreement, and a statement indicating under which state or country's laws the contract is valid. Sometimes (not in this example) there is a *severability clause*, which says that if one part of the agreement turns out not to be enforceable under applicable law, the other parts still remain in effect. And sometimes, the waiver of injunctive relief is reiterated in the last paragraph, because it's so important.

Other Terms

Here are some of the more complicated terms you may encounter in contracts given to you by licensors, such as limitations based on markets and licensing periods.

- A statement that says the licensed material remains the property of the licensor, and that you are only receiving permission to use the material non-exclusively, and subject to the terms and limitations, if any, of the agreement. Such a paragraph will often also demand that after your project is complete, you destroy or return any "raw materials" the licensor gave or sold you. This is fine.

- A section that delineates which rights you are being granted, based on what you negotiated—for example, "worldwide rights in all media in perpetuity," or "streaming rights in North America only for a period of ten years." The rights you negotiated *should* appear in the license agreement you receive from a rights holder. Occasionally, they do not, in which case they should at least be clearly delineated in the invoice you are sent for the licensing fee(s). It's better if it's in the agreement or an addendum to the agreement.
- A statement indicating that you must provide them with one or two copies of the finished work. You can and should provide these, but no more than three, only after the production is publicly released, and only for the licensor's reference. They shouldn't reserve any rights to exhibit or otherwise share your film using these copies.
- A paragraph to the effect that by selling you the materials, the licensor does not take responsibility for any *underlying* or third-party rights. This is standard, as discussed in the next section. Some collections that specialize in concert or sports footage, or footage of celebrities, may have underlying clearances already handled, and that will be spelled out in your contract (and likely reflected in a much higher price) but be sure.
- The warranty and indemnities that you claimed may also be claimed by the licensor, in a statement that provides for various remedies. Suppose you license a clip of a music performance from an archive, for example, but then don't obtain the synch rights for the underlying music. The indemnities clause will protect the licensor from being sued for your error, which is as it should be. In an equitable agreement, there should be a corresponding paragraph that protects *you* from any mistake *they* make, as per note (9) above. Often these two paragraphs are presented one right after the other.

209

Important reminder: don't sign anything until you've checked it out with either your production lawyer or your distributor—or both. Any protections you need to have, as well as all the rights you are obtaining, should be spelled out. Lack of specificity about limitations in a license agreement does not automatically imply those limitations don't exist.

More About Underlying Rights

Underlying rights, sometimes referred to as *embedded rights*, are the rights to any trademarked images, copyrighted sounds or music, performances, sports leagues and logos, or other elements *within* a clip that you're trying to license. These rights usually do not belong to the principal copyright holder—the individual or archive that owns and is authorized to license the clip itself. Instead, the underlying rights must each be cleared separately by you. What kind of materials get overlooked?

- You license a clip of local or national news covering a trial, but no cameras were allowed in the courtroom. The clip you cleared may include the work of a courtroom sketch artist, which in most cases is copyrighted by the artist. If you want to use it, you need to contact the artist (or artist's representatives) to get permission.
- You acquire a news story that includes images and sounds taken from third parties. The news organization used these images and sounds in their immediate reporting of current events and they may have fallen under fair use guidelines. Your re-use of this material, in general, needs to be cleared, which means you'd need to contact the news source to see if they can identify the source of the copyrighted materials included in their coverage. An example of this can be found in audiovisual obituaries. When a famous movie actor dies, it's *spot news* (essentially, news that happened that day), and legitimate media outlets may assemble and present an obituary that includes clips from that person's films without clearing them. Three months or 30 years later, if you're making a project about that movie star, you may *not* include that audiovisual obituary as broadcast, with its clips intact, unless you license them. The only exception to this would be some "fair use," such as your film being a commentary on the obituary itself.

    If you suspect that footage included within a network screener is from another source, *ask*. Networks will often send news stories intact as screeners, only to remove or block third-party materials when you go back to them months later for masters and licensing. As frustrating as that is, it's not that they're trying to make your life difficult, it's just that they only check their paperwork once you ask for a license, and so that's when these issues come to light.
- You acquire footage in which copyrighted works of art appear, perhaps hanging on a wall behind the action. You *may* need to clear this art separately.
    - You want to use clips from Hollywood features that were created under guild contracts that require residuals paid to the Writers Guild of America, Directors Guild of America, and SAG-AFTRA (the Screen Actors Guild and the American Federation

of Television and Radio Artists, which have now merged). As explained in Chapter 15, you will need to pay a fee to those guilds and to the actors directly.

- You want to use a clip from a film in which the mixed soundtrack includes both natural (diegetic) sound and a music track, and you can't access an unmixed track.

These are just common examples. There are many other circumstances where underlying or embedded rights may be an issue.

Underlying Rights in Public Domain Material

If something is truly in the public domain, then usually all underlying rights are in the public domain as well—but that's not always the case. For example, a clip may be from a film that is in the public domain, but elements in the clip are still under copyright, or characters appearing in the clip are subject to trademark protection. An episode of an old television sitcom may have fallen into the public domain, but its well-known theme song may still be under copyright on a stand-alone basis, or its characters may be protected. In rare cases, works may leave the public domain and become protected *again* when a significant copyright encumbrance is discovered. Two such cases involve *Rear Window* (1954), directed by Alfred Hitchcock, and *It's a Wonderful Life* (1946), directed by Frank Capra. In both, it was discovered that although the primary copyright—to the movie itself—had expired, the underlying literary works (short stories) on which the films were based were still under copyright. In the case of *It's a Wonderful Life*, some of the musical score was also still under copyright. Because the short stories were substantially the same as the films (same plot, same characters), the courts concluded that the films were *derivative works*. What this means, according to the U.S. Copyright Office, is that "only the additions, changes, or other new material appearing for the first time in the work"—in this case, the movies—is considered a new work. In other words, without the underlying work, there would be no movie. Therefore, both films had to be restored to copyright protection for as long as the stories were protected.

Types of Licensing Agreements

The Royalty-Free Agreement

As introduced in Chapter 6, there are two primary ways in which commercial copyrighted content is licensed: *royalty-free* and *rights-managed*. When material is royalty-free, you pay a flat fee regardless of how you use the material or how much you reuse it. This should not be confused with *rights free*.

Often royalty-free agreements are spelled out in an online contract, or, even more simply, represented by a few sentences on an invoice. The standard contract (which may be buried on the provider's website, and usually doesn't need to be signed by anyone) is often more like a software EULA (End User License Agreement). Read it carefully, however, because these may include limits that your distributor (or a future distributor) will not accept. You may need to pay a slightly higher license fee to get an *enhanced agreement* or a *rider* that brings their boilerplate language into compliance with what you need.

The Rights-Managed Agreement

With rights-managed materials, licenses are granted for a particular venue or venues, time period, and geographical area, and in addition will impose certain responsibilities. Rights-managed agreements are more complex than either a royalty-free agreement or your own materials release, but they are also the most common.

Who Uses Rights-Managed Agreements?

For the most part, you will be asked to enter into a rights-managed agreement when working with news or commercial (for-profit) archives.

- A *news archive* is a library of footage from a broadcast or print news organization, involving either moving images or photographs. It may be a television network or local station, a press agency, or a newspaper. Some examples of news archives are the CNN Collection (collection.cnn.com) and the photo morgue at the *Boston Globe*.
- A *commercial archive* is any archive that sells, for profit, material from a variety of sources rather than just their own originated material. Getty Images is the biggest and most well-known example of a commercial archive that sells still and motion picture images that originated from a variety of places, including some news agencies. In some cases they've bought the collection; in others, they represent the creators, such as stock shot providers or weather or nature cinematographers. In the case of Getty, they also send their own freelance photographers out to cover subjects.

Variables in Rights-Managed Agreements

When approaching archives that operate on a rights-managed basis, you will have to negotiate which rights you want to acquire. Rights-managed material is often sold for specific uses in specific parts of the world, for specific periods of time. Here are the variables you'll have to decide about, which are discussed in more detail in Chapters 15 and 16.

- *Markets.* What are the markets, or *modes of delivery* you think you may want to explore when your production goes into distribution? Some examples include theatrical and educational markets; film festivals; streaming services; broadcast (commercial or public); home video DVDs and Blu-rays; and internet download or stream.
- *Term.* Sometimes your rights to use the material in your film are limited by time. After this term is up, your film cannot be distributed without re-licensing the clips or stills.
- *Geographic areas.* Where do you want your film to be shown? Worldwide? Only in North America?

Clearing Newspapers

If a newspaper headline is used as a visual intended to forward your narrative—in other words, to convey information that a narrator or voiceover might have conveyed, such as "Mayor Found Guilty"—you may need to clear it. Some organizations will give you a *gratis* clearance, while others will want large fees and may limit (sometimes too severely to be useful) how long the license term is. Many uses of newspapers and their headlines, however, at least in nonfiction projects, fall under fair use. But beware: news *photographs* embedded on those pages will need to be cleared if they are visible in your film, especially if the camera focuses on them—again, unless your use is a fair use.

Logos

Logos, such as on magazine covers, are trademarked. Time, Inc. vigilantly protects *LIFE* magazine's red box logo, as well as *Time* magazine's logo typography. You may not use this distinctive branding without permission. Trademark violations are especially serious when they involve a fake version of a well-known magazine cover or newspaper front page. If your fake version is to be considered satire, courts may consider whether you are satirizing the publication itself (a stronger fair use argument) or another subject, such as the person whose face you inserted onto the fake cover.

If you need to create a false magazine or newspaper for use in a fictional dramatic film, you must obtain permission from the publication and credit them. Sydney Pollack's film *Tootsie* (1982) created an entire montage out of fake covers of well-known magazines to signal the rising popularity of its main character. They got permissions from the publications, and there are specific credits at the end of the film regarding those publications.

Clearing Visual Art

Art can pose special clearance challenges for filmmakers because, as with music, there are often two *parallel* clearances you must obtain:

- Copyright to the artwork itself *if* it's still under copyright; and
- Copyright to the *reproduction* of the artwork (such as a poster of a painting, or a photograph of a sculpture) if that's the source of your image. (There are some exceptions, and certainly some gray areas in the copyright law and legal precedent regarding reproductions, to be discussed later in the chapter.)

214   Artwork clearance depends on when the art was first created, and where or when it was first published, such as in a book or handbill. Pre-1920s fine art is likely to be in the public domain, although you should confirm that, especially if it wasn't created by an American. (Other countries' copyright protections may be longer and may also involve *moral rights*.) If the work *is* in the public domain, you need only obtain a copy you can use, such as a digital file or transparency. Otherwise, you'll need to clear the work.

Working with Museums

Museums may purchase artwork, but only in very rare cases does that purchase convey to the museum or collection the copyright to that artwork. Most often, that copyright is retained by the artist or the artist's estate or foundation, until the work enters the public domain. Thus, museums almost never have a copyright claim based solely on their physical ownership of an artwork, and this is especially true if the work is in the public domain. Clearances with museums are usually only necessary if you are obtaining a print or transparency of an object from them. They own the rights to the *reproductions* they lend you (such as a scan from a transparency) and can therefore charge hefty fees for them. If a museum insists they own the copyright to a particular piece of artwork in their collection, it might be a special case; work with them to determine what rights, if any, they actually have.

In addition, be aware that some large museums may argue that you *must* acquire transparencies of works in their collection only from them and credit them accordingly. This is not the case. If you can find an alternate source that isn't just another copy of the museum's own reproduction, you can generally use it. Be careful that the cheaper illustration is of high enough quality to suit your needs, and that it accurately represents the original artwork, including any colors (art licenses often require this).

As a side note: there are some legal gray areas concerning photographic reproductions of artwork, depending on whether they are two-dimensional or three-dimensional. Courts generally agree that a photograph of three-dimensional art, such as sculpture, is considered a new artistic expression, because the photographer made choices regarding the camera angle, lighting, and composition. Some courts, however, have found that photography of two-dimensional art (such as a painting) is simply a record copy, not containing any new creative expression from the photographer, and therefore the photographer cannot claim copyright. What this means is that you *might* be able to use a photograph of a painting without permission from the photographer, and only be concerned with copyright regarding the painting itself. It's best to check with your attorney if you plan to do this; courts have ruled differently on this issue. A photograph of three-dimensional art, or specialized or creative photography of flat art, would always need additional clearance unless the photograph itself is in the public domain.

Moral Rights

Moral rights protect an artist's ability to control aspects of their work above and beyond the economic benefits of copyright, such as how and whether it's displayed or altered. In the United States, especially since passage of the Visual Artists Rights Act of 1990, moral rights are seen as adhering solely to the work of visual artists such as painters, sculptors, and fine art photographers, although this varies state-by-state. Moral rights remain with the artist even if the work is sold or the copyright is conveyed to a third party. Be aware that your use of the artwork is generally governed by the artist's moral rights; you may not damage the integrity of the artwork or the reputation of the artist.

As discussed in Chapter 14, moral rights have greater and more expansive power in much of Europe, where they are a central tenet of copyright law and are applied to the work not only of visual artists but also other creators, including authors and filmmakers. Moral rights are viewed as inalienable, and in some countries they *can't* be waived by the creator; the creation is seen as an extension of the individual. Unlike the United

215

States, where moral rights expire when copyright expires, in France and some other nations, moral rights survive in perpetuity.

Personal Rights

Individuals who appear in print or motion picture photography that is intended for publication generally need to sign an *appearance release*, discussed earlier in this chapter. This is because under U.S. law, people have individual rights that fall into two related but different categories:

- The *right of privacy* refers to everybody's right not to be bothered in their private lives, not to be photographed or have images of them or their words or voice used without their permission or against their will. Worldwide, concerns about individual privacy have intensified under the pressure of new and ever-more invasive technologies.
- The *right of publicity* protects individuals from the unauthorized use of their name, likeness, or persona for commercial purposes; it involves the right of each person to control and profit from the commercial use of their own name and likeness. The right of publicity grew out of the right of privacy, and while it applies to everyone, it most often is used in reference to high-profile personalities.

Right of Privacy

When it comes to using third-party visuals, the fact that you did not photograph or record the individuals yourself does not shield you if you violate their rights and they therefore pursue legal remedies. Also note that even if the licensor has gotten signed appearance releases from people that allow for the transfer of footage to you, *your* use of these images may not extend beyond any limitations set out in the initial releases.

Not all appearances require signed releases. When people are present at an event at which media coverage can reasonably be expected (such as news coverage of a fire, crime scene, or sports or political event), there is an understanding that their consent to being filmed is *implied*. If they *were* filmed, their image or voice did not have to be cleared by the original maker, nor do you need to clear it, at least not for documentary use. However, you may only use this footage in its original context. For you to imply that someone cheering at a sports rally is now cheering for a political candidate would be actionable, meaning there is likely cause for the person in question to take legal action. Likewise, you may not use generic images of people to imply specifics that are not true. If you have a shot of three anonymous young women on a public basketball court, you may not add any element, such as narration, that implies to an audience that these are high school dropouts, sex workers, or Mensa members, if you don't know that to be the case. Lastly, your use of this type of footage without an appearance release cannot be commercial, which includes use for advertising purposes or dramatic, fictional films.

If people are filmed clearly against their will or without their knowledge, in the absence of circumstances that would lead a reasonable person to assume they might be recorded, there is no implied consent. You need to disguise their identities or seek permission.

Right of Publicity (Right of Personality)

Before they'll license a clip, still, or poster to you, Hollywood studios will demand that you clear the *likeness*, or *right of publicity* (also sometimes known as the *right of personality* or *personality rights*) of an actor or other recognizable celebrity. Right of publicity keeps people from exploiting the name and reputation of famous people—living and dead—in ways not approved by them or their representatives. In the United States, these rules vary by state, including whether the right of publicity expires upon a person's death or continues in perpetuity. (The law applied is determined by the state that served as the subject's primary residence at the time of death.)

217

Another aspect of right of personality involves *passing off*. This is any variation of an attempt by someone to imply an endorsement or relationship (usually a business relationship, usually with a celebrity) that doesn't exist. In the United States and many other countries, *any* use of famous personalities for marketing or advertising will require clearance, and implied endorsement without it is highly actionable.

Elected politicians and those who seek or hold public office are considered to be exempt from the right of publicity, especially while serving the public but often afterwards as well. Thus, if you license an archival excerpt from a press conference of President Barack Obama, or a scene of President Ronald Reagan at the site of the Berlin Wall, you don't need to clear rights of publicity. Beware, however, of underlying copyrights that may affect this exception. Some famous speeches were copyrighted *after* they were given in public, and the likenesses of many historical individuals are protected. The estate of the Reverend Dr. Martin Luther King, Jr., for example, guards the rights to both his image and his words very carefully and has copyrighted many of King's speeches as literary works, including the famous "I Have a Dream" speech, given at the March for Jobs and Freedom in Washington, D.C. in 1963.

Trademark as Well as Right of Publicity

When trying to clear the use of celebrity images, you may encounter both trademark and right of publicity issues. Sometimes the same entity owns both. CMG Worldwide, for example, represents over 200 clients, living and dead, according to its website, and its clientele includes not only humans but also animals, such as Waffles the Cat, named a "Top 10 Pet Influencer" by *Forbes*. CMG is also the exclusive business representative for the Estate of Mark Twain, including the image of his signature—but they don't hold the copyright to his works.

Reality Check

Given the complexity of this licensing maze, you may be thinking, *This is nuts*. If you are, you're not alone. It can be. The intensifying "clearance culture" and the absence of a system of copyright and licensing appropriate for the digital age has proven burdensome not only to media makers but also to anyone creating work that references the past. We have a wonderful, powerful, moving, and important legacy of audiovisual materials dating back more than a century, crossing international boundaries, and offering a dauntingly complex view of the human experience from the macro to the micro level. Yet more and more, media makers can't touch it, whether for reasons of access or expense. The parsing out of markets and time frames is also highly problematic. Attorney Anthony Falzone, former director of the Fair Use Project at Stanford University's Center for Internet and Society, put it succinctly when he said to us, "This is the only kind of property we treat this way. When you go to buy a table, you don't have to tell the guy at the furniture store what room you want to put it in, whether it's going to be next to a white couch or a brown couch. And by the way, what if I want to put it in my cabin at Lake Tahoe? Let's go ask the guy who made the legs, because we might not have the rights to use the legs in the cabin at Lake Tahoe."

Errors and Omissions Insurance

Throughout this book, you'll see references to a form of insurance known as *Producers Errors and Omissions Liability Coverage*, usually shortened colloquially to *E&O insurance*. E&O is one of a handful of insurance policies that film productions need to have, and it's the one that primarily covers rights issues. In general, you need to have applied for E&O coverage *at least* a month before any scheduled presentation.

E&O is there to protect you, as well as those who have agreed to distribute, broadcast, or otherwise present your film, against claims that you've violated another party's rights, including their copyright or other intellectual property rights. The companies that offer such policies work with you to ensure that you've done everything in your power to secure all necessary releases, licenses, and contracts for your film, or that you can document every case in which your use of third-party material without a license is allowed because you have performed due diligence to try to locate the copyright holder, the material is in the public domain, or the way you've used it legitimately constitutes a fair use.

As always, consult with an experienced lawyer before entering into any legal arrangement. An archival researcher can be very useful in helping to negotiate with the archives, and, depending on their expertise, helping you to understand the license terms they're offering—but that does not replace an attorney.

Sources and Notes

Information about copyright renewal is from Copyright Law Revision (Washington: U. S. Govt. Print. Off, 1961). Mark Twain is quoted in "Twain's Plan to Beat the Copyright Law," *The New York Times* (December 12, 1906). Attorney Chris Sprigman is quoted in "The Mouse that Ate the Public Domain," *FindLaw Legal News and Commentary* (March 5, 2002). Duration of copyright information can be found at www.copyright.gov/circs/circ15a.pdf. Cornell University also has a good general chart about copyright terms, https://copyright.cornell.edu/publicdomain. The U.S. Supreme Court's decision in *Eldred v. Ashcroft* can be found at www.law.cornell.edu/supct/html/01-618.ZO.html, with additional information at www.copyright.gov/docs/eldrdedo.pdf. The interview with Lawrence Lessig was conducted for the first edition of *Archival Storytelling*. The Stanford University Libraries Copyright & Fair Use page is https://fairuse.stanford.edu/overview/faqs/law-changes/. Copyright issues for *It's a Wonderful Life* are summarized in a 1999 article by Matt Alsdorf for *Slate* magazine, www.slate.com/id/1004242/. A *New York Times* article about the *Rear Window* case is at http://query.nytimes.com/gst/fullpage.html?res=9C0CEFD7143DF936A15757C0A966958260. Copyright Office information about derivative works can be found at www.copyright.gov/circs/circ14.pdf. Cases involving reproduction images of fine art include *Bridgeman Art Library v. Corel Corporation* and *Eastern America Trio Products v. Tang Electronic Corporation*. Right of privacy information comes from www.law.com. Information about state variations in privacy laws can be found at https://iapp.org/news/a/us-state-comprehensive-priva cy-law-comparison/. State-by-state rights of publicity laws can be found at the National Council of State Legislators' website, www.ncsl.org/pro grams/lis/privacy/publicity04.htm. The quote from Anthony Falzone is from the first edition of *Archival Storytelling*. An excellent source of information about copyright, fair use, and much more can be found at www.nolo.com; relevant materials on this site draw on Richard Stim's *Getting Permission: How to License & Clear Copyrighted Materials Online & Off* (Nolo, 2007). Also see Michael C. Donaldson and Lisa A. Callif's *Clearance & Copyright: Everything You Need to Know for Film and Television*, 4th Edition (Silman-James Press, 2014).

220

CHAPTER 12

Public Domain

Under U.S. law, not all third-party materials are subject to copyright. In some circumstances, people seeking to incorporate others' copyrighted work into theirs may claim a fair use, as discussed in Chapter 13. There are also many cases, especially with older audiovisual materials, in which there is no need to seek permission because the material is not, or is no longer, protected by intellectual property laws. When this happens, the material is described as being in the *public domain*. This means the public has free access to use and reuse the intellectual property contained in the material *ad infinitum*. Not only can you incorporate the material or elements of it into your new work (or works), but others can too—the right is nonexclusive.

Copyright law is specific to each nation and can be further complicated by the existence of other limitations on use, such as *moral rights*. This chapter, therefore, is focused primarily on works created in the United States, unless otherwise noted.

How Do Works Enter the Public Domain?

Some U.S. works are in the public domain because they were never eligible for copyright protection. For example, films, stills, audio recordings, and other types of materials (such as some books), if created with U.S. government funding, are not generally subject to copyright—the public technically owns the material. In part for this reason, the U.S. National Archives and Records Administration (NARA) and the U.S. Library of Congress (LC), which house a lot of government material, can be a tremendous resource for media makers. Along the same lines, decisions made in public courts and records of public court trials, unless they are sealed, are also in the public domain.

Tornado approaching Canadian city, July 8, 1927. NOAA'S National Weather Service Collection.

Other materials have entered the public domain because the rights holders failed to meet the copyright requirements in place when the works were created or published. Material may also be in the public domain because its copyright term has expired, either because owners failed to renew or because the renewal period has also ended.

Failure to Renew

In 1992, changes to U.S. copyright law made the *renewal* of *existing* copyrights automatic for works that were first copyrighted between January 1, 1964 and December 31, 1977. For works up for renewal before January 1, 1964, however, the proper paperwork had to be filed or the work entered the public domain. As of this writing (the year 2020), this means that works created after January 1, 1925 and before January 1, 1964 might be in the public domain, if the copyright holder failed to renew during the 28th year after publication. This includes mainstream films for which the renewal date was missed. All of the following—Rudolph Maté's film noir classic, *D.O.A.* (1949); the Warner Brothers' animated satire of Walt Disney's *Fantasia*, entitled *A Corny Concerto* (1943); Francis Ford Coppola's 1963 cult horror film, *Dementia 13* (1963); and from that same year, Stanley Donen's comedy/suspense classic, *Charade*—did not have their copyrights renewed by the studios that produced them.

Failure to Register

Until 1978 (when the Copyright Act of 1976 went into effect), an *initial* copyright was only granted if creators took the necessary steps to register their work and also displayed an application *mark* or statement on the work itself, showing that it was protected. Until about 1960, most studios neglected to copyright movie trailers (previews of coming attractions). In the years after that, they began to copyright all publicity materials. If you want to use an older, uncopyrighted movie trailer, make sure it's clearly identified as a *trailer* within your project, either by context or by identifying it onscreen, so your audience isn't led to believe it's watching a clip from the (in most cases copyrighted) film itself.

Works created from 1978 onward, as discussed in Chapter 11, are *automatically* granted copyright, and so even if the creator fails to register their copyright, they are still protected. This and other changes to copyright law (notably including various extensions to the copyright period) have had the effect of limiting the public domain. (As noted in that chapter, it's still worth registering your own work with the U.S. copyright office.)

How Do You Know if Something is in the Public Domain?

Because of changes to U.S. copyright law, especially the overhaul of 1976 (which went into effect in January 1978) and the Copyright Term Extension Act of 1998, a significant amount of material that would otherwise have entered the public domain instead continues to be protected. As this book goes to press in 2020, the year 1925 is considered to be the line of demarcation. If something was "published" before 1925, it is pretty safely in the public domain. Absent any new legislation, that boundary moves up one year every year: in 2021, works created before

1926 enter the public domain; in 2022, works created before 1927 enter the public domain, and so on. But for all of the reasons explained in this chapter and the previous one, you can't *presume* anything, as the song "Happy Birthday to You" demonstrates. The tune dates to 1893 (as "Good Morning, Dear Teacher") and thus has been in the public domain for many years. However, the "Happy Birthday" lyrics were first published in the 1920s and copyrighted in 1935, and so the overall song was considered protected. As a result, "Happy Birthday to You" was a major—if controversial—source of income for its rights holder, most recently Warner/Chappell Music. In June 2013, filmmaker Jennifer Nelson brought a class action lawsuit against Warner/Chappell on behalf of media makers and others who'd paid fees to license the song rather than face legal action and financial penalties. (Nelson herself had paid a $1,500 synchronization fee.) The judge found that Warner's predecessor had "never acquired the rights to the Happy Birthday lyrics," and that therefore Warner/Chappell, as "purported successors-in-interest, do not own a valid copyright in the Happy Birthday lyrics." The parties reached a settlement and in June 2016, "Happy Birthday to You" officially entered the public domain.

Researching Copyright

If you want to know the copyright status of an item registered prior to 1978, probably the least expensive way to find out is for you or a researcher to consult the copyright reference card catalog at the Library of Congress. Any U.S. title from that era can be looked up for registration and renewal dates, and if it was not registered originally or was not renewed before 1963, it is now in the public domain.

If the item was registered (or has been registered) since January 1, 1978, you can use an online database at the Library of Congress's records website to search by title, author, and a variety of other tags that should send you in the direction of the last known copyright holder. But because formal registration was no longer a requirement as of 1978, you'll only find copyright holders who took that step. A work missing from this list is *not* necessarily—or even likely—in the public domain.

Asking the Library of Congress to Research

You can pay the Copyright Office to research a copyright for you and their report should satisfy your E&O insurer and distributor. You initiate the process on their Records Research and Certification Services (RRC) page; the current fee to request a search *estimate* is $200 per hour or fraction thereof, with a two-hour minimum. The more details you can give them about the item you're researching, especially the years in which they would most likely have been registered, the less expensive the search is likely to be. The Copyright Office does not offer an estimate of its response time, but for an extra fee you can request an expedited search, and they'll let you know if they can accommodate you.

Alternatively, if you're in a hurry and have the resources, you can hire an intellectual property law firm to do some digging for you. Some advertise this specific service, and often they do a very thorough copyright check. They will probably be able to track the changes of ownership that have taken place over the years and provide contact information for the current copyright holder, if any. They also have the advantage of being able to write a formal legal opinion for your files if they have determined that something is in the public domain.

An excellent quick reference as to what is and is not in the public domain worldwide, or how long something will be protected for, is available at the Cornell Copyright Information Center website (copyright.cornell.edu/publicdomain).

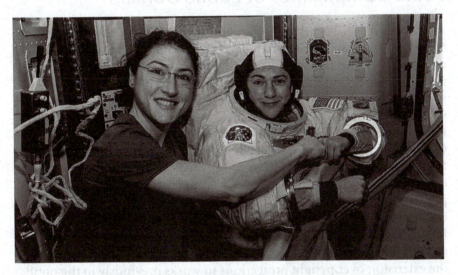

Astronauts Christina Koch (left) and Jessica Meir prepare for their first spacewalk together inside the U.S. Quest airlock, October 18, 2019. NASA/ Johnson.

Public Domain and U.S. Works

If the work was first published and created in the United States and is in the public domain in the United States, the "public domain" is international; anyone in the world can draw on this material. However, for works created *outside* the United States different rules apply.

- Most foreign works, if they were published in their home country before 1924 and are in the public domain in that country, are in the public domain in the United States.
- Foreign works published outside the United States between 1925 and 1977, and then published in the United States, might enter the U.S. public domain if a) they fell into the public domain in their country of origin as of January 1, 1996; and b) when they were published in the United States, they did not follow U.S. formalities, such as registering for copyright or carrying a copyright notice.
- Most foreign works that don't fall into the two categories above are protected for 95 years after the date of first publication in their own countries. As always, consult with an attorney if unsure.

Some Complexities of Public Domain

As discussed in Chapter 11, copyright holders have occasionally sued to have works (such as *It's a Wonderful Life*) removed from the public domain after the fact. This is most likely if it can be demonstrated that these works *significantly* depend on underlying works that are still protected by copyright, in which case, the *entire* work is deemed to be still under copyright. This is not a clear-cut issue, especially regarding foreign works. For example, in *Golan v. Holder* (2012), the U.S. Supreme Court ruled that copyright protection *could* be restored after a work had fallen into the public domain in the United States. Both parties in the case, as well as the justices, cited Russian composer Sergei Prokofiev's popular children's piece, *Peter and the Wolf* (which was restored to copyright as a result of the decision). The majority opinion, written by Justice Ruth Bader Ginsburg, determined that the "limited Times" language of the copyright clause of the U.S. Constitution did not preclude the extension of copyright protections to works previously in the public domain.

Here we discuss a range of reasons why your use of public domain materials may not be as straightforward as you might expect.

A Work Was in the Public Domain but It's Been Modified

In the 1970s, *colorizing* films with computers was explored both as a novelty and as a way of changing public domain films into "new works," and thereby newly subject to copyright. If you can locate a black-and-white version of a public domain film that was subsequently colorized, you may use the black-and-white version on a public domain basis (as long as there are no lingering underlying rights issues, of course). It's a bit more of a gray area when it comes to using the colorized version, or in fact a restoration, as many restored versions of films (and "director's cuts") may have additional scenes or a different edit, and most have a new copyright. Court rulings on the extent to which colorization and restoration are "significant changes" worthy of a new copyright have varied, so always check.

Material Is in the Public Domain but Expensive to Acquire

Just because something is in the public domain and therefore not subject to licensing fees doesn't mean there are no costs involved in its use, even beyond duplication costs. Whoever owns the actual physical materials (an original film print, for example, from which you may need to make a copy) can charge a fee for allowing you to use it, and you may have no choice but to pay if it's the only surviving print. A reasonable charge seems fair, as the cost to restore, preserve, maintain, and house archival materials can be substantial. (As explained in Chapter 6, the same public domain materials may be held by multiple agencies, so shopping around for the best rates or seeing if a copy exists that you can access for free is sometimes an option.)

Material Is in the Public Domain but Your Use or Access Is Restricted

If you can only access the physical copy through a single owner, that owner can set whatever fees they want. They can also restrict or forbid your use, even when the material is in the public domain. This can even occur when rare materials are donated to a public archive, such as the National Archives or Library of Congress. The donor has the right to put restrictions on use of the donated physical material, and the Library must honor those restrictions. This often leads to a situation where tax dollars are paying for vaulting a private entity's materials (such as vintage prints from Hollywood studios) without the tax-paying public having access.

The Copyright Has Expired in One Country but Is Still in Force Elsewhere

Copyright terms vary country by country. Wherever you plan to release your film, make sure that work you believe to be in the public domain is clear in all of those countries.

Orphan Works

Orphan works are not strictly in the public domain, but rather in a gray area that results from an inability to identify the copyright owner or to even know if one exists. Especially since 1978, when creators or owners no longer had to actively register their copyright, it's possible to find material you want to use and, despite your best efforts, be unable to locate the owners. This is one of the most distressing aspects of the 1976 copyright law—without registration, locating the owner can be a nightmare.

Due Diligence

Due diligence (or *best efforts*, as it's sometimes known) is a way of establishing that you've done your best to locate the copyright holder, in order to show that you meant no malice in not licensing the material involved. To that end, as you explore the copyright and attempt to find the copyright holder of a problematic piece of material, *keep a log of everything you do, everyone you talk to, and all efforts you make to locate the rights holder.* Keep track of every phone call you make, when you made it, and with whom you spoke. Send letters "return receipt requested" and keep all returned letters; print out all emails and faxes and keep them in a file identified as due diligence for that particular item. Also, it's a good idea to put some money, representing a reasonable license fee, into escrow. If the rights holder does eventually come forward and you've done your due diligence, the onus is on them, at that point, to prove ownership. If they do, you should be able to satisfy the rights holder's claim using the money you put into escrow, without additional penalties. Fortunately, such claims seem to be rare—but be prepared, in case.

Public Domain Music

Public domain applies to aural as well as visual materials, and there is a wealth of public domain aural content available.

Recorded Music and Sound

There is some very early material in the Edison Collection at the Library of Congress that covers recordings made between the 1890s and the 1920s. These include popular songs, like "Aba Daba Honeymoon" (1914), "The Bells of St. Mary's" (1920), and "Santa Claus Hides in Your Phonograph" (1922). The Edison Archives at the Thomas Edison National Historical Site contains 48,000 early Edison recordings, many

228

on cylinders. Besides music, this collection includes turn-of-the-century comedy and spoken word recordings.

Traditional Music

What about music that is frequently sung but predates commercial recording? Many African-American spirituals, for example, are in the public domain, as are traditional church hymns, such as "Onward, Christian Soldiers." (Neither of these are to be confused with gospel music, which emerged in the 1920s and is generally subject to copyright.)

You can't assume that because a song is traditional it is in the public domain. In the early years of the 20th century, "song collectors" traveled widely, using existing technology (often, bulky wax cylinders) to document traditional music that they not only recorded in the field but also transcribed and copyrighted. An example is folklorist John A. Lomax, who toured the American South in the 1930s with his son, Alan, with equipment provided by the Library of Congress. In 1933, he "discovered" a guitarist and singer named Huddie Ledbetter, better known as Lead Belly. The singer performed some of his own songs but also adapted traditional material he'd learned while growing up along the Texas/Louisiana border. Many of these songs had been shared by performers for years and weren't copyrighted. When collecting and publishing them, the Lomaxes also copyrighted some of them. (Also, just because recordings are in the collections at the Library of Congress doesn't mean they're in the public domain.)

New Arrangements of Public Domain Music

Another thing to remember is that almost all music should be held under suspicion of being copyrighted because a new arrangement is covered by a new copyright. Thus, although the hymn "Onward, Christian Soldiers" dates from before 1925 and is not under copyright (in the United States, at least), almost any *arrangement* you can find is likely to have originated later, and to be under the arranger's copyright.

Voluntary "Public Domain"

In a world marked by strong intellectual property restrictions, and in light of concerns that the creative endeavor of artists, scholars, journalists, scientists, and others is being inhibited by these restrictions, there is a growing number of creators who want to make their work available to the public for certain uses. These creators are not giving up the rights to their work. Instead, they are hoping to inspire new works by making their own works available, generally for noncommercial purposes, through special licenses or agreements, and/or under certain conditions. Two examples:

- The Denshō website (www.densho.org) was created in 1996 to "preserve the testimonies of Japanese Americans who were unjustly incarcerated during World War II," according to the site, and has grown and evolved in the years since. An extensive collection of oral histories (many of them videotaped), original documents, and donated photographs relating to Japanese-American history can be found here. A simple, free registration is all you need to access these works for scholarship, personal, or educational use.
- Creative Commons allows the owner of a copyrighted work to make it available for use under certain licensing conditions to which the user must agree. As of the beginning of 2020, over 1.6 billion works covered by Creative Commons licensing had been posted by their creators on sites including Flickr, Wikipedia, YouTube, Internet Archive, and Vimeo. The Massachusetts Institute of Technology has made its MIT OpenCourseware subject to Creative Commons licensing, and the Brooklyn Museum and Metropolitan Museum of Art are just two examples of organizations that have posted images under CC licenses.

Sources and Notes

The U.S. Copyright Office website is www.copyright.gov/. The saga of "Happy Birthday to You" has been extensively covered. See Robert Brauneis, "Copyright and the World's Most Popular Song," *Journal of the Copyright Society of the U.S.A.*, posted in 2008 and updated in 2013, online at https://papers.ssrn.com/sol3/papers.cfm?abstract_id=1111624. Also see Eriq Gardner, "'Happy Birthday' for All: Filmmaker Aims to Free Song from Copyright Grip" (June 13, 2013); "'Happy Birthday' Copyright Ruled to be Invalid" (September 22, 2015); and "Warner Music Pays $14 Million to End 'Happy Birthday' Copyright Lawsuit" (February 9, 2016), all in *The Hollywood Reporter*. The Associated Press reported on the final settlement in *Maclean's* (June 28, 2016). The LC's online database for items registered in or after 1978 is at https://cocatalog.loc.gov/cgi-bin/Pwebrecon.cgi?DB=local&PAGE=First. The Copyright Office's Records Research and Certification Services Page is at www.copyright.gov/rrc/. For information about orphan works, see www.copyright.gov/

orphan/orphan-report.pdf. A fiction film about the rigors of capturing traditional music in the field is Maggie Greenwald's *Songcatcher* (2000). (MIT OpenCourseWare terms can be found at https://ocw.mit.edu/terms/. Information about the Brooklyn Museum's use of a Creative Commons License is here: www.brooklynmuseum.org/copyright. The Metropolitan Museum's sharing of public domain works via a "Creative Commons Zero" license can be found at www.metmuseum.org/blogs/digital-underground/2017/open-access-at-the-met.

231

CHAPTER 13

Fair Use

As discussed in Chapter 11, American copyright law was written into the U.S. Constitution to "promote the Progress of Science and useful Arts, by securing for limited Times to Authors and Inventors the exclusive Right to their respective Writings and Discoveries." The founders of the United States also wrote a Bill of Rights, including a powerful 45-word First Amendment: "Congress shall make no law respecting an establishment of religion, or prohibiting the free exercise thereof; or abridging the freedom of speech, or of the press; or the right of the people peaceably to assemble, and to petition the Government for a redress of grievances." Free speech principles form the basis of an important exception to U.S. copyright protection, known as *fair use*.

The "Metaphysics of the Law"

Fair use was first introduced as a factor in U.S. copyright law in 1841, in *Folsom v. Marsh*. The Reverend Charles W. Upham, a member of the Massachusetts House of Representatives, had written a two-volume book about George Washington. The book drew heavily on Washington's letters as collected, published, and already copyrighted by scholar Jared Sparks in his 12-volume *The Writings of George Washington* (published between 1834 and 1837). While more than forty percent of Upham's book—353 out of 866 pages—were letters from Sparks's collection, those letters represented less than four percent of Sparks's overall book. It was a difficult case, Circuit Justice William W. Story noted. "Patents and copyrights approach, nearer than any other class of cases belonging to forensic discussions, to what may be called the metaphysics of the law, where the distinctions are, or at least may be, very subtle [*sic*] and refined, and sometimes, almost evanescent." The judge argued that "the question of piracy" may depend "upon a nice balance of the comparative use made in one of the materials of the other; the nature, extent, and value of the materials thus used; the objects of each work; and the degree to which each writer may be fairly presumed to have resorted to the same common sources of information."

In establishing some of the principles of what would become known as fair use, the judge wrote, "no one can doubt that a reviewer may fairly cite largely from the original work, if his design be really and truly to use the passages for the purpose of fair and reasonable criticism. On the other hand ... if he thus cites the most important parts of the work, with a view not to criticize, but to supersede the use of the original work, and substitute the review for it, such a use will be deemed in law a piracy." In the end, the judge ruled against the Upham publication, finding no bad intent on Upham's part but worrying that if one author could use 319 of Washington's letters (protected under Sparks's copyright), what would stop other authors from using more, or even all of them? Furthermore, the copyrighted letters gave Upham's work "its greatest, nay, its essential value" and without them, the book would "fall to the ground." The case may not have defined fair use, but scholars agree that it helped initiate a conversation that is still underway some 170 years later.

U.S. Copyright Law: The Four Tests

Section 107 of the U.S. Copyright Act of 1976, "Limitations on exclusive rights: Fair use," includes a list of the various purposes for which the reproduction of a particular work may be considered fair, including "criticism, comment, news reporting, teaching (including multiple copies for classroom use), scholarship, or research." Section 107 also states that in determining whether or not a particular use is fair, "the factors to be considered shall include—

1. the purpose and character of the use, including whether such use is of commercial nature or is for nonprofit educational purposes;
2. the nature of the copyrighted work;
3. the amount and substantiality of the portion used in relation to the copyrighted work as a whole; and
4. the effect of the use upon the potential market for or value of the copyrighted work."

In evaluating a fair use claim, courts consider all of the tests, although the individual nature of each case means that the relative weight of a particular test may vary significantly.

Test 1: The Purpose and Character of the Use

The first test, regarding "the purpose and character of the use, including whether such use is of a commercial nature or is for nonprofit educational purposes," is often misunderstood by people who conclude from it that only nonprofit or educational projects can take advantage of fair use. This isn't true; many commercial projects and products have been successful in their claims. Nonprofit or educational (in its broadest definition) purposes may count a small additional amount toward a successful consideration of fair use, but are not determining factors, based on actual case law. Furthermore, even within the category of films that are nonprofit and/or educational, the range of styles, approaches, and uses of third-party materials is quite broad; this also helps to argue against any effort to more clearly delineate how either term (nonprofit, educational) is defined.

One key factor in consideration of *purpose* is the question of whether or not your use of the original work is *transformative*. "At issue is whether the material has been used to help create something new or merely copied verbatim into another work," explains the "Copyright & Fair Use" site of the Stanford University Libraries, https://fairuse.stanford. edu/. It continues: "When taking portions of copyrighted work, ask yourself the following questions:

- Has the material you have taken from the original work been transformed by adding new expression or meaning?
- Was value added to the original by creating new information, new aesthetics, new insights, and understandings?"

In addition, an aspect of transformative use often looked at by the courts is whether the new use *is for a different purpose* than the original use, as illustrated by some of the case law described below.

Parody and Satire

The Stanford explanation should also help to explain why parody or satire are considered transformative and generally protected as fair use. In addition, these forms of speech perhaps most clearly shine a light on the First Amendment roots of fair use doctrine. As explained on the website of the Washington, D.C.-based First Amendment Center, www. freedomforuminstitute.org/first-amendment-center/, both parody and satire "have served for generations as a means of criticizing public figures, exposing political injustice, communicating social ideologies, and pursuing such artistic ends as literary criticism." To inhibit such speech runs counter to the basic tenets of democracy.

Test 2: The Nature of the Copyrighted Work

In this case, the "copyrighted work" referred to means the work that is being borrowed or derived *from*; the protection of certain works may be stronger than others. For example, when the courts consider whether a violation has occurred, they may grant more protective weight to works that spring from someone's creative imagination (such as screenplays, films, art, photography, poetry, prose fiction) than to works that offer a synthesis of existing research, such as a scientific journal article, or that recount a true story, such as a magazine article.

Test 3: The Amount and Substantiality of the Portion Used

Case law has repeatedly shown that the courts weigh this test heavily in their decision-making. If you take too large a portion of someone else's work (over-exploit it), it can be quite damaging to what might otherwise be a strong fair use case. You should only use as small a portion as is necessary to illustrate your point or accomplish your purpose. The case of *The Definitive Elvis*, discussed later in this chapter, is a good example of this, and is also an illustration of how the purpose of the new use may not be considered *different enough* from the purpose of the original use to merit consideration as fair.

Test 4: The Effect of Use on the Potential Market or Value

Looking back at *Folsom v. March*, a determining factor was the judge's concern that if Upham could use 319 of Washington's letters, what would stop another author from using even more? At what point would the letters be so widely available that Sparks's copyright would be meaningless, and there would be no reason to purchase his set of books? In a case from 1998 that illustrates two of the tests, Castle Rock Entertainment succeeded in stopping Carol Publishing Group from marketing *The Seinfeld Aptitude Test*, a trivia quiz book. Carol argued fair use, but the Second Circuit Court of Appeals ruled that Carol's publication of the book impeded Castle Rock's ability to publish its own book of that nature, and furthermore, the use was excessive: Carol's book relied completely on characters and plots that belonged to Castle Rock.

Legal Challenges

Each fair use claim is weighed on its own merits against the four tests, and as the Stanford University site notes, "the only way to get a definitive answer on whether a particular use is a fair use is to have it resolved in federal court." Here are some examples of case law that supported, and in one case, denied, fair use claims against complaints brought by copyright holders.

The Wind Done Gone

In her 2001 novel, *The Wind Done Gone*, author Alice Randall built on events in Margaret Mitchell's 1936 classic, *Gone with the Wind*, to tell an original story from the perspective of the enslaved people at Tara, the fictional plantation in Georgia owned by the white O'Hara family. Although Randall invented her main character and never specifically identified any of Mitchell's characters, the Mitchell estate claimed copyright infringement and successfully blocked publication. Subsequently, however, a court of appeals ruled that the injunction amounted to "unlawful prior restraint in violation of the First Amendment." The book was published (with the words "The Unauthorized Parody" on its cover), and the parties reached a settlement.

It's interesting to note that in countries with strong *moral rights* laws (see Chapter 14), a fair use case such as this would be far less likely to succeed. In France, for example, an author's moral rights survive in perpetuity, giving heirs the ongoing right to protest new works that draw in any way on the originals. Occasionally they are unsuccessful, as in 2001, when the heirs of French author Victor Hugo tried to prevent an author from publishing a novel that borrowed characters from Hugo's 1862 novel, *Les Misérables*, arguing that only Hugo had the right to create a sequel. The French court refused the suit, and, according to *The* (London) *Independent*, "pointed out that Hugo was an ardent defender of freedom of speech and believed that all literature should be in the public domain, after a writer's death."

"Pretty Woman"

In 1990, the group 2 Live Crew and their record company were sued over their song "Pretty Woman," a commercial hit that drew significantly on Roy Orbison and William Dees's 1964 classic, "Oh, Pretty Woman." The first court to hear the case agreed with 2 Live Crew's argument that their work had been intended as a parody of the original. The fact that it was a commercial success did not alter its claim to fair use. After a later court reversed the decision, the case went to the U.S.

Supreme Court, which noted in its ruling that "parodic use" was not "presumptively fair," but instead, "like any other use, has to work its way through the relevant factors, and be judged case by case, in light of the ends of the copyright law." After consideration of the four factors, the Supreme Court reversed the previous decision, deciding in favor of 2 Live Crew.

The Grateful Dead: The Illustrated Trip

In *Bill Graham Archives v. Dorling Kindersley Publishing, Inc.* (2006), the Bill Graham Archives sued a publishing company over its reproduction of original concert posters in their book, *The Grateful Dead: The Illustrated Trip.* The book used seven small photographic images of posters advertising concerts at Bill Graham's venues as part of a printed collage showing scenes from the years when the Grateful Dead, an American rock band, flourished. The courts ruled in favor of the publisher, determining that the posters had not been overused (they appeared quite small in the collage), the book didn't depend on them, and the original posters were transformed from items publicizing a concert into artifacts that contributed to the telling of social history.

238

'85: The Greatest Team in Football History

In this 2019 case, Red Label Music Publishing, Inc., the owners of a 1985 song and music video performed by the Chicago Bears, called "Super Bowl Shuffle," sued Chila Productions for their inclusion of excerpts of the music video in their 2016 documentary, *'85: The Greatest Team in Football History.* The decision by the federal court in the Northern District of Illinois decided in favor of the production company and agreed with their fair use claim.

Applying the four tests, the court found that Chila's use of the music video was transformative; the original purpose was for entertainment, but the filmmakers' purpose was to provide evidence that advanced a historical narrative about the team's 1985 season and victory at the 1986 Super Bowl. Additionally, they had been careful not to over-exploit the music video: they used 16 separate clips, totaling 59 seconds—roughly two percent of the song and 17 percent of the music video—but were careful not to use the song's title or distinctive chorus. This speaks to the court's consideration of *which* particular excerpts were used—whether the "heart" of the original work was used—as well as their length.

The Definitive Elvis

In this case, a documentary production company, Passport International Productions (a.k.a. Passport Video) *failed* to convince the courts that their use of Elvis Presley material constituted a fair use and not, as plaintiffs argued, copyright infringement. Passport had produced and sold a DVD box set, *The Definitive Elvis*. The 16-hour series was advertised as "brimming with classic film clips, rare home movies, never-before-seen photos," according to the court record. The filmmakers promoted it as containing "Every Film and Television Appearance … as well as Rare Footage of Many of Elvis' Tours & Concerts." In arguing that their use was fair, the filmmakers noted that the work was a biography of the singer (1935–1977) and included some 200 interviews they had shot, along with clips. However, the clips, from both film and television appearances, were long and in many cases represented most of the original. Nearly all of Elvis's appearances on *The Steve Allen Show* were used, as well as appearances on *The Ed Sullivan Show* and in theatrical films. Had the filmmakers licensed these clips, the rights might have cost them upwards of $10,000 per minute, not even including the cost for clearing the music.

Limited, selective, and careful use of *some* material might have warranted a fair use claim, but courts determined that the overall project didn't pass the four tests, including the fourth test: the product was in direct competition in the marketplace with products produced by several of the copyright holders whose rights had been violated. Most important, the use was neither transformative (just like the original purpose, the product's main purpose was entertainment), nor did it avoid over-exploiting the original material—in fact, its advertising announced and made use of the over-exploitation. In February 2007, after a five-year legal battle, the U.S. District Court in Los Angeles awarded plaintiffs $2.8 million in damages and attorneys' fees, to be paid by Passport and its owner.

Myths about Fair Use

Much of intellectual property law, but particularly fair use, is filled with shades of gray. This is both by necessity and by design, because intellectual property and its many uses can be difficult to categorize. The law is believed to work best when challenges can be considered on a case-by-case basis, and even judges hearing cases may disagree (at times quite vehemently) about which party should prevail and why.

While the lack of specificity may be beneficial, it has also led to some common myths about what constitutes fair use. All of the following are *false*:

- You may quote up to 50 words of text.
- You may quote up to eight bars of music.

- Spot news coverage is always protected by fair use.
- If you want to claim fair use, keep it a secret; never go to the copyright holder.

Filmmakers may only claim a "fair use" of certain copyrighted materials subject to the four tests and their interpretation by the courts, period. An understanding of what fair use is—and what it clearly is not—can help as you make decisions about which third-party materials you use, and how you use them. Additionally, it protects you as a creator of copyrighted materials when others try to claim that their use of your work constitutes a fair use, for which they do not need to secure licenses.

Fair Use and Filmmaking

Prior to 2005, many if not most independent filmmakers in the United States, especially independent documentary makers, were reluctant or unable to claim fair use for a number of reasons. There were questions about how to apply the four tests to their specific circumstances, for example, and filmmakers' legal counsel nearly always recommended the "safe" approach, which was to license everything unless it was clearly in the public domain. Additionally, failure to license all copyrighted material jeopardized a project's chances of reaching mainstream venues, including festivals, broadcast and cable television, and theaters, because those venues required evidence that filmmakers had errors and omissions (E&O) liability coverage. To qualify for such coverage, filmmakers had to show that they'd cleared all rights to third-party materials in their films. Without such proof, they could not get distribution for the film.

But everyday life is filled with images and sounds that are copyrighted, trademarked, and otherwise owned. They are so omnipresent that filmmakers may not even notice them until after the shooting's over and they're in the editing room. Suddenly they see the posters on the teenager's wall that feature artwork, models, rock stars, or sports heroes. They see the logos on the family's clothing and gear, hear the radio playing in the kitchen, the ring tones on characters' cell phones, the TV shows playing in the background. No matter where we go, the rights-protected world is inescapable.

What could filmmakers do? Previously, many suspected that the use of some images and sounds didn't need to be licensed but instead qualified as fair use. But the David versus Goliath nature of such challenges tended to pit small, independent filmmakers against large and powerful rights holders. Unable to afford either legal counsel or the time

240

necessary to go through a court trial, no matter how justified their claim of fair use, many filmmakers felt they had no choice but to pay high licensing fees or remove or replace copyrighted material, sometimes altering the truthfulness or accuracy of the original scene.

Frame grab from *Sing Faster* (1999). *The Simpsons* was playing on TV, and Jon Else caught four seconds of it while filming backstage. Faced with a $7,000 license fee to FOX, and unable to fight a last-minute legal battle over fair use, he digitally replaced those four seconds with public domain footage of a nuclear test. Today, the FOX snippet would clearly be accepted as an "incidental capture"—a fair use.

Best Practices in Fair Use

Help came in November 2005, when the Center for Media & Social Impact (CMSI, https://cmsimpact.org/) at American University released the *Documentary Filmmakers' Statement of Best Practices in Fair Use*. Created with funding from The Rockefeller Foundation and the John D. and Catherine T. MacArthur Foundation, the statement was jointly authored by a handful of media organizations in consultation with two academic organizations (including CMSI) and a legal advisory board. The statement "makes clear what documentary filmmakers currently regard as reasonable application of the copyright 'fair use' doctrine." It includes a preamble and background information and offers some common misconceptions about fair use. The statement itself is "organized around four classes of situations that [documentary filmmakers] confront regularly in practice," with a look at the principles and limitations involved for each.

- ONE: Employing copyrighted material as the object of social, political, or cultural critique;
- TWO: Quoting copyrighted works of popular culture to illustrate an argument or point;
- THREE: Capturing copyrighted media content in the process of filming something else;
- FOUR: Using copyrighted material in a historical sequence.

In other words, the statement applied the four tests to the specifics of documentary filmmaking and offered the greater community—including legal, insurance, and industry executives—a common understanding of where fair use was relevant. The document helped to articulate an industry standard and thus offered (and continues to offer) consistent and credible support for independents who want to claim fair use.

Fair Use and International Distribution

Fair use is unique to U.S. law. While some nations have similar-sounding doctrines, such as "fair dealing" (see Chapter 14) they're not the same. What this means for filmmakers who want to distribute internationally is that they need to educate themselves about the laws in those other countries. An intellectual property lawyer under your retainer should be able to tell you which countries will recognize your fair use, and for which countries you may need to either clear rights or remove materials to enable foreign distribution.

Fair Use in Action

If your use of a copyrighted image or clip or song is a fair use—meaning that you and your attorney(s) feel confident that if challenged, your argument for fair use holds up—then you don't need permission from the rights holder. With that said, there are reasons why you may want or need to be in contact with the rights holder.

Notifying Rights Holders about Fair Use
Even if they do not need to rely on the rights holder to secure masters because they've identified an alternative source, some filmmakers may

still want to notify the rights holder that they plan to make a fair use of their material. For example, if the rights holder concurs that you have a fair use, they may be willing to provide a *non-objection letter*, stating in writing that they will not sue you for your use of their clip. If you must obtain a master directly from the rights holder, and they're sympathetic to your claim, they may agree to furnish you with the master for a reasonable fee that represents their time and effort as well as lab costs. More likely, though, they'll dismiss your claim to fair use, and it will be up to you to decide how to proceed.

Isn't It Risky to Notify the Rights Holder?

"A lot of people will tell you—and I'm afraid some of these people are even lawyers—that if you ask permission, you lose somehow all or much of the merit of your fair use claim, despite the fact that the Supreme Court has said exactly the opposite," said Peter Jaszi, a co-author of *The Filmmakers Statement of Best Practices in Fair Use*.

> When I give anybody advice about this, I always encourage people to get in touch with the copyright owner unless they're absolutely sure that they're going to have a door slammed in their face. And even then sometimes it's worth going through the exercise because in fact nothing helps your fair use argument more than being turned down on a content-based objection. If someone were to actually say to you, "I'm not going to license you that footage because I don't like your project," that's bankable.

For example, Kenn was asked to clear rights for a feature-length documentary about American economist Robert Reich, *Inequality for All* (2013), directed by Jacob Kornbluth. The film used many clips from both historical archives and entertainment programming. The entertainment clips chosen were short, and they were used to illustrate points Reich made during his filmed interview with Kornbluth; most qualified as fair use. One piece Kenn intended to license was a short interview clip with then-Viacom C.E.O. Philippe Dauman. The clip was part of an interview that the *Wall Street Journal* (*WSJ*) had streamed on its internet channel. In it, Dauman discussed his decision to lay off workers and fretted about the difficulty they would face finding new jobs, while also arguing that the cuts were necessary for the company to survive. Over this 17-second clip, the producers of *Inequality for All* superimposed Dauman's astronomical annual compensation; he was, at the time, the highest-paid CEO in the United States.

At first, *WSJ* seemed prepared to negotiate, but suddenly Kenn was told that it was "not in *WSJ*'s best interest to license the clip." The producers then felt free to fair use the clip, and E&O insurers agreed.

As another example, consider producers Bonni Cohen, Jon Shenk, and Richard Berge's *An Inconvenient Sequel: Truth to Power*, a 2017 update of *An Inconvenient Truth*, the 2006 Academy Award-winning film about the climate crisis. To illustrate resistance to established science, the producers wanted to begin the film with an audio montage, using Fox News hosts and guests, as well as members of Congress, as they called the issue a hoax. Despite the fact that permission was not likely to be granted, Kenn went through the exercise of contacting Fox News. They said they wouldn't license any clips that included the voice or likeness of their on-air talent, who appear in almost all of their programming. But because the clips were available from other sources, the project didn't have to rely on Fox News for clean masters. After double-checking with their attorney, the filmmakers proceeded to use the audio as a fair use.

Does This Mean That Any Time I'm Turned Down by a Rights Holder, I Can Claim Fair Use?

No. This only applies to materials for which you have a legitimate fair use claim; your other use of copyrighted material must be with the permission of the rights holders. They can and sometimes do refuse to grant that permission, or they set fees or conditions that effectively prohibit your use. Although frustrating, this refusal alone does not grant any kind of "fair use" status.

What If I Decide Later That My Use is a Fair Use?
As in the *WSJ* example above, it is possible that you could try to license footage, get turned down, and then realize that your use of the footage should fall under fair use, or perhaps you edit your film to better justify a fair use claim. In that case, the refusal by the rights holder to license the work does not alter your claim to fair use, if it's legitimate.

Getting Materials from Rights Holders

You sometimes have no choice but to get materials you need (a screener, master, or digital scan, for example) from the rights holder. At what point, if at all, do you tell them that while you want their materials, you don't intend to license them because you're going to claim fair use?

You almost never need to say anything, especially in the early stages of editing. You're still just gathering materials and honestly don't yet know what you'll end up using, or how. You pay whatever fees might be necessary to obtain a rough copy to cut with, and get the information you need about whom to contact when it's time to negotiate rights, and you leave it at that.

When it comes to masters, you're in a more difficult place. You can try to get the rights holder on board, as previously discussed. But as you might expect, in many cases the copyright holders will be intractable, saying they don't believe in fair use or that your use isn't fair. They have also probably expended time, effort, and expense to locate the clip for you and/or digitize a screener, and were prepared to make you a master. Not unreasonably, they may have anticipated recouping these expenses through the license fee. In that case, you have a couple of choices. If there is only one source for the material you need, you may have to abandon the fair use claim and license the material. If you can find the material elsewhere, and you're confident in your claim of fair use (with a legal opinion to back you up), then you might go ahead and use it from the other source and take your chances.

In Chapter 6, we discussed Internet Archive (archive.org) and its searchable Television News Collection. Increasingly, media makers are turning to that source not only to research clips by transcript, but also to rent DVDs of those broadcasts and make master files, at least for news broadcasts from approximately 2012 onwards. Although mostly in standard definition, these masters can serve in cases where filmmakers are confident that their use is a fair use. Similarly, while we warn against taking clips from YouTube because of provenance issues, in situations where you know your use is a fair use, YouTube might be a viable source, quality allowing.

When Agreements Tie You to Licensing

Very occasionally, an archive will require you to sign an agreement, even as you order screeners, certifying that you will purchase from them whatever you use. In that case, the agreement is binding and overrides any fair use claim.

Don't Claim Fair Use as an Excuse to Cheat

Don't claim fair use just because you don't feel like paying. And don't agree to pay and then cheat someone at the last minute. It can seriously damage trust, not only between the rights holder and you, but also between that rights holder and any other producer who contacts them down the line looking for material.

Incidental Capture: Documentary vs. Dramatic Filmmaking

With documentary filmmaking, copyrighted images or sounds that are inadvertently captured in the course of filming real life do not need to be cleared, as their appearance falls under "incidental capture." Thinking of this in a different way, to change or mask the actual location or situation—to tell your subjects that they need to change their clothing, turn off the ringtone on their phone, or redecorate the room in which you're filming, for example—would misrepresent the reality that you're documenting.

If, however, you are *setting up* or *art directing* scenes for any kind of film—for example, building and decorating a set, costuming people, or re-arranging the background for an interview—incidental capture *does not apply* and clearances must be sought. This most often applies to fiction filmmaking, and was clarified in a landmark 1997 case, *Ringgold v. Black Entertainment Television, Inc.*

Ringgold v. Black Entertainment Television, Inc.

Faith Ringgold is a visual artist who works primarily in fabrics, often creating works that tell stories of the African-American experience. One of her pieces, "Church Story Picnic Quilt" (measuring roughly six feet square) was commissioned and is housed at the High Museum of Art in Atlanta, which describes it as a "painted 'story quilt.'" Ringgold retained the copyright to the work, but she granted permission for the museum to publish and sell a poster of it, which they did.

In 1991, *Roc*, a television sitcom produced by Black Entertainment Television (BET) and HBO, premiered on the Fox Television Network. In a particular episode, the poster was used as part of the decor for a scene that took place in the hallway of a church. The poster was on screen, in the background of a handful of shots, for a total of just under 27 seconds, but no identifying information or credit was included in the show.

In 1995, Ringgold saw the show in a re-broadcast and sued for copyright infringement. Initially, the court agreed that the producers' use of Ringgold's work was a fair use. But Ringgold appealed and won, because the purpose and character of the work's use in the show (decoration) was not transformative; because the entire work was on screen for a substantial amount of time; and because a market to license the poster for use on film sets existed—and Ringgold had previously refused to agree to such a license.

The 1997 decision galvanized Hollywood, because it created a strong precedent that there is no such thing as incidental capture when it comes to a fictional film, television show, or other media project. After the Ringgold decision, every piece of set decoration in dramatic works, even when they are filmed in real locations (for example, city streets, parks, coffee houses), had to be cleared. So-called "on-set clearance" people became a part of every crew. Every poster, every logo, *absolutely everything*, needs to be carefully selected based on whether it can be cleared. This doesn't mean that fair use doesn't exist in fiction film—it absolutely does—but not in the context of incidental capture.

Architecture

Clearing architecture, as well as buying and using archival shots of iconic buildings, can be a gray area for filmmakers, both fiction and nonfiction. While some older architecture is protected in the United States, most isn't, but all new architecture *is* protected, as is all public art.

U.S. copyright law regarding architecture changed in 1990, so that *any* building created in the United States on or after December 1, 1990 is automatically protected by copyright. In addition, many iconic pre-1990 buildings, such as the Chrysler and Empire State Buildings in New York City, are trademark protected against commercial use without permission. This means that if you are producing a fiction film, while you may be able to include the building in an aerial or wide shot of the New York City skyline, you will likely need permission if the building itself is your primary focus. And if you want to use the image of one of these iconic buildings—or *any* building erected from 1990 onwards—for commercial purposes (which might mean your movie poster or film publicity), consult a lawyer first. This use would probably be considered *merchandising*, which is even more problematic.

There is also a distinction made between architecture that can be viewed from a public location and that which can't. For those shooting documentary, the rules of incidental capture generally apply. But remember, *fair use is a defense against a copyright claim*. It's better to avoid the claim by being conservative when using images of buildings and public art, whether you shoot them yourself or use archival visuals—it should be evident that you didn't mean to capture that building or work of art; it was truly *incidental*For those shooting dramatic/fiction works, there is no "incidental capture" defense. One good way to gain some clarity about art and architecture when shooting a fiction film on location is to talk to the film bureau from which you're getting your shooting permits. They're likely to know, or be able to find out for you, what is and isn't protected at your location(s).

Outside the United States, the laws regarding architecture differ substantially. For example, the famed Eiffel Tower in Paris can be shot by any filmmaker during the day, because it's not protected. However, shooting the tower at night is problematic, because the design of the lighting that illuminates the tower is under copyright to the artist, and it can be very expensive to license. Kenn ran into this while clearing rights to *An Inconvenient Sequel*. The documentary producers wanted to use a 2013 archival shot of the Eiffel Tower at night, available from a commercial stock footage company. But the company would not issue a license until rights to the lighting had also been cleared, adding an unanticipated and significant hit to the budget.

Public Art

Like architecture, public art—such as sculptures that appear in the courtyards of buildings, or murals on public walls—are also usually protected. For example, Calder's famous "Flamingo" sculpture, which sits in the plaza outside the Kluczynski Federal Building in Chicago, Illinois, would require clearance from Calder's estate if it was seen in a shot in a fiction film. If the same sculpture was truly incidentally captured by a documentary crew in the process of filming some other main action, it would not. But again, the documentary capture needs to be *incidental* to be a fair use. If you're following your characters as they enter the Federal Building and they walk past the sculpture, great. But if you're just showing the building with the sculpture to establish that it's Chicago, or because you think the sculpture is visually interesting, that could be problematic. As always, the advice of a knowledgeable attorney should be sought.

Sources and Notes

For more information about fair use in documentary filmmaking, we strongly recommend Patricia Aufderheide's and Peter Jaszi's *Reclaiming Fair Use: How to Put Balance Back in Copyright*, 2nd edition, published by University of Chicago Press (2018). The report of William W. Story, Esq. on *Folsom et al. v. Marsh* (1841) can be found at the Caselaw Access Project, Harvard Law School, https://cite.case.law/f-cas/9/342/. More information about U.S. copyright law and fair use can be found at www.copyright.gov/fair-use/more-info.html. For an excellent overview of copyright and fair use, go to the Stanford Copyright & Fair Use Center website, http://fairuse.stanford.edu/Copyright_and_Fair_Use_Overview/chapter9/9-a.html. The Stanford quotation about whether or not a use is transformative is from https://fairuse.stanford.edu/overview/fair-use/four-factors/. The First Amendment Center's website is www.firstamend

mentcenter.org. The suit over *The Wind Done Gone* was settled in 2002, and the publisher made a donation on behalf of Mitchell's estate to Morehouse College. For more on the Victor Hugo suit, see John Lichfield, "Hugo Family Lawsuit Rejected," *The Independent* (September 13, 2001). The 2 Live Crew case can be read online here: https://caselaw.findlaw.com/us-supreme-court/510/569.html, and a copyright office summary of the case's history can be found here: www.copyright.gov/fair-use/summaries/campbell-acuff-1994.pdf. *'85: The Greatest Team in Football History* (102 minutes, 2016) was directed by Scott Prestin. Information about the case, *Red Label Music Publishing v. Chila Productions*, can be found at www.copyright.gov/fair-use/summaries/redlabelmusicpublg-chilaprods-ndill2019.pdf; see also the summary from Loeb & Loeb LLP, www.lexology.com/library/detail.aspx?g=fdc3887a-1422-4b82-9699-4202edc4db82. For further information on *The Definitive Elvis* lawsuit, see https://caselaw.findlaw.com/us-9th-circuit/1173854.html. To download a copy of the *Filmmakers Statement of Best Practices in Fair Use* and find other resources, visit https://cmsimpact.org/code/documentary-filmmakers-statement-of-best-practices-in-fair-use/. Information about *Ringgold v. Black Entertainment Television, Inc.* can be found at https://caselaw.findlaw.com/us-2nd-circuit/1054870.html. Information about artist Pierre Bideau's Eiffel Tower lighting, first revealed on December 31, 1985, can be found at www.toureiffel.paris/en/the-monument/lights. (The engineer of the tower, Gustave Eiffel, died in 1923, so the structure itself entered the public domain 70 years later, in 1993.)

CHAPTER 14

Fair Dealing, Moral Rights, and More: A Conversation with Hubert Best

While "fair use" is unique to U.S. copyright law, there is a related concept, "fair dealing," especially among member states of the Commonwealth of Nations. Primarily, fair dealing applies to spot news (the ability, for instance, to quote the work of someone in the course of broadcasting an obituary), quotations or citations, parody and certain classroom and educational uses. No country in the world is more permissive than the United States when it comes to fair use, largely because of its unique constitutional protection of speech.

However, while fair dealing is often quite limited, in European Union countries it may be further trumped by "the moral rights of the author," or *droits moral*, a concept that originated in France. This legal concept gives tremendous creative power to whoever is considered the "author" of a work regarding how the work is used by others. Moral rights differ from copyright. When it comes to film, in the United Kingdom as in the United States, the producer generally holds the copyright to the film. However, among E.U. countries, while the producer of a film maintains economic rights—called "related rights," as distinguished from copyright, including the right to exploit the film, get it distributed, etc.—the "author," for purposes of moral rights, is generally considered to be the film's director, and occasionally other creative participants. Therefore, E.U. film employment contracts customarily ask each member of the crew other than the director to agree not to enforce their moral rights to their own contribution to the overall work. By law, moral rights can't be waived or assigned, but one can contractually agree not to enforce their own moral rights. The practical outcome of this is similar to "work-for-hire" contracts in the United States, in which crew members relinquish claims to copyright in their own work.

To better explain the non-U.S. rights landscape, we spoke with Hubert Best, an internationally recognized expert in intellectual property and media law, particularly the exploitation of audiovisual and music content in new media environments. Trained at the Royal Academy of Music, but "seduced" (his word) by copyright law, he only recently retired to pursue his music. He hasn't let copyright go entirely, however, at the time of this interview, he was preparing a lecture (illustrated with music) about 19th century German composer Felix Mendelssohn. As he explained, Mendelssohn was the first author to overcome the national limitations of copyright protection, long before the 1886 Berne Convention.

Best, who was born in South Africa and spent much of his career in England, moved to Sweden in 2000 while working on intellectual property issues for the opening and closing ceremonies of the 2004 Athens Olympics. How now divides his time between Stockholm and London. In Stockholm, he is a former partner at ENN Advokatbyrå, and he has for many years been an international legal advisor for the Federation of Commercial Audiovisual Libraries International, Ltd. He spoke with Kenn for the first edition in 2008, and they again corresponded in September 2019. At that time, the Brexit deadline was October 31.

What is the history of copyright in the United Kingdom, and are there any major philosophical differences between how it's viewed there as opposed to in the United States?

In terms of the philosophical and historical origins, it's the same. After all, it was English copyright that made its way across the Atlantic, originating from the Statute of Anne in the beginning of the 18th century.

[The Statute of Anne, 1710, was "An Act for the Encouragement of Learning, by Vesting the Copies of Printed Books in the Authors or Purchasers of such Copies, during the Times therein mentioned."]

Of course, there were earlier origins, but that's generally taken to be the real beginning. Curiously enough, our first integrated copyright statute, in which the copyright in all the different kinds of works (or different kinds of uses) was assembled into one statute, was our Act of 1911, which is more or less the same time as your Act of 1909. I think this was partly in response to the general commercial things that were happening, but very largely in response to the coming into being of the Berne Convention [for the Protection of Literary and Artistic Works] at the end of the 19th century. Of course, there were some crucial differences. Your law very clearly preserved common law copyright, which of course it still does. But you've now adopted the Berne Convention arrangements.

Before we get into actual copyright terms, and fair dealing, could you talk briefly about whether and how public domain differs in countries other than the United States?

There is a bit of a trans-Atlantic divide in understanding about "public domain." I think it stems from the former U.S. provision, taken from the U.K., that when an unpublished work was first published, formalities had to be observed to entitle it to continued copyright protection as provided by the statute, without which it entered the public domain. [Until 1978], that arrangement continued for much longer in the U.S. than it did in the U.K. The reason for this was the Berne Convention, under which no formalities could be required by a member state's copyright laws for a published work to be protected by copyright. The U.K. as a founder-member therefore changed its copyright provisions with the 1911 Act, so that it was no longer necessary to register a work at the Stationers' Hall (equivalent of your Library of Congress). On publication, a qualifying work was automatically protected for—in those days—the life of the author plus 50 years. So, for more than a century, the U.K. has had a regime in which works can't enter the public domain through failure to register the copyright. Publication doesn't bring about any change in copyright status, which only ends at the end of the copyright term. So, I think we have got used to thinking about "the public domain" in a slightly different way from you.

Unpublished works remained in copyright forever—unless published, when the 50-year rule kicked in—until the 1988 Copyright Act came into force.

That's the Copyright, Designs and Patents Act of 1988.

It abolished "perpetual copyright" and as a "transitional provision" substituted a term of the author's life plus 50 (now 70) years for all works, unpublished as well as published.

Life plus 70 years, whether the work is published or not, or formally registered.

Exactly. Whereas before, the whole issue of publication and registration was totally central and crucial; I suppose that's basically historical now. But nowadays, I think the crucial difference between the U.K. and the U.S. arises from your First Amendment. And also the fact that it's really clearly stated in your Constitution, isn't it? The purpose of copyright is the creation of new works. This really seems to suggest, overall, that it's not generally possible to create, on a large scale, many new works unless one is involving, in some way or other, existing copyright works. Do you see what I mean?

Absolutely. That creative and artistic progress depends on the ability to build new works on the shoulders of prior works.

This really shows up in the whole "fair use" thing [in the United States], whereas here, this is not a part of the concept. Copyright [in the United Kingdom] is there to protect the exclusive rights of authors, full stop. Our copyright grew up from printing; the monarch granting monopolies to print books, music, and the like; giving printers a certain short period of exclusive rights in the works they had printed. When you look at judgments in this area, there seems to be almost a fiction: that it's possible for more or less everything that's protected by copyright to be totally original, unless it contains some acknowledged third-party rights. Obviously, that's not right. It does seem to me that your First Amendment and also this particular Section 8 from Article I of your Constitution does—well, I just think it's more realistic, frankly.

Is the European Union now standardized in terms of copyright protections, and are Eastern European E.U. countries synchronized with Western E.U. countries? What about northern E.U. countries such as Sweden, Denmark, and the Netherlands?

The broad parameters of copyright protection (length of term, kinds of works protected, available remedies) are standardized; "harmonized" is the expression they use. Because each country has its own national copyright statute, there is no single "European copyright law." So even when a particular aspect is "harmonized," it may not be 100 percent identical in all the countries, but it's pretty broadly corresponding. Some areas are not *entirely* standardized, for example, the exceptions to copyright. They are largely standard in the digital sphere, but there are still minor differences in exceptions to copyright in the analog world. A major and continuing force for standardization [is] the European Court, or CJEU [The Court of Justice of the European Union]. National courts refer questions arising in national cases to the CJEU, which acts as an umpire, and its judgments are binding throughout the E.U. So, this has an incremental standardization effect on E.U. copyright law.

And can you explain how authors' rights, or "moral" rights, come into it?

In Germany and France, it's said that the work is inextricably joined to the personality of the author. This idea arose in France, and it's a mainland continental issue. The more southern countries are stronger on that; the more northern countries, like the Netherlands and the Nordic countries, don't take that to such an extreme—they're more like ours. All the former Soviet Union countries—Russia itself, Ukraine, Armenia, Azerbaijan, and all those different countries—have new copyright laws which are very much in line with this moral rights principle. The primary issue is the author's moral right, which is often everlasting and can't be alienated from the author. The economic right, which is what we basically regard as copyright, is for them almost a subsection.

255

In the United States, we don't have authors' rights, per se. We have moral rights, but they only apply to the work of visual artists.

Yes, specifically a painting or a sculpture or something like that. An author of a book or a composer of a musical work has no moral rights in the States. There was a very well-known example, when a John Huston film, *The Asphalt Jungle* [a 1950 classic of film noir, directed by American filmmaker John Huston], was colorized in the States, and he objected to that and got nowhere; they just went ahead and did it. But in France, his heirs took Channel 5 to court. They won on his moral right, on the grounds that he said he hadn't intended [his films] to be seen in color, he'd wanted them to be seen only in black-and-white. So that shows very clearly this whole difference.

But there are differences, for example, between the United Kingdom and France—or were, until efforts were made in the mid-1990s to harmonize copyright throughout the European Union.

Yes. Up until 1996, when a substantial film with decent finances was going to be produced in the U.K., all the rights would have to vest in the producer in such a way that all other contributors' rights—the script

Publicity still from *The Asphalt Jungle* (1950) reflecting director John Huston's dramatic use of light and shadow. French courts held in part that "because HUSTON's renown is based on the interplay of black and white, creating an atmosphere, the said atmosphere would be jeopardized by colorization."

rights, the director, composers of music, actors—all their rights had to be waived. The "author" of a film was considered to be the producer, who had no moral rights, but of course held all the economic rights by contract. The film was protected as a copyrighted work; the term was 50 years from the first publication of the film. It wasn't like a book, where protection was for 50, then 70 years after the death of the author.

So the film producer had a sort of limited author's copyright, derived from the collective work of the production team, but the members of the team waived their moral rights and the producer had none.

Only an author—e.g., a scriptwriter or composer—would have had moral rights. They cannot be transferred *inter vivos*; they stay with the originator of the work until she dies; or, if she waives them, they cease. The producer had no moral rights, nor did performers. In fact, performers had no exclusive rights at all; their consents were needed in some circumstances, which could be given verbally or even by simply taking part in a recording. Whereas in a country like France, a film, an art film, had always been regarded as a work of authorship. And, of course, the author was the director, and so he was the king and he had these moral rights of authorship, and the term of his economic rights was the full 70 years after death.

Now, in order to harmonize the duration of copyrights in films, the U.K. also introduced this term of 70 years after the death of the author. The "author" of a film is now considered to be the producer *and* the principal director. The producer's (or production company's) position is the same as it was, having all the economic rights, but the principal director—as an author in the true sense of the word—has moral rights. Secondly, the performers now have exclusive rights—to permit or prohibit the restricted acts, just like a copyright owner—and they also have moral rights. Of course, the producer/production company will still require all participants in the film to waive their moral rights. It's just accepted in the U.K.

On the *continent*, on the other hand, moral rights are the very foundation of copyright, and they can't be waived. And, in many countries, they last forever. So, it's like a continuum, with France, Germany, and similar countries at one extreme, the U.S.A at the other, and the U.K. kind of sitting in the middle, like it does in so many things.

In the United Kingdom, when the 70 years on a film's last "author" are up, does the film enter the public domain?

Yes. On the expiry of the term of copyright, it goes into the public domain.

At the time of this writing, the United Kingdom is less than two months away from leaving the European Union. How is this going to affect existing copyright and moral rights issues moving forward, do you think?

Anybody's guess. Some significant IP-intensive industries I represent are disadvantaged by the "Fortress Europe" policy and can foresee significant benefits from leaving it. The latest E.U. copyright directive, the "DSM" (Digital Single Market) Directive of 2019, will have wide-ranging impact, ranging from permissions required for news reporting—thus potentially taking the E.U. media even further from U.S. First Amendment freedoms—to filtering technologies required to be implemented by ISPs. Its passage through the European Commission was more contested than any previous copyright directive, with several member states maintaining their vote against different provisions. So it was passed by majority and not unanimously. It must be implemented by member states in the next two years; whether the U.K. will implement some or all of its provisions remains to be seen. I see that U.K. courts are still sending questions to the CJEU about intellectual property cases, even though U.K. government officials have disengaged from E.U. meetings in general in order to concentrate on practical Brexit preparations.

My personal hope is that the U.K. will align itself more with U.S. copyright law, including in respect of fair use and internet/safe harbor issues. Although, as you observe elsewhere, a trend to challenge the latter is also emerging in the U.S.A. In the U.K. copyright community, I believe that my views are in the minority: almost every U.K. copyright practitioner and academic I know believes that an ever-closer correspondence with the E.U. copyright regime is the only conceivable way to go and anything else is madness. I suppose there must be other views out there. I know a perhaps proportionately smaller minority of Swedish practitioners and judges who feel as I do.

In countries such as France and Germany, where moral rights exceed copyright terms, it seems that moral rights give the creator a level of control above and beyond copyright. While copyright is considered to be the economic part of protection (giving authors royalties, etc.), moral rights give authors (or their estates) control over types of uses.

But what they give you a right to do is, to some extent, limited. Different countries have different ones. For example, in France, there's the *droit de repentir*, which is the right to withdraw your work, but it's not commonly exercised; you have to compensate people who've made investments. Mostly, there are two rights: the right to be named as the author [*droit de paternité*] and the right to object to the work being treated in a derogatory way [*droit au respect de l'oeuvre*]. It's still the case in all the continental countries that the real issue with copyright is the economic right, because that's what enables the author to earn the money. But nevertheless, philosophically speaking, they regard that as only a minor extension of the basic moral right.

Are the countries in the Commonwealth of Nations—Canada, the United Kingdom, Australia, etc.—consistent on this?

No, they're not quite. Every Commonwealth country that's a member of the Berne Convention does have to have moral rights, but I would say that they have a different force in the different countries. Canada has been very much influenced by the French, and so Canadian copyright law does have a lot of authors' rights influence in it. An early example of that is a case called Tariff 22. And it was about music, licensing of music rights.

In 2006, SOCAN, the Society of Composers, Authors and Music Publishers of Canada, wanted to compensate its members by charging internet service providers royalties for SOCAN music cached on their servers. The courts eventually said they couldn't.

I think it's fair to summarize the judgment of the Canadian Supreme Court in the Tariff 22 case as being that an internet communication that crosses one or more national boundaries "occurs" in more than one country, at least in the country of transmission and the country of reception. Communication presupposes a sender and a receiver. A real and substantial connection to Canada is sufficient to connect the Canadian Copyright Act to an internet transmission, and relevant factors include the place of the content provider, the host server, the intermediaries, and the end user.

Since then, one has seen a trend for national courts to "reach out" beyond national borders, most often applying their own domestic laws extra-territorially, but sometimes relying on the laws of other countries, in their attempts to police the availability of copyright content online.

But the ISPs, according to the ruling, were not responsible for content if they were merely serving as a conduit.

That used to be the starting point, provided that an intermediary ISP was content neutral—meaning that it does not engage in acts that relate to the content of the communication, and only provides a "conduit" for information communicated by others. If an intermediary ISP ceased to be content neutral—if it had notice or should have known that a content provider had posted infringing material and failed to take remedial action—the intermediary SP might be liable for copyright infringement. However, things have moved, and are continuing to move on. On both sides of the Atlantic, the trend seems to be for ISPs to have to jump ever higher bars to escape liability for infringing—and sometimes even potentially infringing—content in their services. As I mentioned above, the DSM directive will significantly affect ISPs.

Two WIPO treaties, which were meant to supplement the Berne Convention when it came to internet and online stuff, dealt with questions like: *What happens when something is put on the Internet? Is copying happening? Is distribution happening?* But they never produced a conclusion about *Where* is it happening? So this huge issue has been up in the air, and ripe for legislative and, especially, judicial development.

So, we have a global market dealing with national and regional approaches to copyright and moral rights, strongly driven by the American entertainment industry and its perspective.

I find I'm dealing with so many things—music, science, user-generated content websites, and all sorts of things—which have been originated in America by people (including lawyers), who are steeped in U.S. copyright law, and they start from that basis: that copyright is an economic right, which can be traded any which way, as opposed to the authors' rights/ moral rights approach. These things [such as] the "takedown" provisions; this whole question of ISP liability and so on—what for us is completely outside copyright law—have made it (very sensibly) into your copyright law. The business models which are an outworking of the U.S. provisions migrate to Europe, where they just don't fit and don't work anymore.

Can you offer an example?

If you look at YouTube and look at their terms and conditions and the takedown provisions for the user-generated content that's being provided—that if somebody objects, do it like this, and this will happen and that will happen, and it will get taken down—all that is simply a mirror of the U.S. copyright law. That doesn't necessarily work in Europe. Doing all that doesn't necessarily relieve the ISP or the organization of liability for copyright infringement. However, in practice, large ISPs—and not just U.S.-originated or based ones like Google and YouTube—adopt user terms and conditions which are based on the U.S. statutory takedown provisions, and these seem to be universally accepted which is a good sign that they are practical and work in real life.

Are there exceptions to copyright for certain uses, such as satire?

This is taking us on to *fair use* versus *fair dealing*. In the U.S., you have fair use, and this encompasses its four tests and all that. Here, we don't have anything like that. Fair dealing basically only applies in four situations: making copies for private study, copying for criticism or review, fair dealing for reporting current events, and some very specific aspects of educational use. That's it. And in each of those cases, fair dealing is like a little subsection of the exception, where it's saying that you can use it for this very limited purpose, and in addition, it has to be fair dealing. Each exception to copyright has to be very specifically framed in specific terms.

Fair dealing is either for specifically reporting current events, or specifically criticizing or reviewing the work or another work, or quoting from a work or satirizing it. Even then, it goes further than that; it goes on to say that the authors of the original work have to be acknowledged.

Attribution? Even if it's a televised news report?

Attribution is a really important part of it. There is a section which says that if it's news in audiovisual media, if it's impossible—not just inconvenient or difficult—to give an attribution, then that's okay. But that exception doesn't apply to fair dealing for criticism or review. So the issue is, for documentaries like that, in Europe, nearly all the clips have to be cleared. That's the only way.

I think the question of freedom of speech is significant, in itself and as a straw in the wind. The view in countries such as France and Germany—and the E.U. itself—is that copyright legislation, in particular the exceptions, already take the issue of freedom of speech into account. This recently led to a situation where freedom of expression was not a defense to a claim of infringement, because the author of the quote used had not been credited, [which] is a requirement of the E.U.-harmonized citation exception. That a relatively insignificant formal regulation, giving an author a credit, prevails in the face of freedom of expression suggests—at the very least—that the concept of freedom of expression doesn't rank very high in European jurisprudence. As already mentioned, it seems that the DCM directive will take things even further in this direction.

I guess the takeaway is that even if a film succeeds in a fair use claim in the United States, if it's distributed internationally there's a risk that copyright holders could enjoin the film.

Yes, absolutely. And now there's one further distinction which I should make. These fair dealing provisions apply in the U.K. and add a degree of flexibility to the exceptions to which fair dealing applies (mentioned previously). But continental copyright laws don't have that provision. There simply isn't any fair dealing provision in France, Germany, Spain, Italy. So there, one is tied to very specific exceptions, and that's all.

261

And in the United Kingdom, fair dealing also comes into play in educational or classroom use.

Yes. There again, our Copyright Act of 1988 has very specific exceptions which apply to education. Each of those has a good many subsections. For example, the first one relates specifically to any materials used for an examination. And then there's another very specific one applying to sound recordings and broadcasts and so forth. And then it says it's restricted to the person giving or receiving instruction, *and* it has to be accompanied by sufficient acknowledgment, *and* it must be noncommercial, and so on. Now, certain of those educational exceptions are subject also to fair dealing.

So you see, fair dealing is never like fair use is in the States, where it's an overarching concept. Fair dealing is always a qualification—if you like, a further qualification—of a tightly defined exception, in our law. And there are these few cases where it can be used, some educational purposes.

U.S. copyright law is somewhat vague when it comes to fair use, but intentionally so, so that courts can decide on a case-by-case basis. Whereas fair dealing, it seems, is so spelled out that artists may know better where they stand, but their hands are tied much tighter.

It's almost impossible to imagine a situation where an artist could use one of the fair dealing exceptions. Of course they could use it for their private study. But to make a public work of art, the artist would need to rely on specific exceptions, such as reporting current events, criticism or review, quotation or parody. But—say in the case of parody—it would be very clunky, because you would still have to have all those acknowledgments and everything, which would undo a whole lot of the cleverness of what parody or satire usually is.

And yet the United Kingdom is a country that has a rich history of satire.

A specific parody exception has been introduced since our last conversation, ten years ago. Many continental countries also have it. France has it. Sweden has it, not explicitly in the statute, but by judicial interpretation. I must say, even when the U.K. didn't have the exception, satire seemed to thrive. I do so hope that, now that we have a parody exception in the U.K., our satirical wit doesn't become blunted and obvious!

Is it fair to say that fair dealing in Canada and Australia is similar in philosophical underpinnings, but not exactly the same in specifics?

Yes, absolutely. Different interpretation.

Is there anything in fair dealing that covers what we would call "incidental capture," which happens, for example, when a filmmaker documenting reality can't avoid copyrighted material, such as logos or background music?

There again, because of the way our law works, there is a very specific exception for incidental inclusion. It's Section 31 of our Copyright Act. "Copyright in a work is not infringed by its incidental inclusion in an artistic work, sound recording, film, broadcast or cable programme." That's very specific, you see, as to what it can be incidentally included in.

So the law doesn't differentiate between incidental capture in vérité documentary and fictional work? That's an issue here. When studios shoot a dramatic film, for example, and film a chase scene through a real landscape with billboards and that kind of thing, they often opt for clearing, or trying to clear, to take the safest stance.

263

It would be exactly the same here, because the question comes up in every case: What does "incidental" mean? And your example of the billboards in the film: if it's a feature film, an art movie, and not just some piece of news reporting, then I think the answer might well be, "Yes, that's not incidental, because you chose to film there. The billboard was there. You could have chosen to film somewhere where the billboard wasn't."

I remember having to answer this question for one of our news channels back in "pre-history" when Margaret Thatcher was still in power. She was interviewed in Number 10 Downing Street, on the staircase. And behind her was a portrait of Winston Churchill, which was of course still in copyright. And they asked me, "Is this incidental?" I said, "Well, it's a question of fact. Did it just happen that you managed to get her to stop on the stairs, or was she posed? If she was posed, I'm afraid it's not incidental." What we decided was, if it was simple to get the consent—the artist was well known—we would go with that; otherwise we'd think again. And it *was* simple, there was no issue. At the time, of course, it was also subject to reporting current events. I'm talking now about use of it for archival later on.

In the case of the chase scene, a filmmaker might argue, "Well, if we picked another location, there would be four other billboards!"

All I can say is, in the U.K., the courts have always been pretty strict. Incidental does have to be really incidental. I should say that there's a special section excluding music. So, music can rarely be incidentally included; that will always have to be cleared. And that's simply because when the act was framed, the music industry lobbied powerfully.

Another challenging issue involves digital rights. If I buy a music CD or a physical book or a work of art, I can lend or sell it without any additional monies owed to the original creator. The recent case of Capitol Records, LLC v. ReDigi Inc., *clarified that this is not the case in the digital world. ReDigi was offering its digital platform as a place for users to buy and sell legally acquired digital music from others. The courts ruled for Capitol, arguing that users were essentially selling unauthorized reproductions, which is a violation of copyright.*

264 When the digital distribution right was introduced, back in the early 1990s, there was a lot of discussion as to which of the existing copyright-restricted acts it should fall under. Initially some countries viewed it as a kind of broadcast or cablecast. In the end, of course, it was classified as a distribution right, but this introduced the problem of exhaustion (or first sale doctrine), because the distribution right had previously applied to physical copies. Once sold, the author's distribution right in that copy was exhausted; hence, second-hand bookshops didn't need to pay a proportion of their sales to publishers. However, if the *digital* distribution right were to exhaust – chaos! So a provision was introduced, that in the digital milieu, the distribution right would not exhaust.

So, for a library to use CDL—controlled digital lending—for books, it can make available only one digital book for each physical book it must have in its collection, with some exceptions for patrons with special needs.

My impression is that digital contracts are a *fait accompli*, the norm, and the issues are practical. Academic institutions' libraries take all sorts of steps to keep their [transmissions] secure, to assure integrity of registered users' lists, etc. I've done contracts for publishers of journals with academic institutions, and all the security, logging of authorized readers, etc. are carefully stipulated. I've no idea whether any of it really works. I suspect there are probably endless ways around it all, and the publishers try to price that into their subscription charges.

Sources and Notes

The United Kingdom's Copyright Act of 1911 was an "Act to amend and consolidate the Law relating to Copyright." Information can be found at www.legislation.gov.uk/ukpga/Geo5/1-2/46/enacted. The United States' 1909 Copyright Act extended the maximum term of protection to 56 years and made further provisions regarding copyright. See www.copyright.gov/timeline/timeline_1900-1950.html. More information about the Berne Convention, adopted in 1886, can be found here, www.wipo.int/treaties/en/ip/berne/. Information about the Copyright, Designs and Patents Act of 1988 can be found at www.copyrightservice.co.uk/copyright/uk_law_summary. Section 8 of Article I was referred to in Chapter 13. It indicates that Congress has the power to "promote the Progress of Science and useful Arts, by securing for limited Times to Authors and Inventors the exclusive Right to their respective Writings and Discoveries." Based in Luxembourg, The Court of Justice of the European Union is the supreme court of the E.U. in matters of European law. See https://europa.eu/european-union/about-eu/institutions-bodies/court-justice_en. The Turner Entertainment Company aired a colorized version of John Huston's *The Asphalt Jungle* in the United States, over Huston's objections. The photo caption information from *Turner Entertainment Co. v. Huston, CA Versailles*, 1994 is available online, www.peteryu.com/intip_msu/turner.pdf. More information on the 2019 Directive on Copyright in the Digital Single Market can be found at https://ec.europa.eu/digital-single-market/en/modernisation-eu-copyright-rules. For more information on Tariff 22, see the website of the Copyright Board of Canada, https://cb-cda.gc.ca/tariffs-tarifs/certified-homologues/music-musique-e.html. Controlled digital lending, or CDL, is a way for libraries to distribute copies of books they physically own to borrowers via digital downloads that expire when the term of lending is done. See https://blog.archive.org/2019/08/08/librarians-share-benefits-of-controlled-digital-lending/ for more information. For more information about *Capitol Records, LLC v. ReDigi Inc*, see https://copyrightalliance.org/copyright-law/copyright-cases/capitol-records-v-redigi/.

CHAPTER 15

Licensing Visuals

This chapter explores the challenges involved when media makers seek to license not only photographs and footage, but also artwork and graphics. What kinds of licenses are available? Who has the power to license the visuals you need? If you're clearing film clips from Hollywood features and television, how do you also clear the actors, writers, and directors involved in their creation? When should you contact copyright holders, and how much do they need to know about your project? How do they set their rates, and is any of it negotiable?

For media makers, this chapter offers some step-by-step guidance to the process. For audiences, educators, and scholars, it offers what we hope will be an eye-opening look at what's involved in using third-party visuals—including historical photographs and footage—to tell stories to present-day audiences. Licensing is complicated and expensive, and underlying rights to works expire, which is why some of your favorite films and series may no longer be available, and why some filmmakers shy away from the audiovisual historical record, using substitutions—re-enactments, generic visuals, or animation—as a budgetary rather than a creative choice.

Locating the Rights Holder

First, you need to know who *currently* owns the rights to the visuals you want to use. Individual properties and entire archives routinely change hands, so this can be time-consuming (and another reason to consider hiring a professional researcher and/or clearance person). Once you have a license, it remains valid for the duration of the term you've negotiated, even if the copyright subsequently changes hands, because whoever assumes the copyright must honor the terms of all existing active contracts. However, if at some point you need additional rights or an additional time period, then you will negotiate a new license agreement or addendum with the new copyright holder.

Professional Archives

If you're working with a professional archive—exploring clips in the media library at the ABC News VideoSource website, for example, or still photographs on the site of the Chicago Historical Society—finding reliable information about copyright ownership may be fairly straightforward. Except for rare instances where there may be a legal complication, such as a donor restriction or privacy issue, it's pretty safe to assume you'll be able to clear rights from them.

Public Domain Archives

Working with sites whose material falls under the public domain (see Chapter 12) is also generally straightforward. If you are researching and pulling photographs from the U.S. Library of Congress's website, for example, or searching the collections of the U.S. National Archives and Records Administration (NARA), online usage guidelines will provide information on which materials are *unrestricted* (not subject to copyright). On the page for the particular item you are interested in, look for a heading that says "Rights Advisory," "Use Restrictions," or something similar, and see if there are any known restrictions. If not, you're fine. Otherwise, there will be information about any encumbrances that may exist, and you'll have to obtain paperwork from the owner of the copyright before the archive will agree to duplicate that material for you. If a high-resolution copy is available for download right on the website, then there are no rights encumbrances and you can just download the image or footage and use it.

Note that government archives providing public domain materials will not provide paperwork for your files. You should print out the page on which the item was found and keep that printout in your files in lieu of a license agreement or other documentation. The printout should show the ID information for the item, and also include the information regarding its lack of restrictions. This way, you can prove the item is in the public domain.

Some smaller private commercial companies may claim they provide "public domain footage." This may or may not be true; while some companies, such as Critical Past, Footage Farm, Periscope, and Pond5 *do* provide legitimate public domain material, other organizations may simply be marketing old footage from unknown sources that has been curated by collectors looking to make money. These legitimate vendors will provide a *boilerplate* license agreement for your use on a royalty basis, as discussed elsewhere).

User-generated Sites such as YouTube, Wikipedia, or Pinterest

While many filmmakers begin their search for images with general web browsing, and may discover a tantalizing variety of raw materials that might be perfect for their media projects, this method can lead to frustration and waste when it comes time to clear rights. Kenn has seen filmmakers need to start virtually from scratch because their rough cut consisted almost entirely of clips they'd pulled from YouTube or elsewhere on the web, but couldn't trace back to the rightsholders and therefore couldn't license—or use. Even if you're vigilant about keeping track of the URL associated with each clip, the screen names of those who posted them rarely lead to an actual name and contact information. If you do succeed in finding the person, they may have no idea about the original provenance of the material they uploaded.

In some cases, the poster may have at least provided copyright information in a caption or text, along with the material. You need to independently verify that the image or footage has been accurately captioned—visual information is as subject to fact checking as written information—and you need to make sure the copyright holder named was, and still is, the copyright holder. And then, of course, you need to figure out how to contact that entity. Sometimes the footage or image will have carried a watermark or *bug* (logo burned into the image) that will provide a great clue as to who may own it—if so, you're in luck. And sometimes, the YouTube channel is managed by the copyright holder, such as a legitimate news organization, in which case the provenance may be easy to determine.

Otherwise, here are two tricks that might help you locate copyright holders of posted visuals.

269

TinEye

TinEye may help you locate the original source for a still photograph someone has posted, especially if the copyright holder has posted it as well. TinEye (www.tineye.com) is a free search engine that does reverse searches of images. It can be used through their website, or downloaded and installed as an extension for some browsers. TinEye allows you to upload the URL of an image you find on the internet, and, using artificial intelligence, it will quickly find as many websites as possible on which that photo appears, even if it's cropped, flipped, or flopped, or to a certain extent manipulated. If you find a photo you like and the poster is anonymous or long gone, do a TinEye search. It's just possible that the copyright holder (such as a museum, historical society, or commercial archive) has posted the same image and can license it to you. If not, a TinEye search might at least reveal a site that has more information about the image, such as a caption that includes the source.

Viral Media Companies

Certain companies, such as Viral Hog (www.viralhog.com) and Jukin Media (www.jukinmedia.com), serve as agents to internet posters; they license some of the videos found on YouTube, and sometimes in Twitter and Facebook feeds and elsewhere. If you find a video you want to use on YouTube and it's tagged to one of these organizations, see if you can negotiate a deal with them. If they don't represent the rights you require, they can probably put you in touch with the original media creator, so that you can discuss your use with them. These agencies, when they're legitimate (and many are not), can help media makers who post on YouTube and elsewhere earn revenue from what they've created. In doing so, they can be of help in making material that might have been anonymous and unusable available for licensing.

Print Materials

Existing books and articles about your subject are good places to start to search for rights information for visual material. Often, the images are credited, making your search for copyright information easier. There may also be archive or collection information which may lead you to a source for the high-quality reproductions you'll need. Watch out for "from the collection of the author" credits however; this may simply mean the image was in the possession of the author, not that the author owns the copyright.

A Note About Fair Use

In Chapters 13 and 14, we talk about situations in which your use of materials may constitute a *fair use* exception to U.S. copyright law (and some similar but not identical exceptions found in the laws of selected other countries). If your use is a fair use, you don't need to contact the copyright holder. But it is still incumbent on you as an ethical filmmaker to be sure that the material is being used in a way that accurately presents its content. Researching the material's provenance can help confirm that.

When There Are Multiple Rights Holders

In some cases, you will be seeking to license visuals for which you will also need to license *underlying rights* (see Chapter 11). For example, you may want to use a clip from a Hollywood film, such as *Mary Poppins* (1964). That clip will include underlying rights related to the involvement of unionized actors, a director, and writers, among others. You will also need to clear the music, as discussed in the next chapter.

Clearing Third-party Footage Used (and Licensed) by Another Filmmaker

The credits and accompanying websites of other films on your topic may suggest the range of archives and other sources from which those filmmakers acquired third-party footage. But even if you are able to locate the filmmakers, it's likely (Kenn estimates about 75 percent of the time) that they won't remember where specific visuals came from and they haven't held on to (or else aren't willing to share) the relevant paperwork that would provide the answer. If they *can* help, be prepared to pay them for their time, as they may have to dig through old files. If they can't access the shot logs but the film was made for a particular venue or distributor—say, a PBS station, HBO, Netflix, or Focus Features—the legal department of that organization may have copies of the paperwork, dating from when the film's "rights bible" was given to them. With the permission of the filmmaker, you *might* be able to get the information from the lawyers. And again, your arrangement of those visuals must be original to your project; you cannot lift an edited sequence from someone else's work.

271

Start Research Early to Avoid Major Problems Later

Given the complexity of identifying rights holders and confirming the provenance of material you wish to use, the process of licensing material should start as soon as you begin to gather visuals. Try to identify which materials might be most difficult, if not impossible, to clear. In addition to clips that you've found online without any information about where they're from or who can license them, you or your researcher may become aware of potential problems from certain rights holders. For example, the rights you want to license may be controlled by:

■ An individual or entity known for unusual delays and complications in rights negotiations;

- A corporation or individual's estate (heirs and trustees), who may be very protective of reputation, intent on making a large profit, or both;
- An individual or entity embroiled in some activity (personal or medical issues, long-term travel, legal problems, a product launch, or bankruptcy) that is going to make their licensing to you a very low priority;
- An organization, even a news organization, that does not normally store, provide, or license archival material and thus is not prepared to do so. Many, if not most local television stations' news departments fall under this category, as the general downsizing of personnel has meant that archival requests regarding all but their most accessible file footage is often a low priority, or out of the question all together.

Solutions to problematic licensing may exist, but working them out can be time-consuming. For example, for one segment of *Eyes on the Prize* (1987), producers wanted to depend heavily on a U.S. Information Agency film about the 1963 March on Washington for Jobs and Freedom. As a product of the U.S. government, the rights to the footage might ordinarily be in the public domain. At the time, however—the 1980s—U.S. Information Agency (USIA) films could only be distributed and used overseas, and therefore clips couldn't be included in a series for American public television. For that reason, soon after production began, producers worked to get an act passed by the U.S. Congress and signed by then-president Ronald Reagan to have that particular USIA film, *The March*, released domestically. (USIA films can now be accessed in the United States 12 years after their initial release.)

Deciding Which Rights You Need

One of the first things to determine is whether the moving image, clips, graphics or stills you need are categorized by the archive holding them as rights-managed or royalty-free. We discussed these terms earlier, but in this section we go into more detail about how to navigate each type of clearance.

Royalty-Free

Royalty-free means that you pay a flat fee for the material provided. The amount is negotiated between you and the provider, or dictated by them, and there are no further restrictions on how you use the footage, in which markets, or for how long. Often you can even use this material in more than one project, which is strictly forbidden with rights-managed footage. (The license is *not* transferrable to others, however.) In essence, you pay a single fee for a non-exclusive "buy-out."

A word of caution: as with any contract or other legal document, be careful with royalty-free image "boilerplate" agreements. You should find them on the provider's website (sometimes they're a bit hidden) and download, read, and keep that agreement for your files if you purchase material from them. This is important, because some of these agreements seek to limit commercial use of the material in ways that might not work for you, especially if you need all rights. For example, they may not allow publicity or promotion uses, such as a theatrical trailer or television advertisement. Some don't allow you to assign the license to a distributor, which is almost always a necessity. There is also sometimes an issue with the provider's claimed right to *injunctive relief*. (We discuss both assignability and injunctive relief in Chapter 11, where we dissect the elements of a typical license agreement.) To address these issues, the provider may offer a "film rider" or a "premium license," which provides the additional rights you need at a higher rate. The bottom line is that as easy as it is to click and buy, be sure to treat the online license agreement as a legal document, and understand what you're agreeing to. It's on you to let the provider know if you need something clarified or changed.

273

Rights-Managed

It's likely that most of the material you'll need to license will be rights-managed. This means that you pay a negotiated rate per second, per clip, or per image, with the price dependent on where, how, and for how long you plan to distribute your project. Examples of materials that are typically rights-managed include historical footage and photographs, news stories, and photographs of celebrities and special events. Examples of rights-managed archives include the major networks and studios, news organizations such as Reuters and the Associated Press, and both commercial and public television stations in the United States and other countries (such as RAI in Italy, NHK in Japan, the BBC and Channel 4 in England).

With rights-managed footage, you are always negotiating for one-time use; that is, use in only one project and subject to the markets and time restrictions you need. You may *not* re-use rights-managed material in any other projects, including derivative works, nor can you continue to release your project after the initial term has expired, nor can you release it in territories or venues not covered by your agreement, unless you enter into new negotiations to *upgrade* the rights. This means you should carefully determine which rights you want to acquire and which you don't need.

Rights-managed material is usually sold for specific uses in specific parts of the world, for specific periods of time. The variables you'll need to make decisions about include *markets* (or *modes of delivery*), *term*, and *geographic areas*.

Distribution Markets

Most of the time you will be licensing rights for use in specific *markets* (often referred to in license agreements as *media*). This means that you're clearing rights only for the venues that you need. If your film is intended solely for classroom use, for example, you will not need or want to pay the costs associated with clearing rights for streaming or theatrical use.

In general, the primary markets in which your film might be distributed (you might think of them as *modes* of delivery or types of audiences) include:

- Film festivals (this is usually the least expensive rate);
- Noncommercial television (such as PBS, BBC, or other noncommercial and government-related broadcast entities);
- Commercial broadcast; network, independent, or other over-the-air for-profit broadcasters;
- Streaming, through a service such as Netflix, Amazon Prime, Hulu, or another such service;
- Basic (or free) cable, such as the Discovery Channel or Lifetime—essentially any cable station that is part of a basic cable package and usually runs ads;
- Premium cable, such as HBO or Showtime; stations that may be sold a la carte to customers and contain no ads, except for their own programming;
- Educational; for example, classrooms, libraries, or church and community groups. These are often called *nontheatrical audiovisual rights*;
- Theatrical, meaning "wide release" in a large number of movie theaters around the country; although most theatrical films really require "all rights, all media, in perpetuity," as Hollywood films do;
- Limited theatrical, meaning releasing only to art or repertory houses, such as the Film Forum in New York, the Coolidge Corner in Boston, or the Nuart in Los Angeles. Because consideration for Academy Awards involves opening in at least one theater in Los

Angeles or New York, filmmakers sometimes purchase limited theatrical so they can qualify for an Oscar;

- Museums. This would be as part of an exhibit, a lecture, or other screening or display (but selling video copies in the museum bookstore for use at home wouldn't be included);
- Corporate presentations. You may be making a sales film, or a video project for presentation at a stockholder's meeting, or to teach CEOs new management skills. Corporate use is often a fairly expensive right, and like film festival rights, is usually granted for quite limited time periods;
- Television commercials. Archives may differentiate between national and local commercials;
- Home video, which means both selling physical materials such as DVDs or Blu-rays online, or in brick and mortar stores, or unlocking downloadable digital files to individual consumers for private use, as opposed to educational rights, which include permission to show to a group of people in a public place;
- Internet, whether streaming or downloadable from an internet website. If you are specifically purchasing this right, many archives will differentiate between the two, and it may be less expensive to license a visual if it is going to *stream only* or if a still image can't be downloaded and you block copying. Streaming means that you can use a clip or still image on your website (although you may *not* use it as, or in, a corporate logo or anything that could be construed as a trademark), and people who visit your website can thus watch the clip onscreen, even repeatedly, but they cannot copy it onto their computer. Downloadable means that a visitor to your website can click a button and it will copy to their computer's hard drive. Internet downloading rights also would apply to items sold on iTunes, Amazon Music, or other similar sites. (Rights to, say, play an audio clip on Pandora, Spotify, or another such service would normally be considered streaming);
- In-context promotion; for example, using the material in a promotional trailer or television commercial, or using a still image or frame grab on a poster, on packaging or other print-based advertising. Sometimes you can convince a rights holder to let you have in-context publicity rights along with other rights you are purchasing; other times it's decidedly separate and quite expensive. As with television commercials, if you have to clear them separately, publicity rights are often subject to per-cut pricing, and even a purchase of "all rights, all media, in perpetuity" may not include certain publicity uses; you have to double check

275

with the rights holder if it's not specified clearly in your license agreement.

- Merchandising, which includes putting a still photo or graphic on a hat, T-shirt, tote bag, coffee mug, souvenir paperweight, etc., whether to sell or give away, or using that still photo or graphic as part of your signage, logo, or trademark.

Bundled Rights

It used to be that you could purchase these rights in any combination, or bundle. Nowadays, however, most commercial rights holders prefer to sell you a *pre-bundled* collection of rights. In the case of media makers, most often these bundles are:

- Film festivals only;
- All rights, all media in perpetuity EXCEPT theatrical; or
- All rights, all media in perpetuity INCLUDING theatrical.

In-context promotion may be included in the last two categories, or not (requiring an additional fee). If it isn't clear, it doesn't hurt to ask if the licensor would be willing to throw in "in-context promo" so that you can advertise your film without having to work around using their materials in your trailer, for example. Another potential item to discuss with the licensor is whether they would consider allowing "limited theatrical" in the "EXCEPT theatrical" package. If they are filmmaker-friendly and you explain that it would help you qualify for an Oscar, they may allow it, or charge you a small surcharge.

Despite the fact that many of the above rights are now bundled as described, it's important that you understand them individually because this knowledge is always helpful; it may well come up not only in your licensing discussions with rights holders, but also in your negotiations with distributors.

Option Windows

If you ask them to, many rights holders will allow you to include an *option window* in your license agreement. This is a negotiated amount of time during which you can upgrade the rights you bought with additional ones, but priced as if you'd bought them as part of the initial bundle. For example, suppose at picture lock that you purchase and license only film festival rights. This gives you the master material you need to finish your film without costing a fortune, but leaves you vulnerable if you get a distributor, because they will need you to have broader rights. Instead, it's possible that a clause can be added to your license agreement that locks in the rate to *upgrade*—add additional specified markets within a limited period of time, generally three months to a year. Ask for the longest window you can get; this will allow you to show in festivals, and/or pitch your film to distributors. Once you've attached a distributor, the fee the distributor pays to you can help pay the upgrade costs.

Often, filmmakers sell distribution to different entities for different markets. If you receive enough from one distributor to upgrade your rights to clear all markets, then any money you get from additional distributors may go to you, your investors, your debtors, or toward publicizing the film and selling it even wider.

Archives won't go out of their way to offer option windows; you need to *ask* for them. If the option is granted, make sure you have the agreed-upon upgrade rates written into the initial licensing agreement. This allows you to budget for the upgrade and you'll know immediately whether or not you can afford to accept a distributor's or broadcaster's offer should it come later on. There's no fee or penalty for negotiating an option period; it's just a question of whether an archive will do it.

Time Limitations

Time periods (*terms*) for licenses vary. Unlimited time is called *in perpetuity*. This means the rights will never expire. In contrast, some rights holders grant permission for just a few years of use, which filmmakers may agree to if they're only seeking to show their work at film festivals; the assumption is that you will enter a cycle of festivals over a short period of time. In general, producers seeking broadcast or educational rights, while they would ideally seek those rights in perpetuity, may agree to somewhere between five and thirty years of use.

Normally, you will be charged less for a shorter licensing term, which in some cases can be helpful. For example, a two-year license that allows for festival use may appeal to cash-strapped filmmakers. But the drawbacks of a limited time license can be considerable. In the first place, it may be that you simply don't have a choice: a limited term is the only way the rights holder will let you use their material at all. If they insist on a very limited term, say five or ten years, this is likely to become an issue later on, but at least you can finish your film, get your E&O insurance, and start getting it in front of audiences. The risk is that when the rights to even a single third-party element of your film expire, the entire film can no longer be distributed, unless you renew the rights or re-edit the film to remove the expired material. For that reason, even if you have no choice but to agree to a very limited term, make sure

277

the license agreement clearly indicates that the term is *renewable*—but understand that renewing rights may not be as straightforward as it sounds.

Imagine, for example, that you released your movie seven years ago, and now the rights from one or two licensors have expired, but there's still a market for your film. You're probably involved in other projects by now, or juggling media projects with other employment. Now you're supposed to go back into your seven-year-old files, figure out which rights have expired or are about to expire, relocate the rights holders (who may have sold their collection to someone else by now), figure out who the current contact person is, negotiate to renew the rights, and find the money to pay the renewal fees. In a competitive funding environment, it may be challenging raising funds to renew a seven-year-old film that's not likely to attract new press or win new awards.

Certainly, make sure that you get at least as much time as you need for existing commitments, and don't sell your film short. Two years may be standard for film festival or museum use. Even less is likely sufficient for a corporate presentation. In general though, ten years is a good minimum for most other uses and nowadays many distribution channels require perpetuity. A negotiating trick: sometimes rights holders are unwilling to sell you anything "in perpetuity," but "for the life of the film" is a phrase that for some reason makes them more comfortable. It amounts to the same thing from both your perspective and that of potential distributors, so ask for that language if the licensor balks at "perpetuity."

If you do have expiration dates, try to synchronize them, including both primary rights (such as the film clip) and underlying rights (such as music embedded within that clip). There's no point in having mixed time frames; remember that your film must stop distribution until you renew, and renewing different pieces at different times will be stressful and time-consuming.

Geographic Limitations

Although it's less prevalent these days, you or the rights holders may want to carve up geographical regions, such as *North American* home video or *worldwide* broadcast. As with time-limited licensing, there are benefits to this segmentation because it allows you to pay for only those markets you need and/or can afford. But there are also drawbacks to limiting the geographical area. For example, if you clear U.S. rights only, and your film catches the attention of Netflix (which is international), you will need to go back to rights holders to expand the geography of your license. The upgrade may be easier to afford once you've gotten a commercial backer, but that's not always true. Most companies want filmmakers to deliver their projects free and clear, with the necessary rights *already* negotiated *and* paid for, so at least make sure you have an option window during which you can upgrade easily.

The Fine Print

Per-Second and Per-Cut (or Clip) Minimums

We cannot repeat too often the maxim that you should try to use *the most material from the least number of places.* Not only does that give you some negotiating power, as mentioned above, but it's also important for another reason: most rights-managed archives charge minimums—sometimes simply per project, but often per individual moving image clip. To explain:

- *Per second.* Most archives charge rights holders a 30-second or 60-second minimum per project. This means that if you want anything from the archive, even if it's a single second, pricing starts at 30 seconds' worth at the negotiated rate. If you need less than 30 seconds total from the archive, you lose out. You should expect this from most archives, and avoid using just a few seconds of material from any source.
- *Per cut.* Instead of, or even in addition to an overall project minimum, some archives charge you a minimum per clip or per shot. The most common per-clip minimum is ten seconds. This applies to runs of footage furnished by the archive online or otherwise; each edit you make in an original archival clip or shot, whether it's one second or ten seconds long, will cost you the same. (The only time this isn't true is if the original shot is short; they won't penalize you for a shot that was shorter than the minimum when they gave it to you.) So at a hypothetical price of $10 per second, a three-second cut from an archive with this pricing structure will cost you $100, as will a ten-second cut. For this reason, be careful, especially when using archival to create a *montage.* Fees for a cut that runs *longer* than ten seconds will be calculated at the per second rate; in this example, a 12-second shot will cost you $120.
- *Per clip.* Similarly, archives that put clips online (which may run 5–30 seconds, on average) are likely to charge by the clip and sell

279

you a clip for a flat rate—but often that's misleading. A "clip" for licensing purposes may be defined as only ten seconds long, so if the online clip is longer than that and you use more than ten seconds, you'll pay an additional ten percent of the clip rate for every extra second you use (in other words, a pro-rated amount). Say you negotiate a price of $1,000 per clip. You find an online clip that's 20 seconds long, but you may only be able to use ten seconds of it for that $1,000. You may need to pay an extra $100 for every extra second of the original clip beyond ten seconds that you use—and of course you don't pay less than the $1,000 if you only use four seconds of the clip. Make sure you ask archives if their per-clip price is really "per clip," or if it's actually "per ten seconds."

The complexity of per-cut and per-clip licensing structures can make it difficult to accurately assess the archival costs of your film, because "screen time" may differ from the duration for which you'll be billed by the archive. Again, you may be especially penalized for creating quick montages, so editors cutting sequences from this material should try to let individual shots play longer, if possible. Producers interested in montages and fast cutting should focus on approaching archives that do not have per-cut or per-clip minimums.

How Much Will Rights Cost?

For historical filmmakers, whether working in documentary or period drama, the use of archival material can be one of the largest production expenses, depending upon how much you need. Rights holders nowadays are far less flexible when setting fees than they once were, in part because increasingly centralized archival collections have become big business. Clips have become "assets," and whole collections are constantly being bought and sold for profit.

While licensing rates can be prohibitive, it's important to keep a couple of things in mind. First, visuals archives continue to be more willing to negotiate than music publishers and record companies. Second, many visuals archives, even commercial ones, will often be more negotiable with projects that use a substantial quantity of their material. This is why we recommend you buy your archival material from the least number of sources possible. The strategy is likely to save you time, hassle, and money.

280

Communicating with Rights-Managed Archives

Unlike royalty-free images, which you can generally search for, download, and license without interacting directly with the provider, rights-managed agreements often require direct communication with people at the archive. It's a good idea to make initial contact with them as soon as you have a sense of the material you might need from them, and then stay in contact with them at various points during your postproduction process. It's especially important to keep the lines of communication open at the beginning and end of the editing period, to avoid finding out too late that material is unavailable or that you'll never be able to afford it.

When you first approach them, most rights-managed archives will want some basic information, such as:

- *The name, phone, and email of the contact person they will be dealing with.* Do your best to avoid having multiple people from the same project contact the same archives about the same footage. Designate one "point person," whether a professional archival researcher, an associate producer, or yourself, to follow through with a particular archive (or all archives) for the duration of the project. Don't have other members of your staff contact that archive directly unless there's good reason. A production manager arranging payment, or an editorial person or post supervisor addressing technical questions are both good reasons, but many professional film researchers also have the knowledge and experience to deal with these issues.

- *The project.* They'll want to know the name of the project and whether it's a stand-alone program or a multi-part series. They'll also want to know generally what the film is about—its storyline or subject—and whether or not the film already has a distributor. The best way to handle this is to prepare a document in advance that you can save and send as a pdf file. In two to five short paragraphs, describe the project and any coproduction or distribution deals in place, and explain which markets you plan to reach. This all can be updated as the project moves forward of course, but, for now, the archive simply needs to set up an account for your production company and project.
- *The rights you anticipate needing.* Generally, it's best to provide archives with your most conservative but truthful guess regarding the rights you think you'll need. If you've already committed to a distributor and/or broadcaster with known market requirements,

let them know. Otherwise, go with festival or educational rights as appropriate.

- *The licensee.* You—or your production company, distributor, or broadcaster, depending on circumstances—are, for the purposes of contracts and agreements, the *licensee*, seeking to license the rights to the material owned by the *licensor*. Often the licensee will be a limited liability company (LLC) established by you or your production company as a legal entity responsible for an individual film. You should discuss with a lawyer whether there's a good reason for you to set up an LLC for a film you're producing, separate from your company, if you have one.

You should plan to ask the archives a few specific questions up front as well. These might include:

- Are there any limitations on their rights to license the kinds of clips you'll be looking to get from them?
- What is the *book rate* (the list price, or non-discounted rate) for the rights that you think you may need, based on your current estimate of the markets you're hoping to reach. Will they be open to any discounts based on quantity?
- Do they have any minimums or additional fees? Most archives do charge a fee for providing you with master files of the shots you ultimately license, and some will charge you per-project or per-cut minimums as described above.

When you're beginning a relationship with these rights holders, it's important to regard and treat them as allies. Experience shows that many archive owners welcome your excitement about your subject and dedication to your film; they love film too. Some account managers, even at commercial archives, will ask up front what budget constraints you have. If you're honest in your conversations with them, they'll try to accommodate you, within reason. It's also important to present yourself as a qualified professional who knows how to *accurately* assess what your budget allows for and what your film's market potential will be.

Rough Cut: Begin Negotiating Prices
Rough cut is the stage of editing where your film is beginning to take its final shape. A one-hour film may still be three hours long, but you have a sense of its story and structure—and ideally, you have a sense of your third-party materials, both what you have and what you need. Of course, changes will be made right up until picture lock, but at this point you

may want to be in touch (again) with your sources. At minimum, let them know that you're considering their footage and are still editing. By staying in touch, you maintain credibility, and the archives will know to keep your file open, since some editing cycles are long.

Rough cut is also a good time to check on your archival progress. Is your use of third-party material in line with the style and goals of your film, or could it be cut back? For example, are you using too many archival news reporters to provide information that could be provided more effectively by a few pieces of narration or another interview? Alternatively, are there archival "holes" for material you still haven't found, and are you concerned that you might not find it? If you had to prioritize the archival elements used to this point, what is your "must have" material? Such a priority list might be useful as you go back to rights holders with a more accurate estimate of how much footage, and which specific footage, you anticipate including in the final film.

By rough cut, you might have a clearer picture of which rights you'll need as well. You can keep the archives informed without locking anything down. You and the rights holder might even begin to be able to develop some purchasing scenarios, such as a discount depending on the amount of their material it seems you might ultimately use. Footage for which you haven't found the rights owner—a YouTube video, for example—might never be useable, and it may be time to search for alternatives.

One additional word about contacting personnel at rights-managed archives: even if an archive is set up for online purchasing, unless you are only using a few shots, *contact the archive by phone anyway*. Establish a relationship. You may be very happily surprised at how much money you might save, just by telling them about your film, your budget, and your needs. Always assume you can make a better deal than the list price you're seeing online.

Picture Lock: Report Material Used

A film is "picture locked" when visual editing is complete but the film has not yet been color-corrected or sent for *track work* (sound editing and mixing). You don't want to wait until this point to find out that footage is unobtainable or unaffordable. Instead, it's time to obtain clean master files of third-party footage and stills, to replace any screeners still in the cut.

At picture lock, you must report to each rights-managed archive exactly what footage you used. As we explained in Chapter 11, online clips for editing purposes will have timecode numbers or other identifiers burned into the picture area. Make sure you report all this information to the

283

archive, and *be accurate to the frame*. If the archive doesn't have their own reporting form (and many do), create a spreadsheet including each shot you are ordering, with a visual description, whatever identifying numbers appear onscreen or in any log sheet provided to you, the displayed timecode in and timecode out, and the total length of the shot in seconds and frames. You can help the archives make your master if you provide the shot list in timecode order for each separate ID number, *not* the order in which the shots appear in your film. When you submit the list, remind the archive that you've given them exact cues, but you need *handles* at the head and tail of each cue for editing. It's *extremely* important not to forget to include any frames necessary to cover both ends of any effects, such as dissolves, wipes, or split screens, or you'll end up without important master content just when you need it most urgently.

Special Effects

Archives require you to pay for their footage as it *actually appears on the screen*. This means you should annotate and report any effects that you have performed, such as slowing the motion or freezing the frame: if two seconds of a clip is slowed down to ten seconds on screen, you owe the archive for ten seconds of use. You might have some success negotiating with an archive about this if it's extensive, so make separate notes about the varying durations of shots that are used for special effects.

Reporting Per-Cut and Per-Clip Minimums

Along the same lines, keep track of any shots or clips that have a duration that is less than the archive's per-cut or per-clip minimum, if relevant. When you create those footage reports, show both the *actual* number of screen seconds and the *billable* number of seconds, not only for your sense of what the footage will cost, but also because it may be useful for negotiating purposes.

Archives rarely will lower or waive their per-*project* minimum, but often, if you use enough of their material and aren't a big-budget film, you may get a waiver of per-cut or per-clip minimums. If you're using a Hollywood clip, you may be able to convince the owner to lower their per-clip minimum from one minute down to 30 seconds. If you are paying $7,500 to $15,000 per minute and using 25 seconds, this can be a significant saving.

How much material do you need to acquire from a single archive to get them to consider a discount? It varies. You might be able to get a discount for as little as one minute of footage, and definitely you should bring up the possibility of a discount if you're negotiating with one source for two to three minutes (or more), or for three or more clips or stills. Most archive managers *expect* to be asked by producers for a discount, but *you* have to ask.

Sound Only

Don't forget that your editor may have used archival sound without corresponding picture (or audio-only archival). You'll need to include those timecode cues on the log as well. Most archives want to charge you the same rate whether you use picture, sound, or both. You might be able to talk to them about a discount for sound-only clips if you have those totals ready, and happen to hit the archive manager on a good day. (If you don't need sound for something, let them know—it may save them and you time and expense when they prepare your master.)

As an aside, some producers don't order masters of sound-only clips, but rather use the sound from their screeners. Technically speaking, this is a violation of the clip's copyright, because you are not reporting and licensing the total amount of material (including the copyrighted sound) that you're using. Don't do it.

Picture Lock: Pay Licensing Fees

In most cases, the archive won't release masters until you've signed and returned a licensing agreement, and this won't happen until you've negotiated and paid the license fee, along with any costs the archive charges for producing the master. Remember that your license fees and contract terms correspond directly to the shots you need, which is why accurate reporting is so essential. Avoid returning to an archive because you've forgotten a shot, or miscounted frames, once you've reported to them.

If you have a distributor by this point, you'll know exactly which rights you need to license. If you don't, remember that you will get the best deal on license fees by purchasing the largest package of markets, in the widest geographical area, for the longest term that you can. Again, if cash flow is a problem, choose the film festival or educational market, which are some of the least expensive, but don't do this if you know you won't be exploiting those markets. Often filmmakers secure festival rights when they plan to shop their film at festivals, such as Sundance, in hopes of picking up a distributor.

Negotiating with Individuals and Smaller Archives

Sometimes individual collectors and smaller archives are willing to accept a high-quality copy of their material (produced by you from their original, in a format of their choice) as full or partial payment for rights. This often happens when individuals have holdings you want but they are in an obsolete format. You will need to digitize or convert those items anyway; offering the owner a digital copy of their old Super 8 home movie or ¾" U-matic videocassette can be a win-win. (This won't work for commercial archives, as you won't be given access to the originals, only a copy they've made specifically for you.)

Special Consideration: Hollywood Clips

As mentioned, most Hollywood studios charge based on a 60-second minimum per clip. Because the minimum applies to each individual clip, if you need four clips from one movie or television show, and as edited in your film they last 15, 30, 35, and 45 seconds each (a total of two minutes and five seconds of material), you'll pay a license fee for four minutes. If you interrupt any one of these clips—say you cut away to something else in your film—each segment of the interrupted clip is usually considered a separate clip. Sometimes, if it is a simple one-shot cutaway and your production is low-budget, the studio may consider the clips on either side of the cutaway as one; it's worth asking.

If you are producing a dramatic feature or documentary for a major studio (such as Paramount) or streaming service (such as Netflix), you may discover that the organization has a cooperative arrangement with certain "sister" or affiliated studios. Always ask about these arrangements, because you may be eligible to use clips from those studios at a discounted price. And as studios merge, you may find yourself working for a studio that actually has the same parent company as the one you want to license from. For example, 20th Century Fox is largely now the same company as Disney. NBC is the same company as Universal. Note, though, that these arrangements are for the clip rights only; they don't affect guild fees or underlying rights (see the section on guild clearances below).

Maintain the Integrity and Order of the Shots
Don't ever change the order of the shots *within* one Hollywood film clip. None of the studios allow this, nor should they: it's an ethical breach, because you are destroying the artistic integrity of the original film.

Maintain the Integrity of the Soundtrack
Many studios also have rules about changing the soundtrack of the film, although you can usually strip the sound out completely. If you add any audio over a motion picture clip—such as voiceover narration—it must

be absolutely clear to your audience that the sound they're hearing is not from the original movie. To alter the soundtrack itself is a serious ethical violation.

The same is true of the film's musical score. Filmmakers often want to strip out a film clip's musical *underscore* and replace it with other, cheaper music, implying that it's the original music from the clip. Don't do this. It's considered unethical and probably violates your contract with the studio. If you add your own musical score, it should be established before the clip, run through it, and continue past it. Don't mix in other elements of the original film's soundtrack, such as the dialogue, with your music.

Guild Clearances: Directors and Writers

When seeking to license a clip or still from the entertainment industry, remember that there are a few levels of rights that need to be cleared, including rights to the clip or still itself and rights to underlying elements, such as music, personalities, or background art. In the case of Hollywood films, some of these underlying rights include clearing entertainment industry guilds representing directors (Directors Guild of America), writers (Writers Guild of America), and actors (SAG-AFTRA, the Screen Actors Guild and the American Federation of Television and Radio Artists, which merged in 2012). *Guild clearances* most often apply to features released in and after 1960 (with some exceptions) and to *all* television programming. If you're licensing a clip from an entirely non-union film or television show, however, guild clearances probably won't apply.

Directors Guild of America

The DGA (www.dga.org) requires a payment for all films produced after May 1, 1960, and all television show excerpts, regardless of when the shows were made. These payments are *residuals* for the director. Rates are *stepped* (*tiered*), based on the duration of the clip(s) you're using. It costs a certain amount to clear clips of up to 30 seconds, a larger amount to clear clips from 31 seconds up to two minutes, and so on. In addition to that fee, if the director is still living, you must pay a surcharge, that is, a percentage of the guild fee to cover pension and welfare (P&W).

Rates differ depending on use, with the price primarily determined by whether the work you're excerpting *from* was a theatrical film or a television show (rather than how, where, or for how long *your film* will be shown). For example (all rates are as of the time of this writing):

- A theatrical film clip to be licensed for your television program (*theatrical in television*) or for your theatrical film (*theatrical in theatrical*) will cost the same price. A clip or clips of up to 30 seconds in length will cost you $238 plus 12.5 percent P&W. Using a theatrical clip or clips that total between 30 and 120 seconds will cost you $683 plus P&W.
- A television clip to be included in either a theatrically released or broadcast project (*television in theatrical* and *television in television*) is always charged at a higher rate than a feature clip. At present, a clip or clips from television totaling 30 seconds or less will cost $433 plus P&W; television clips with a total running time of between 30 and 120 seconds will cost $868 plus P&W.

Check the guild's website for the most current rates *when the time comes to pay these fees*, not at the beginning of your project. If a new union contract has gone into effect, the rates may have gone up even while you were producing your film.

Writers Guild of America

The WGA (www.wga.org) must be paid if the clip you want is from a feature film made after 1960 by most studios, or produced by United Artists or Universal after 1948, as well as from any television show, regardless of when it was made.

Writers Guild payments are very similar to DGA payments, structured in the same tiers based on the total number of seconds used (1–30 seconds, 31–120 seconds, etc.) and on whether the original work is a feature film or a television show. The main difference is that there is no P&W surcharge.

Paying the DGA and WGA

Payments to the DGA and WGA are *one-time flat-fee payments*. You don't need to go back to clear additional markets, to lengthen a term, or expand to a different geographical area. You pay the guilds directly after you've finished your production and know exactly what clips you're using. Send a letter to the contact person and address on the guild website, explaining what your project is (the name, producing entity, distributor, and how it's being released). Indicate what clip(s) you are using, the total length of each, the price you are paying the guild for them, the name of the writer(s) or director(s) as applicable, what kind of use(s) category (theatrical in theatrical, theatrical in TV, etc.). Add P&W based on 12.5 percent of the total for Directors Guild payments only (and note that you've done so in your cover letter), and mail the letter with your check made out to the proper guild. Their mailing addresses are available on their websites, as are the names of the contact people to whose attention you should direct your correspondence. The guilds are always glad to answer any phone or email questions you have; they want to get their members paid.

Multiple Writers and/or Directors

You don't pay any more to the guilds if there are multiple writers or directors for any particular work you're excerpting, but you do need to name them all in the cover letter. The guild will distribute the fee among the beneficiaries.

Guild Clearances: Actors

If you are using a clip from a feature film made before 1960, it's unlikely you'll have to clear the actors, unless they are stunt performers. Otherwise, you need to clear actor appearances through SAG-AFTRA (www.sagaftra.org). Clearing actors is tricky; the fees aren't set. Instead, you must negotiate with each actor individually.

SAG-AFTRA

SAG-AFTRA has much more stringent requirements for clearing actors than either the DGA or WGA has for writers and directors. You must locate each and every actor (except extras) who appears in the clip(s) you want to use, *whether or not their faces can be seen*. Anyone seen *or heard* in the clip (or both) who has an onscreen credit as a particular character (even "Android Number Three" or "Worker in Alley") must be cleared. The credit is what differentiates them from extras and, of course, allows you to identify them. When you find actors, you must obtain signed in-clip appearance releases from them for your files, for which you will negotiate a fee (usually through a representative or, if the actor is deceased, through their estate).

Some actors' estates are actually represented by SAG-AFTRA, in which case the negotiations may go more smoothly. *The fact that an actor is no longer living does not mean that the appearance does not need to be cleared.* Furthermore, other trademark and right to publicity issues may apply (see Chapter 11). And be warned: negotiating with a deceased actor's estate can be extremely difficult. Estates and their lawyers are notorious for keeping you waiting and charging outrageous sums.

Appearance Releases

The appearance releases you create for clip use can be almost identical to appearance releases you use for anything else. Put a header at the top of the form specifying the actor's name, the name of the show or movie in which they appear, and the name of the character they play; for example: *Clip Appearance Release for Rachel Brosnahan, playing "Miriam Maisel" in the Amazon Studios show, The Marvelous Mrs. Maisel, Season Two, Episode 7, "Look, She Made a Hat."* Remember to specify that you want all rights, all media worldwide in perpetuity for the appearance. If your wording isn't broad enough, or if a certain actor refuses to grant you rights that wide, then you *will* have to return to those actors if your distribution expands beyond what the release allows. Perhaps surprisingly, the better known the actors, the more likely they are to assign you all rights. The question is: what will they charge?

Notifying SAG-AFTRA
When negotiations with actors are complete, send a confirming letter to SAG-AFTRA. Tell them which actor(s) you've cleared, for what clip(s), from which film or television show, and how much you've paid to each. If there were extras or crowd scenes in the clips you used, note that fact and that you didn't clear those. You do not have to send the guilds actual copies of the releases; these are for your files and use. Note that you do *not* make payments directly to SAG-AFTRA (see the following section).

Actors appearing in foreign films likely also require guild clearances, because of course there are acting guilds outside the United States, just as there are independent, non-guild productions. The foreign studio or the production company you buy the clip from should be able to tell you about any underlying rights, including guild rights, that you may need to clear.

Actors' Right to Privacy and/or Publicity
One benefit of the otherwise cumbersome process of contacting actors and clearing rights to satisfy guild requirements is that, by having them sign a clip appearance release, you are also clearing rights to privacy and/or publicity for those individuals and so you do not have to pursue those separately. However, it won't clear rights to a trademarked character if that's relevant to the clip (see Chapter 11).

Finding Actors
How do you find the proper person to contact for, say, Marlon Brando's estate, or the agent or publicist of actor Lupita Nyong'o? This is where SAG-AFTRA is a great resource; it's their job to see that actors are employed and that they're paid residuals. The guild has a hotline and email address through which you can access the contact information

(generally the actor's agent, publicist, or lawyer) for the actors you hope to find. They will usually ask you to limit yourself to three actors per call or email, but then they respond very quickly. You can also access their new online database if you register (for free); then you can research as many actors as you want 24/7. The contact information you receive is *never* to be used for fan mail or anything else not related to employing or paying actors.

Once you get the actor's representative on the phone, explain your needs. Hopefully, the person you reach can handle the clearance, but if not, they're likely to know who else has been retained by the actor. (If you're referred to a large agency, such as Creative Artists Agency or William Morris, there will be an "agent locator" inside the company who can direct your call to the proper person.)

Be prepared for any and every response imaginable. Agents might say, "No problem," but then turn the matter over to lawyers, and suddenly you're faced with a crippling quote and a three-page contract asking you to promise things you can't deliver. Some representatives never get back to you—keep at them! Agents are often quite cooperative, since they stand to make a percentage, but even if everyone has the best of intentions, their client may be on location halfway around the world, so you might have a significant wait before you get a signature. Occasionally a publicist will say, "I'm sure so-and-so would be pleased to have that clip used in your project. Email me your release; I'll have her sign it when we meet for lunch and send it back to you before the day is out." Some actors (including some that are well known) will call you back personally. You just never know.

Hitting a Dead End

Sometimes the information SAG-AFTRA gives you is incomplete or out of date, or they have no contact information. Perhaps the actor is no longer in the union, or has failed to notify SAG-AFTRA about a change in address or representation. Or they are deceased (check IMDB) and no estate information was given to the guild. If the contact information you've been given isn't working and they aren't deceased, try calling a few of the bigger Hollywood agencies to ask if they have more recent information. Use IMDb to find out what some of the actor's most recent movies or TV shows were, and try calling the production companies listed—they might be able to help. Often if an agency no longer represents an actor, their former agent there knows who does. If all else fails, put some money in escrow and, when you send your letter to SAG-AFTRA, indicate that this particular actor was untraceable.

Paying Fees to Actors

Actors can ask for as large a fee as they want in exchange for signing your release. Start negotiations by offering the equivalent of the current union scale for a day (as of this writing, around $800), plus ten or fifteen percent to cover the representative's fee. Be prepared to replace the clip if the quote you're given is unreasonable—and don't be surprised if the agent or manager suddenly decides to cooperate once you tell them you'll drop the clip. After all, it's just a signature (and exposure for their client), so whatever fee you can afford, provided it's at least a single day's scale, is better than no fee at all for their client and themselves.

Exceptions to Clearing with SAG-AFTRA

There are a few cases in which you do not have to clear actors.

- If the feature film you're licensing material from was produced by a studio other than Universal or United Artists before February 1, 1960. But note that this cutoff date does not apply to *stunt performers;* you must notify SAG-AFTRA about any stunt performer(s) who appear in clips you're using from films released on or after August 1, 1948. There is no cutoff date for television shows.
- If the production you're licensing material from was not a signatory to the guilds *and* the actors in the clips are either not members

Frame grab from *Good Night, and Good Luck,* its set replicating the 1950's studio of *See It Now.* On the monitors: an original episode, a 1950's Alcoa commercial, and the in-studio feed of actor David Strathairn as Edward R. Murrow. Note the CBS branding on the camera (L), which also required clearance.

of SAG-AFTRA or, if members, they had a waiver to do the film outside of their union contracts.

■ If the clip you are using is in the public domain or your use of the clip legitimately satisfies a fair use exception to copyright.

Fee Exception for A-List Actors

In a last, interesting twist, if the actor(s) in the clips you want to use are considered to be *A-list*—an industry term that reflects their fame and marketability—you still must get them to sign an appearance release, but they are allowed by SAG-AFTRA to waive the fee if they want to. Who's an A-list actor? It's always a matter of opinion. However, if you're negotiating with "stars," it doesn't hurt to explain why your project will benefit humankind or give them good exposure, and ask if they'll sign the release *gratis*. If you are doing a documentary and interviewing a big star (in addition to using clips in which they appear), you might be able to get them to waive payment and sign your clip appearance release in person along with your appearance release for the interview.

Note that SAG-AFTRA rules *prohibit* actors who are not on the A-list from waiving their fees. Frankly, as with musicians, you should try to pay them at least the day rate, out of professional respect for those engaged in difficult and often uncertain work. Actors *can* request as little as they want to, however, and if a cause is close to their hearts, they might seek only a nominal fee. But that should be their decision, not yours.

293

Special Consideration: Television Commercials

Many archives sell copies of television commercials (particularly older ones), and may charge a hefty clip fee, but you should additionally get written permission from the company whose product is being advertised, if they are still in existence. Often this permission will be granted for free; explain the situation to someone in the company's public relations or press department and ask them to sign a materials release or to write a short, official letter (on letterhead) granting permission. They can mail it to you, or email it as an attachment. If you feel you are being turned down by a company because you want to use their advertising in a way that's critical or analytical and they don't approve, you probably have a case for fair use. (Note that clips from old cigarette advertising, which was banned from U.S. airwaves in 1971, *automatically* fall under fair use, so there's no need to contact the tobacco company). Finally, remember that companies buy each other. If you think a company is out of business, make sure another company hasn't bought them – if they have, go to the parent company. Sometimes companies may refer you to the ad agency that created the ad, but it's usually better to get the company to sign, since in most cases the advertising agency was creating the ad for the company as a "work for hire."

Special Consideration: Sports Footage

Obtaining and clearing sports footage and stills poses some unique challenges, and some film researchers specialize in this. Most of the time, you need to license material not only from the copyright owners, but also the teams and the entities they operate under. In the United States, for example, you may find yourself seeking clearance from the National Basketball Association, National Football League, or Major League Baseball, in addition to getting clearance from individual teams (which usually also covers the appearance of their players and what are usually trademarked uniforms). If the footage you want is from the Olympics, you'll need permission from either the National or the International Olympic Committee. You may also need to clear *branding*, such as a trademarked NFL logo or the Olympic five-ring. (That logo usually costs a minimum of $10,000, according to the International Olympic Committee, so try to avoid shots that include the logo on-camera, if you possibly can. IOC rates are usually non-negotiable.)

Obviously, these layers of licensing can get expensive, and you can generally count on paying at least double the normal archival licensing rates for any such footage you use. You must also put very specific credits (dictated by your agreements with these entities) at the end of your film. However, many commercial archives that handle sports footage can also do the league or team clearances for you, because they have ongoing relationships with these entities. Sometimes all those underlying rights are pre-cleared by the archive, saving you a virtual nightmare of clearance issues. Although their rates are high, working with these specialized archives is usually a better bet than trying to clear sports footage on your own.

Note that Olympic Committee clearances are only necessary for footage of events *inside* the athletic venues. Clearance of footage for a related news event, such as the kidnappings at the Olympic athletes' dormitory in Munich in 1972, requires permission only from the news source. A newsworthy event that happened *in* the Olympic stadium, however, would still need to be cleared with the relevant Olympic committee(s) unless you're making a fair use claim.

Vintage Sports

Older sports footage—from the 1950s and earlier—in many cases doesn't have the encumbrances that newer footage does. If you just need generic "old baseball," "old football," or "old boxing" footage, and you don't much care who the players are or what specific game you're showing, newsreels—and especially the Universal newsreels at the National Archives—can be good source of (black-and-white) sports footage.

Special Consideration: Fine Art

As discussed in Chapter 11, in the United States, fine art is subject to the same copyright terms and issues as any other kind of material, and in addition, art created in other countries may be subject to what are known as *moral rights*. What follows are a few strategies for locating the rights holder and/or the artist whose permission you need before using their work in your film.

Finding Artists

The copyrighted work of many artists of the 20th and 21st centuries is represented by one or more international agencies that collect fees on the artists' behalf. In the United States, these agencies are the Artists Rights Society (ARS) and Visual Artists and Galleries Association (VAGA), both in New York City. Sometimes ARS or VAGA represents everything an artist has done, but sometimes they only represent some works, and for others you must go to the artist's foundation, agent, gallery, or estate. Each piece of art can provide its own unique clearance issues.

Both ARS and VAGA are related to "sister organizations" in other countries. If you get worldwide clearance through ARS, you are then cleared for the same work if it is represented by DACS in the United Kingdom, ADAGP in France (ARS itself also operates in France), VG Bild-Kunst in Germany, and similar organizations elsewhere. Likewise, if you are in another country and you buy world rights from these organizations, you're covered, regardless of what other organizations represent that work elsewhere. VAGA has similar arrangements with other international organizations. In addition to representing artists, VAGA represents some other assets, such as the right of publicity for Ernest Hemingway's image.

If a Work is Not Represented by ARS or VAGA

If neither of these two organizations represents a work, they can usually give you good leads on who does. They have reference works at hand with lists of artists' agents and galleries and are usually glad to consult these for you over the phone. Often one gallery will have exclusive representation rights to a contemporary artist's work even if multiple galleries sell it. If the artwork was created in the United States and published before the current copyright cutoff date, the artwork itself is in the public domain. You don't need to clear it, but you may need to clear a specific reproduction of it that you're using.

Obtaining Suitable Reproductions of Artwork

You can sometimes obtain digital or physical copies of art directly from artists, in which case this is part of your negotiated deal with them. There are also organizations that sell or lease out images of artwork, including Art Resource (which works closely with ARS) and Getty Images (which represents the Hulton Archive, the Andy Warhol Foundation, the Hermitage Museum, and many others). The fee for these reproductions can be steep, even for works that are in the public domain.

In some cases, you may have to create (or hire someone to create) a photograph of a work of art. At times, this may include shooting an environmentally placed piece, such as a statue in an outdoor plaza. In that case, you still must secure permission from the rights holder, if any,

John Trumbull, "Declaration of Independence," oil on canvas, commissioned 1817. Photo courtesy of Architect of the Capitol.

for the artwork, *and* you may need to get a permit or, if the work is not on public property, a signed location release. Be especially careful if you're filming and *incidentally* shoot a copyrighted piece of art, whether it's outdoors or indoors. The moral rights of the artist may trump any "incidental capture" fair use claim, especially outside the United States.

Remember also that *architecture is* art: more than a hundred famous buildings and structures (such as the Chrysler Building in New York) are trademarked or otherwise rights-controlled in certain situations. And for some public domain structures, even more complex restrictions apply: as noted, the Eiffel Tower's design is not trademarked, but the design of its lighting is. You may use daytime footage of it without encumbrances, but to use footage of it that you filmed at night or are licensing from an archive, you must obtain separate permission.

Museums

You may find yourself needing to acquire an image of a piece of art from the museum that owns it. As discussed in Chapter 11, if you can get a suitable quality reproduction of the artwork from another source, it often makes sense for you to do so; many museums charge high fees and make extensive demands regarding the use of materials in their possession, whether or not they hold the copyright. As we've mentioned, you are not obligated to lease the transparency from a museum simply because the physical object is located there, as copyright rarely transfers with the physical object unless a special arrangement was made at the time of transfer or donation.

Documenting Non-Licensed Material

If you are using material that your research shows is in the public domain, or material for which your lawyer supports a claim of fair use, you will need to create your own documentation for your lawyer and/ or for your files, as we describe below. This is so that if an issue comes up years later, or someone else has to access the rights files to your film sometime in the future, it's clear what the status of the item is. You won't be left wondering what happened to the license agreement, if it was ever cleared, or who owns it.

This raises an important point about having complete documentation as a producer. Filmmakers sometimes think of this as the "if you get hit by a bus" scenario – and as gruesome as that sounds, it's good practice. If you suddenly disappear from the scene, or many years go by, could someone else carry on with the film, reconstruct what you did,

297

or develop the same knowledge *you* had? That should be a goal as you organize your documentation throughout your career.

Fair Use

If you are claiming fair use, you need to obtain a written legal opinion in support of this claim and place a copy in your files along with a memo to accompany whatever documentation you have about the original material as well as your use of it. This is required when you apply for E&O insurance (see Chapter 13).

If you have fair use claims, at picture lock, create a form or spreadsheet in which you list (in the order they appear in your film) every shot you believe should be considered fair use. Have columns for the timecode cue where the shot appears in your film, the duration of the shot, a brief description or descriptive title, and in the final column, your reasoning regarding why you think the use is fair. This form should be given to your production lawyer along with a copy of your picture lock with burned-in timecode. Your lawyer will use these to review your film and write a formal legal opinion for your files and for your E&O insurance, certifying that they agree these items fall under fair use. If they disagree, they'll discuss those instances with you, and together you'll end up with a final list of fair use claims, attached to the lawyer's letter. Keep this in a safe place, with all your other releases and contracts (your *rights bible*) and submit it along with everything else to your insurer.

Some production attorneys will ask you to include public domain items on the same spreadsheet they use to evaluate your fair use claims, so they feel confident the items don't need clearance. If so, list those items and present any printouts from websites that indicate there are no rights encumbrances, as described earlier in the chapter.

Breaching Archival Agreements

What happens if you license footage for festival use and then start distributing your film in some other venue? What if you continue to make your film available for sale via the web a year after some of your underlying rights have expired?

The obvious response is, *don't*. You are breaching a contract and subjecting yourself to potential legal action that could cost you a significant amount of time and money. If you were not able to get waivers of injunctive relief (see Chapter 11), rights holders may be able to *enjoin* your film, keeping it from being made publicly available. In addition, this dispute may trigger an arbitration clause, often found in licensing agreements, that gives a neutral third party control over important decisions about your film, such as whether or not it can be released or distributed.

It's possible that you could find yourself in breach for reasons beyond your control, due to actions taken by others without your knowledge or intent. This is partly what E&O insurance is for. If such an issue comes up, discuss it with your insurer and your production lawyer.

Sources and Notes

Information about clearing through Artists Rights Society (ARS) in the United States is at www.arsny.com/procedures.html; you can search their database of artists represented at www.arsny.com/complete.html. At VAGA's home page, www.vaga.org/, is a list of most of the artists they represent.

299

CHAPTER 16

Licensing Music

Licensing music ("clearing music rights") can be one of the most frustrating, difficult, and expensive tasks a filmmaker faces when dealing with third-party materials. Because of this, growing numbers of independent filmmakers are forgoing the use of prerecorded music entirely, relying wholly on hired composers or music libraries. This is unfortunate, particularly with films that explore the past. A filmmaker's creative and content choices should not be unreasonably limited by logistical or financial issues. Music is part of our lives, culture, and history. When the music of a time period is used by filmmakers as an archival artifact (just like archival visuals), or to help place the audience in a specific time and place, the music track is usually a crucial element.

With that said, what does it take to include someone else's music in your project? What follows is an overview of the entire process, intended to help whether you're doing limited licensing on your own or working with a professional, which we strongly recommend. A professional music supervisor can significantly streamline the process and save you money in the long run. "If you don't have someone clearing these rights who has enough experience to really understand the rights that they're clearing, what's feasible and what isn't, and how to negotiate, you're going to end up with costs that are just sky high," explains Patricia Shannahan, a former music industry executive who now clears rights through her company, My Forté Music Industry Services, in the Los Angeles area. Simply getting a response from music executives can be challenging, she notes. "You may get a voice mail at these large companies that gives you instructions on how to fax your request to a general number and then you never hear back from anyone." Especially if music publishers and record companies think you're a low-budget production, they couldn't care less about ever following through on a request—which can leave you hanging. Because music supervisors have contacts in these organizations, they can get through these barriers and get licenses done.

The 369th Infantry Regiment band, led by Lt. James Reese Europe, entertains patients from the courtyard of Paris hospital, 1918. U.S. Army Signal Corps, from the U.S. Library of Congress.

Synchronization and Master Use

If you want to use copyrighted music in your film, usually you'll need to explore both *synchronization* (or "publishing") rights and *master use* rights. The first refers to the composition (music and lyrics); the second to any preexisting recording you may want to use.

- If you include a copyrighted song in your film but either perform it yourself or have someone perform it for you, you'll need to secure synchronization (or "synch") rights to compensate the people who wrote and published the song. If you don't perform the music yourself, you will also need a release, similar to an appearance release, from the performer you hired, giving you permission to use the performance.
- If you want to use a specific preexisting recording of a song, you will need to secure synch rights *and* master use rights to compensate not only the song's authors and publishers but also the musicians who recorded the performance you want to use *and* the record label that released it.
- If you're using *underscore* music from a Hollywood film or television show, you'll usually need to clear synch rights and sometimes master rights separately from the clip.

Featured, Background, or Credit

The rights holder will want to know more about your project, including what it's about and how much of the song(s) they own will be used—meaning the number of separate musical cues (often called *needle drops*) and how many seconds each cue lasts. In addition, for each cue, they will want to know the type of use, whether *featured*, *background*, or *credits*.

- *Featured*. You film Hootie and the Blowfish performing on stage, or you film a group of teenagers performing a Hootie and the Blowfish song. The song is *featured* in the film. (As an added complication, note that if your film's subject is an individual or a group of people in the audience of a Hootie and the Blowfish concert, and you never show the band, the issue of whether the use is featured depends on what country you are producing in; more on this later.)
- *Background*. You have a scene showing your subject dying, and you think it would be great to put the Blue Oyster Cult song "Don't Fear the Reaper" on the soundtrack. The music is not being performed onscreen; instead it has been added to the soundtrack.
- *Credits*. Music is played on the soundtrack over the opening or closing titles of your film; this type of use will usually cost you more than background use in the body of the film. Sometimes you'll use a song as background, but then return to it in the end credits. You'll need to clear each cue for its individual use.

As mentioned, definitions of *featured* and *background music* vary. In Canada and the United Kingdom, music is *featured* if the people in the scene would hear it (thus, if we see someone put a CD into their stereo, the music they and we hear is considered to be featured). In the United States, the criterion for *featured* music is whether its *live* source appears in the scene's visuals. Thus, in this example, the CD music would *not* be considered featured in the United States because we don't see the musician(s) performing; it would be considered background. Use the definition that applies to your film's country of origin.

Intended Markets

When clearing music rights, the markets you intend to reach are essentially identical to those described in detail in Chapter 15: educational, broadcast and/or cablecast (free or pay), theatrical or limited theatrical, home video, streaming services, museum use, film festivals, corporate presentation, etc. As with clearing visuals, you will also probably request a time period (term) and geographical area for your rights.

Options

304 What if you don't yet know which markets you'll need and only have enough money on hand to clear a minimal license? Sometimes, as with visuals, you can get an *option window* to expand your rights in the near future. Option windows for music may run 12–24 months. If you want this, *ask*—rights holders will seldom offer. But despite the additional cost, the hassle of clearing less rights up front, and going back later is often not worth it.

These days, broadcasters, distributors, and streaming services interested in a filmmaker's work often want the filmmaker to have cleared third-party licenses that grant all rights in all media, worldwide, in perpetuity, or at least "for the life of the film." Even if the distributors or venues asking for such broad rights (although rarely if ever offering to pay for them) don't actually *need* them, it's just easier for them to know that everything is cleared. It's a tough scenario, and cash-strapped indie filmmakers are often caught in the middle.

Clearing Synchronization Rights

Most often, you clear synchronization rights through a song's publisher or publishers (there are often more than one). They represent the song's composer(s) and lyricist(s), if applicable. If you are using a particular arrangement, the arranger is also treated like a composer in this regard and often is credited along with other composers and their publishing companies. In this regard, remember that although you might be using a song in the public domain, such as a 17th century madrigal or a tune from the Civil War era, the synchronization rights to any copyrighted *arrangement* of that music needs to be cleared, just as if it were a recent song.

Identifying the Publisher

The first step in identifying the publisher may be to look on the liner notes of the CD (or LP), if you have one. Often the publisher is listed for each song, and it's indicated whether they are members of a *performing rights organization*, such as the American Society of Composers, Authors, and Publishers (ASCAP), Broadcast Music, Inc. (BMI), or the Society of European Stage Authors and Composers (SESAC). Composers and publishers join these organizations because they help promote and sell their music, stand with them when litigation arises, and keep a watchful eye on relevant trends, pending legislation, and other issues.

Each of these groups has an online database (www.ascap.com/ace, www.bmi.com, and www.sesac.com/repertory/repertory_main.asp) that allows you to search for contact information about a song's authors and publishers. If you don't know which group is affiliated with the song you want and the liner notes don't tell you, it's easy enough to search each database directly by song title (although you need to know the *exact* title of the song) or by composer. If you use music you downloaded from a service such as iTunes, and don't have liner notes, it can be helpful to go to a music store, find the album, and take notes off of the back of the jacket or jewel case.

Some songs, because of the number of artists involved, will be on more than one site. For a really complicated example, look on the back of Beyoncé's album, *Dangerously in Love* (2003). The CD is copyrighted by Sony Music Entertainment and manufactured by Columbia Records. The first track, "Crazy in Love," is credited as: "Beyoncé Publishing/ Hitco South all rights admin. by Music of Windswept (ASCAP)/EMI Blackwood Music Inc. obo [on behalf of] itself and Dam Rich Music (BMI)/EMI April Music Inc. obo itself and Carter Boys Publishing (ASCAP) Unichappell Music Inc. (BMI)." In fact, additional research will reveal that some of this information is outdated (since publishers buy and sell *catalogs*, or holdings, all the time). Check the liner notes to find out who the original publishers were, but don't be surprised if the ASCAP and BMI sites indicate that they've changed—as in this example.

Where to Start?

In this case, the online databases do tell us that some of the publishing companies have changed since the record was released. In fact, the ASCAP database includes 119 results for "Crazy in Love," including two for songs coauthored by Beyoncé and three other writers (one is the *a capella* version). The other entries are for other songs that have the same title or possibly for the same song but in different copyrighted arrangements.

ASCAP indicates that their publishers own 12.51 percent of the song. There are two ASCAP-affiliated writers (Beyoncé and Shawn C. Carter), but there are three publishing companies listed: Beyoncé Publishing, Lil Lu Lu Publishing, and WB Music Corp. Look closer at the contact information for the first two, and you'll see it's identical to the third, WB Music Corp./Warner-Chappell Music, Inc. (the music publishing division of Warner Brothers, one of the biggest in the world). So, you might be able to clear three of the publishing companies and two of the composers by contacting one big conglomerate. Sounds as if it might not be too hard (although expensive).

But remember, that only covers 12.51 percent of the ownership; the ASCAP database tells us that the rest is owned by BMI-affiliated publishers, which represent the other two composers of the song, Richard Christopher Harrison and Eugene Booker Record. So you then must go to the BMI database, to see whom you need to contact about this majority portion of the ownership. The BMI composers are represented by EMI Blackwood Music, Inc. (for Mr. Harrison) and Unichappell Music, Inc. (for Mr. Record). Does that second name look familiar? The contact information for Unichappell turns out to be the same as for WB Music/Warner-Chappell, the ASCAP publishers. Unichappell is owned by that same conglomerate, but is a BMI-affiliated publisher. Does that mean you can clear the portion of the song that represents the three publishers representing three of the four contributors, Record, Knowles, and Carter by talking to one person at WB Music? Maybe, maybe not. You would have to call them at the contact information listed on the database(s), explain who the three publishers are, and find out from them how to proceed.

Finally, you're going to need to negotiate separately with EMI Blackwood (owned by Sony) for Mr. Harrison's portion of the royalties. Since the BMI database doesn't offer information about percentages of ownership, the publishers will have to tell you which publishing company owns how much. Publisher contact information is available on both sites by simply clicking on the name of the publisher (just about the only simple thing about the process).

Theoretically, the synch rights for three or four publishers of a single song should not cost significantly more than if there was a single publisher. However, it sometimes doesn't work that way. If you have to approach multiple publishers, you may end up paying more for the song than if there were only one or two.

The Good News

The good news is that sometimes you don't need to contact and negotiate with all of the publishers involved. When a copyright is shared, specific percentages are assigned to each copyright holder, as illustrated above. If you're lucky, one primary publisher (often the one with the largest percentage ownership) *may* have the right to collect license fees on behalf of the other publishers as well. Perhaps "Crazy in Love" can be cleared entirely through WB Music, Inc., and they will then distribute the appropriate percentage of the license fee to EMI Blackwood. However, this multi-publisher payout varies on a case-by-case basis, so you may or may not have to track down each publisher.

The Bad News

The ASCAP, SESAC, and BMI online databases only cover publishing rights for the United States. If you anticipate wider distribution, you must ask the U.S. publisher(s) that you contact if they own, or know who owns, publishing rights in other countries. And while we indicated that publishers listed on the liner notes may be out of date (because catalogs of titles are sold all the time), the database information may *also* be out of date, if the parties involved didn't provide the update to ASCAP, SESAC, or BMI. Also, be aware that with catalogs changing hands and consolidating, there may be times when publishers claim not to own songs because they didn't used to, when, in fact, they now do.

"I find that many times, I have to tell them they own the material," Patricia Shannahan said. "There are all kinds of complications. The people at each company don't know what they have because of sheer volume. They have to find ways to combine databases; if they can't look it up on the computer, they have no idea whether they have it or not, and this gets worse as time goes on and the volume increases. You end up being a victim of the technological problems they're having, and the lack of staff with any historical knowledge of the songs, recordings, or artists."

Further compounding this issue is the complexity of a global music industry still working with nationally based copyright laws. "All these major companies now have worldwide organizations, and their needs are different in each country, in each territory," explained Shannahan.

"They're not only trying to find ways to combine with other companies here, but [with] their whole worldwide groups, and everybody has their database system based upon their own peculiar needs in each country. So it's a very complex matter."

Needless to say, identifying, contacting, and negotiating with the correct publisher(s) can take months. *Leave yourself plenty of time, and always have an alternative track as a Plan B.*

Another Wrinkle

Suppose you look up a song, find a single publisher listed (at least for the United States), get hold of that publisher right away, and the publisher still owns the rights to the song. *You need to ask if they are the only publisher to hold that copyright;* it's possible that there are others and they're not listed or not yet listed. Conversely, you need to do your own due diligence. People may adamantly (and even abusively) claim ownership they don't actually have, such as the publisher who insisted to a colleague that he owned half of *world* rights to a classic soul tune when, in fact, he owned half of *U.S.* rights.

Clearing Synch Rights for Multiple Songs

308

Organize your music "shopping list" and needs ahead of time. That way, if you've got several songs owned by the same publisher (often one of the larger companies like EMI or Warner Bros.), you can group this information and make a single phone call. You should ask for a discount for clearing multiple songs, although it's not likely you'll get one. Generally, the price is the price, although, again, music supervisors can often get publishers with whom they have relationships to soften up a bit—another reason to strongly consider hiring a professional.

Clearing Master Use Rights

What if you want to include not only the song but also the song *as recorded* at a specific time by a specific artist (or group, symphony, etc.)? For this, you will need not only publishing rights but also *master use* (also called simply *master*) rights for the actual sound recording.

In other words, with the Beyoncé song previously mentioned, so far we've only addressed clearing the synchronization rights; you (or someone else on your behalf) would have to perform the song. If you want to hear Beyoncé and fellow performers, including Jay-Z, singing "Crazy in Love" on the soundtrack of your film, you'll need to clear the master as well.

Identifying the Master Rights Holder

To get a master use license, you need to contact the owner of the specific recording (the *master*) of the song you want to use. Usually this means contacting the record company (or its parent company) that released the specific version to request rights and negotiate a fee. Be sure to have the exact title of the song ready, along with the name(s) of the composer(s) and performer(s)—very important in the case of master rights—as well as information about the recording, such as the name of the album, the label (which, again, is sometimes a subsidiary of a larger label) and the recording number (for example, "Warner/Elektra 250683"). Also be prepared with the length of each cue you want to use and the total length of all the cues from that song. The label will come up with a quote based on this information, taking into consideration the markets and term for which you want the license.

Public Domain Music, Copyrighted Performance

With classical music, such as a Beethoven symphony, it's possible that both the composition and (Beethoven's own) arrangement are old enough to be in the public domain. In that case, there would be no synchronization rights to worry about, but in most cases, you will still need to get a master use license for the recorded performance you want to use. This would also include paying union fees for orchestra musicians.

Paying Union Fees

The master use license almost always will require that you pay a fee to the American Federation of Musicians of the United States and Canada (AFM; www.afm.org), the world's largest musicians' union. This fee provides additional payment for the musicians—generally *other* than the featured performer or performers—who are involved in the recording, from back-up vocalists to a full-piece orchestra, plus a fee to the union's pension fund. The fee is based on the project budget and is per player, so while the cost per individual is relatively low, if there are many people involved (such as an entire orchestra), the fee can become prohibitively steep.

Nowadays, most record labels demand that filmmakers provide proof that AFM fees have been paid before issuing the master use license. In any case, avoiding this fee, as some filmmakers boast of doing, is both risky and unethical. It likely will put you in violation of your master use license, for which there are legal penalties that may cost you money and hamper your film's distribution. Furthermore, the fees provide relatively minimal compensation for individual musicians who face ongoing professional challenges, including sometimes unsteady employment. Pay the fees because it's the right thing to do.

Clearing Synch and Master Use Rights for Embedded Music

In some cases, filmmakers want to use third-party footage that includes music already, whether it's part of a film's on the soundtrack (such as composer Danny Elfman's score for the feature *Silver Linings Playbook*) or an onscreen performance (such as a clip of Bob Dylan singing in the *vérité* classic *Dont Look Back*). This underlying or "embedded" music almost always needs to be cleared separately from the visuals; in fact, very occasionally, the music may need to be cleared even if the film is in the public domain.

Hollywood Studio Films Before the 1960s

When dealing with feature films made by the larger American motion picture studios, especially in the decades prior to the 1960s, the licensing of the underlying musical score can be relatively straightforward. This is because in that era, the so-called "majors," such as Metro-Goldwyn-Mayer (MGM) and Paramount, employed composers and musicians on staff. The film scores they wrote and performed were thus "works for hire," owned outright by the studios. There are exceptions; sometimes "big name" composers were able to retain publishing rights to their music, or a song written for the title sequence or end credits of a film. In general, though, when you buy a clip of an older film from a studio, the clip clearance person will refer you to their own music division for both master use and synch rights to the score.

Studio Films Since the 1960s

Beginning in the 1960s, the major studios no longer kept composers and musicians on payroll. Then, as now, producers and directors usually hired independent, outside composers who maintained copyright to their music and controlled any usage beyond inclusion in the film score. These composers are represented by publishing companies also.

Clearing Cues from Soundtracks

An example of a successful, contemporary film composer is Mark Isham. According to his official online biography, Isham has scored more than 400 movies and television shows. Each *cue* (or music track) from each movie he's scored is listed separately as a composition on ASCAP's ACE database. Combined with Isham's concert works, this means that there are more than 1,800 compositions owned by him and controlled by various publishers, some related to the studios for which he composed specific film scores, and some not. A filmmaker wanting to use one or more pieces of music from an Isham film score would need to identify the particular cues they're interested in clearing, and treat each individually. The names of the cues often relate to the screen action ("Danny comes home"), and you can usually discern them by checking the tracks on the original soundtrack recording, if there is one.

When a Film's Soundtrack Includes Third-Party Music

You need to make sure that what appears to be the underscore in the clip you're using is not taken from yet another original source. Feature films may include prerecorded music from an earlier era (as when a character in a 1990s story plays a Rolling Stones album from the 1970s, for example; or when films feature a large list of preexisting hits on their soundtracks). Cartoon music often "quotes" other popular music, and each copyrighted song that's quoted needs to be identified and separately cleared, even if it's just a snippet. Navigating all of this is your responsibility.

Can You Clear Music on a Market-by-Market Basis?

In the past, filmmakers with limited budgets would be able to divide up markets, similar to how archival visuals are licensed—for certain territories, periods of time, and media or venues. For the home video market, producers had a choice: to purchase music rights for up to a certain minimum number of units (DVDs, etc.) sold or to do a buyout. These choices are now no longer possible, according to Patricia Shannahan. "Licenses for films are [now] always done on a flat fee basis. The license is needed in perpetuity, [or] for as long as the film has a life. All media rights now known or hereafter devised are licensed, including DVD and digital rights. [These are] licensed on a non-exclusive buyout-of-rights basis." Occasionally, you might be able to purchase only film festival rights, but it's rarely worth it; in fact, Shannahan won't do that for her clients. You'll pay a lot for film festival rights, and then if you can't afford the additional rights you need, you'll have to remove the song and your film festival fees will have been lost. However, *step-deals* are possible: in this case, you negotiate for and

311

commit to all rights, all media, worldwide in perpetuity, but the license specifies that you can pay portions of the fee over time, as you exploit different markets.

Clearing Music for American Public Television

If you are making a film specifically for American public television (PBS), a different situation applies. Because of a *compulsory license* arrangement in the copyright law, producers don't clear synch rights for a PBS broadcast. A compulsory license (in this case) legally compels a music entity to accept a certain predetermined fee for use, and this is paid by PBS, not you. In the United States and elsewhere, compulsory licenses are written into copyright law.

What this means is that if you *only* want to clear music for PBS broadcast, you're all set. Following certain guidelines (pertaining, for example, to the amount of a song used per cue), all you need to do is fill out and submit a PBS Music Cue Sheet, with information researched as you would if you were going to clear these rights yourself. List performers, performing rights societies, publishers, and the songs used; provide information about how and in what quantity songs were used and exactly where they appear in your show. PBS's legal department then clears *synchronization* rights under the compulsory license. In addition, because another section of U.S. copyright law is presently interpreted by PBS as an exemption that allows for *master use* rights, the legal department will take care of those as well. (In the United Kingdom, the BBC has a somewhat similar compulsory license for music use, as well as cue sheets for producers to report use.)

As liberating as this may seem for PBS producers, be aware that there are limitations, and anything not covered by the compulsory license must be separately negotiated and paid for by you.

- The compulsory license does *not* include recordings of spoken word that might include a literary copyright (such as a recording of a Martin Luther King, Jr. speech that is copyrighted) and it doesn't include dramatic works, such as recordings of plays, radio dramas, and the like—because, again, there are multiple underlying copyrights, and you are responsible for them.
- The compulsory license and master use exemption does not cover music acquired through a *production music library* (see the end of this chapter). If you can find the same recording(s) streaming or on CDs available to the public, however, then you are in luck.

- Many PBS producers' contracts require that you obtain permission for a variety of other rights from all rights holders (including those covered by the compulsory license agreement). These may include educational rights (use in institutions such as schools and libraries); home video rights, if PBS Home Video is going to distribute the film on disk; and online streaming rights. In fact, before you sign your PBS producers' contract, make sure you understand which rights you will be required to clear for all third-party materials. Increasingly, these contracts require clearance of much more than just PBS broadcast rights. Negotiate to make sure you don't need to pay to clear music and visuals in markets that will, in the end, only benefit PBS.
- And finally, the most important thing to remember about this: *the compulsory license and exemptions only relate to the PBS broadcast.* Presentation in other venues, including festivals and distribution to educational, theatrical, home, or other markets, needs to be cleared by you, under terms you mutually negotiate with the publishers and record companies.

One option that filmmakers sometimes exercise is to include commercially-recorded music for the film as broadcast on PBS only and then remove or replace that music for all other distribution channels. Even Hollywood films have occasionally changed their soundtracks. It's a sad reality, because usually the original score reflects the filmmakers' true intentions.

313

Music Clearances in the United Kingdom

Music clearances in Europe are philosophically similar to the process in the United States, but overarching groups that represent a number of member composers, music publishers, and other parties help to consolidate some traditional rights clearances for producers. In the United Kingdom, PRS for Music—an alliance between two agencies, the Performing Rights Society (PRS) and the Mechanical Copyright Protection Society (MCPS)—can be an enormous help in clearing a song. They can usually streamline the process for filmmakers seeking to obtain synch licenses, for example, as well as the mechanical and performing rights needed for internet distribution. However, some music publishers retain the synch rights, in which cases the filmmaker will be directed to them. Still, filmmakers commissioned by major broadcasters can often rely on the "blanket licenses" which the broadcasters have in place with PRS for Music, provided the filmmakers use music in the extensive PRS repertoire, thus avoiding the need to deal with copyright clearance altogether. Master rights are still held by the individual record labels.

Deal Making and Distributors

Any distributor interested in your film will need to know that the appropriate music rights have been cleared and paid for. In general, unless the distribution deal is negotiated otherwise, filmmakers are responsible for both negotiating and paying for all the third-party rights needed. Even when the filmmaker uses money from a distribution deal to purchase these rights, which often happens, it is still a payment from the filmmaker—in other words, the filmmaker's responsibility.

Most Favored Nation

One of the most difficult structural and strategic aspects of music clearance work is that, almost always, publishers and record labels demand what is known as *most favored nation* or MFN status. This means that while you may be able to negotiate separate deals with each rights holder, those with MFN status can't be paid less for *like use* than the rights holder who is getting the most.

For example, suppose you get publishers of three songs to agree to a "most favored nation" arrangement of $5,000 each for the synch rights to cover all the markets you need. What happens when a fourth publisher, who controls a song you *really* want to use, won't go along with that deal? This publisher wants $7,500 for those same rights, not $5,000. Under MFN, you have the choice of either dropping that fourth publisher's song or paying *all* the publishers the higher amount.

As stated, MFN should be done on a "like use" basis, which is supposed to consider quantity. For example, if your total rights fee to use a two-minute cue from one publisher is $1,000, another publisher (or record company) *shouldn't* try to charge you the same $1,000 for a music cue that's only 20 seconds, citing MFN. Some rights holders *will* accept this fairer interpretation of MFN and adjust your total fee for the cue based on its length. But many publishers and record companies won't. In their view, a cue is a cue, a cut is a cut. Try to get them to prorate when you can; they're not going to offer, so it's up to you to ask.

MFN can be the bane of music rights clearance. "It's become worse and more binding," says Patricia Shannahan. "It's a nightmare because what you're dealing with is a house of cards; you try to add one, and they just all fall down." MFN arrangements can wreak havoc with your budget, in part because you can't know what you'll need to pay for music rights until you're finished negotiating with all rights holders. The worst music deal you negotiate—the one that costs you the most and gives you the least freedom—is retroactively applied to every other MFN deal you've negotiated.

Most Favored Nation Across Publishers and Record Companies

Another wrinkle: in the past, MFN deals went across publishers *or* across labels. In other words, the practice used to be that publishers used MFN to charge the highest synch fee paid to any one publisher; record companies used MFN to charge the highest master fee paid to any one record company. Nowadays, however, a record company or publisher is just as likely to ask for an MFN deal based on the most money you are paying *either* another record company *or* any publisher (often referred to as *MFN across all songs and masters*).

This "crossing the line" between publishers and record companies can be a worst-case scenario because now *all* the music entities you are negotiating with are subject to the same (highest) payment for the same rights and negotiated time period. "You're dealing with people who don't understand what they're doing to the [filmmaker's] budget," Shannahan says. "They simply have a mandate. The game has completely changed now by virtue of the fact that you have only a few companies owning everything, for the most part. You're dealing with assets, as far as they're concerned."

You need to avoid the MFN trap if you possibly can by dropping whatever piece of music is throwing off the rest. That's why it's very, very important that you remain flexible with your music choices. *Have backup choices.* The more flexible you can be, the more you can use MFN to your advantage. If everyone insists on being paid the same, keep "the same" as low as possible. With a Plan B for each cue, you have the power to refuse a deal that doesn't work for you.

Additional Music Rights

You may hear about another type of music license, for *performance rights*. Filmmakers rarely, if ever, get involved in these; they are fees paid— usually to the performing rights societies, annually—to clear the performance of a list of songs or music in a particular venue. For example, a jazz club or theater or a radio station will pay a fee annually to clear all the music that has been played by or in that venue over the course of a year, based on play lists or logs that are kept by the venue.

You may also hear about *mechanicals* or *mechanical rights*, which we briefly mentioned earlier in relationship to the internet. This relates to making an original soundtrack recording of the music used in your film—in other words, a derivative product from your film. If you plan on releasing a soundtrack album, you will additionally need mechanical rights for this specific use, and they *are* based on how many units you sell. These are the easiest of the music rights to negotiate. In the United States, mechanicals to *most* songs are handled by the Harry Fox Agency in New York (www.harryfox.com). In the United Kingdom, they are handled by the alliance between MCPS and PRS (prsformusic.com). If these organizations don't control the mechanicals to the music you need, they almost certainly will know who does. In addition, there's a published statutory rate for mechanicals (currently 9.1 cents per unit sold), which does not change often. There's a little bit of wiggle room, as it's customary to try to negotiate for 75 percent of that rate, if the publisher and record company agree. Although this is just pennies per unit, remember that when negotiating for mechanicals, you are still likely to run into a most favored nation situation—so saving a few cents per unit on one song could lead to that same discount on all of them. Multiply that by the number of units you expect to sell, and you may save some real money.

Alternatives to Pre-Recorded Music

Filmmakers reluctant to research and pay licensing and master use fees can still include music in their work through a variety of means. You can hire a composer and musicians and negotiate a flat fee to "buy out" the rights to the recording they make. Many composers of scores don't even need musicians. They perform the entire score themselves using *MIDI*. These scores consist entirely of computer-generated music that imitates specific instruments, including the human voice, and they are increasingly showing up, even on mainstream feature films. You can also work with an undiscovered group whose original music you like but whose work is still low profile (known in the industry as a "baby band"); this is the choice of many indie filmmakers. The band might be eager for exposure and therefore be willing to give you a good rate on performance and licensing fees. Composers and performers can also create *soundalikes* to order for you—work that emulates but does not copy the original. Make sure they and you know where the line is between a new composition and an infringement, and be sure to pass the result by your attorney.

And finally, you can also purchase music from a music library.

Music Libraries

Also called "sound libraries" or "production music libraries," music libraries are somewhat akin to stock footage and stock photo houses in that they offer a catalog of choices which they own outright, thereby simplifying the clearance process considerably. In the past, music libraries provided generic music that would fit a mood but not really have any personality of its own, but that's changed. "Libraries are getting a lot more deals now and are handling a lot more contemporary music than they did before, making deals with producers and helping them with their music supervision and getting a lot of exposure for their catalogs; this seems to be the new trend," Patricia Shannahan said.

Shannahan works closely with Hadley Murrell, who owns an entire catalog of *covers* (songs recorded by performers other than those who initially made the song famous), as well as *soundalikes*, which are original songs that evoke specific copyrighted songs but are different enough to avoid copyright issues. Either of these can serve as an alternative to filmmakers on a budget.

Although libraries may hold material that they have licensed from others, such as recordings of classical music, you only need to license it from them. Some libraries advertise their music as royalty-free and/or copyright-free. Remember that if you purchase clips from a sound library, you must negotiate with them in good faith, and the PBS exemptions do not apply. One of the largest production music companies is APM (www.apmmusic.com). They recently provided additional cues for such films as *Toy Story 4* and *Star Wars: The Last Jedi* (both of which, of course, also had their own primary composers).

Some libraries also offer sound effects, and often you can negotiate one flat fee for the use of anything in a library's catalog and cover all of your film's needs, thus saving you uncertainty, hassle, and cost. They will happily inundate you with recordings from which to choose.

Plan Early, Be Flexible

If your film depends on clearance of specific pieces of music or you intend for music to play a significant role, the earlier you begin to narrow your choices (with backups in mind), the better off you'll be. This is especially true if you find that you simply can't do it yourself and need to hire a professional. "If [filmmakers] come to me in time—which is frequently *not* the case—I know a lot of companies that have catalogs over many, many decades of music that we can work with to give them a good replacement at a good cost," Shannahan said. "But a lot of times, time has become a major issue. So that makes it more difficult."

Sources and Notes

For ASCAP, BMI, and SESAC databases, see www.ascap.com/ace/, www. bmi.com/licensing/, and www.sesac.com. Section 253.7 of the Code of Federal Regulations, addressing music licensing for PBS and NPR, is reproduced at Bitlaw, www.bitlaw.com/source/37cfr/253_7.html. BBC's music reporting form can be found through their commissioning page at www.bbc.co.uk. The MCPS/PRS Alliance can be found at www.prs formusic.com. Hadley Murrell can be contacted regarding covers and soundalikes at madley1@aol.com or by phone in Los Angeles at (323) 697–2947.

318

ADDITIONAL MATERIAL

CHAPTER 17

Afterword

Too often, filmmakers impose a kind of self-censorship when thinking about producing projects that might involve complex or costly rights issues. Perhaps they back away from tackling subjects that would necessitate a focus on corporate giants or stars in the entertainment and sports industries; perhaps they shy away from using cultural or historical materials—images, music, and sound—because to do so puts both schedule and budget at risk. While understandable, this is a trend to be rejected, not only by filmmakers but also by the public they serve, including the educators, scholars, community leaders, families, and individuals whose lives have been and should continue to be enriched by a vibrant and diverse tradition of filmmaking, including archival filmmaking.

Think back to those projects that first inspired you to study media, become a maker or curator, use films in your classroom, or draw on the archival record for your own research into the past. For a generation of Americans, *Eyes on the Prize* (1987, 1990) was an introduction to a civil rights movement hard-fought by their parents, grandparents, and now, great-grandparents. Others may remember watching *The Civil War* (1990) as young children, sitting up late with their parents and wondering at the power of its storytelling. More recently, consider Rob Epstein and Jeffrey Friedman's feature documentary *Linda Ronstadt: The Sound of My Voice* (2019), or Ezra Edelman's documentary series, *O.J.: Made in America* (2016). Archival materials play a key role in theatrical drama as well, such as in Ava Duvernay's *Selma* (2014), Bryan Singer's *Bohemian Rhapsody*, and Barry Jenkins's *If Beale Street Could Talk* (2019).

Others, from Hollywood producers to cell phone filmmakers, may want to make use of third-party content not because it evokes the past but because it captures and lets them explore the present. The cross-pollination of sounds, images, music, and ideas—across borders, disciplines, technologies, and ideologies—can help us to better understand ourselves, each other, and the world in which we live.

Films *matter*. They are not, as some might argue, poor substitutes for books. They are *different* from books, and powerful and effective in their own right. And they are different from each other. Two films may purport to be about the same subject, such as the 1989 protests in Tiananmen Square or the 2019 youth climate protests worldwide. Each of those films might unfold over the course of an hour; each might include third-party materials and talking heads and perhaps narration. But one of those films might be based on skilled journalism and exceptional storytelling, while the other is merely noise and light. One might selectively use news footage to distort and disguise facts (as those facts might reasonably be understood and agreed upon by diverse and knowledgeable parties), while the other will not. There is nothing wrong with criticism or a strong point of view, even in documentary. There is *everything* wrong with lying—including by omission—as a means of convincing your audience.

The rules for Hollywood dramas are different; there is room for invention, even when it comes to telling stories built from the historical or scientific record. But there is also responsibility, as these are the films most likely to reach the broadest possible audience, worldwide, and introduce them to these stories. Consider *Hidden Figures, Apollo 13, and Bohemian Rhapsody*, or television series such as *Good Girls Revolt, The Crown*, and *Chernobyl*. Research, including audiovisual research, plays a key role in grounding these works, even when stories within them may be fictionalized to varying degrees.

Issues of Access

As discussed throughout this book, the extension of copyright terms and skyrocketing licensing costs are two ways in which access to important archival materials has been blocked, not only in the United States but also throughout the world. Yet there are other issues to consider, including media venues purchasing exclusive access to materials that had previously been more widely available, or governments imposing restrictions on footage that was not previously restricted.

Internet Access

Internet neutrality (or "net neutrality") has been and continues to be a hot issue in the United States and worldwide. As defined on the website of the National Conference of State Legislatures (NCSL.org), "Net neutrality is the concept that all data traffic on a network should be treated indiscriminately, where internet service providers (ISPs) would be restricted from blocking, slowing down or speeding up the delivery of online content at their discretion." The ISP providers—massive telecom and cable corporations—oppose regulation. Without it, they are able to profit by giving priority to their own online advertisers, search engines, entertainment content, and more—which would limit *your* freedom to browse when and where you want without hindrance.

There is worldwide public support for net neutrality. Yet in the United States, both the Federal Communications Commission and the courts have legislated in favor of the ISPs. A saving grace, for now, is that individual states are able to enact their own regulations on internet providers, and as of October 2019, the NCSL reports that 29 states "have introduced net neutrality legislation in the 2019 legislation session." Groups including the Electronic Frontier Foundation (www.eff.org/) are working to keep corporate profits from compromising the integrity of the internet.

Extending Copyright, Shrinking Public Domain

In the United States, many of those immersed in copyright reform issues hope that the public will also get involved if and when the U.S. Congress is again pressured to extend copyright terms. Powerful rights holders—individuals and organizations often far removed from the actual creators—have a vested interest in preserving their private commercial interests. But what about the public's interests?

Think of a vast expanse of open forest, public lands. Private interests might *want* to develop the land and exploit its resources for profit, and sometimes there is a public benefit to growth. At the same time, however, the public and its leaders have long recognized the value of environmental conservation, including placing key tracts of land into a common trust for ongoing, protected, public use. As others have argued, the public domain is in no less need of conservation. It is the repository of our shared creative, cultural, scientific, and historical past and even much of our present. The loss of this public good can only partially be offset by the growing efforts of those who voluntarily put their work into the public domain, or release it under Creative Commons-style licenses.

The Future of Ideas

Some people see intellectual property as no different than physical property, a good to be privately held and passed on for generations. Others feel that by its very nature, creative work needs to be shared and built upon. However *you* feel about this issue, chances are that if you've tried to use third-party materials in your own media works—tried to incorporate the music that filled your characters' lives, past or present; tried to illustrate the past or include real life in the commercial culture that is now inescapable—then you understand why many hope to find some reasonable middle ground in this debate.

Copyright both supports and deters creativity. It *supports* creativity because it offers an incentive to create by giving you exclusive control over your work and the exclusive right to profit from it for a certain (and generous) period of time. You can give others permission to use your creation or not, but it's your choice. You can punish those who use it without your permission, if you choose. But copyright *deters* creativity, including your own, because creative acts stand firmly on the shoulders of those who came before. Explore the works of William Shakespeare, Walt Disney, Stephen Sondheim, and pretty much anyone else, and you'll be able to trace an ancestry to earlier creators and times. Culture does not spontaneously emerge; it builds and borrows, grows and changes, reconsiders and explores.

Creative artists can and do have the right to protect their work and to earn money from it. But unchecked copyright laws inhibit what Lawrence Lessig calls "the future of ideas"—the ability of tomorrow's creators to study, analyze, reprocess, and especially to take inspiration from our shared cultural heritage.

Moving Forward

We hope this book has offered a bit of guidance as you work your way through the maze of archival use. We also hope it's made you aware that you're not alone in your struggle, and that in fact, you are a critical part of a centuries-old tradition of reexamining and reusing cultural materials to create something new, unique, and important.

We also hope to influence those around you. Perhaps, by helping to raise awareness of the obstacles you face, this book will gain you greater support from those who set budgets and timetables—those who need to understand that some projects *require* both time and money to be done right. Perhaps it will provide a wider array of tools with which educators, librarians, and others can evaluate media intended to be educational. Perhaps we can gain the attention of policymakers who too often don't understand the importance of archival work and the necessity of ongoing access to archives by filmmakers and scholars. Today, more than ever, information is shared through pictures and sounds, at least as much as words. Today, more than ever, it's important that creators of media have access to the pictures, sounds, and words they need.

About the Authors

Sheila Curran Bernard is an Emmy and Peabody Award-winning filmmaker and consultant and the author of *Documentary Storytelling*, a best-selling guide to story and structure in nonfiction filmmaking, now going into its fifth edition and available in Portuguese, Polish, Chinese, Japanese, Korean, and Arabic. She has taught master classes and served as a jurist at film festivals in the United States, Norway, Belgium, and Poland. Her film credits include the series *Eyes on the Prize; I'll Make Me a World;* and *School: The Story of American Public Education* (and companion book, Beacon Press); and *Slavery by Another Name*, based on the Pulitzer Prize-winning book by Douglas A. Blackmon. Bernard has been a fellow at the MacDowell Colony for the Arts and the Virginia Center for the Creative Arts, and in 2016 was awarded a New York Foundation for the Arts named fellowship in playwriting/screenwriting. A former Anschutz Distinguished Fellow in American Studies at Princeton University and Dorothy M. Healy Fellow in American Studies at Westbrook College, she is now an associate professor in the Department of History (and the Documentary Studies Program) at the University at Albany, State University of New York. Her web address is www.sheilacurranbernard.com.

Kenn Rabin a consulting producer and an internationally recognized expert on the use of archival materials in film storytelling, has worked on more than 100 theatrical and documentary films and series. His credits include *Selma* (Ava DuVernay), *Milk* (Gus Van Sant), *Good Night, and Good Luck* (George Clooney), *The Good German* (Steven Soderbergh), as well as Al Gore's *An Inconvenient Sequel* and Amazon Studios' *Troop Zero*. He was associate producer and co-writer of Barry Levinson's *Yesterday's Tomorrows* for Disney/Showtime, and co-produced and co-wrote PBS's *The Storm that Swept Mexico*, a centennial history of the Mexican Revolution. In addition, Rabin was project archivist for the acclaimed PBS series *Eyes on the Prize* and *Vietnam: A Television History*. Kenn has led master classes at the Miami Film Festival and Seoul International Film Festival and for Women Make Movies, the Broadcast Education Association, and others, and has been a guest lecturer at the Woodrow Wilson Center at the Smithsonian Institution, Stanford University, Northwestern University, the UC Berkeley Graduate School of Journalism and elsewhere. His web address is www.fulcrummediaservices.com.

Note: The authors of this book are not attorneys and do not intend for information they provide to replace the advice of legal professionals.

Index

329

331

335

339

341